STRIPPED

RSA·STR
THE **RSA** SERIES IN TRANSDISCIPLINARY **RHETORIC**

Edited by
Michael Bernard-Donals *(University of Wisconsin)* and
Leah Ceccarelli *(University of Washington)*

Editorial Board:
Diane Davis, *The University of Texas at Austin*
Cara Finnegan, *University of Illinois at Urbana-Champaign*
Debra Hawhee, *The Pennsylvania State University*
John Lynch, *University of Cincinnati*
Steven Mailloux, *Loyola Marymount University*
Kendall Phillips, *Syracuse University*
Thomas Rickert, *Purdue University*

The RSA Series in Transdisciplinary Rhetoric is a collaboration with the Rhetoric Society of America to publish innovative and rigorously argued scholarship on the tremendous disciplinary breadth of rhetoric. Books in the series take a variety of approaches, including theoretical, historical, interpretive, critical, or ethnographic, and examine rhetorical action in a way that appeals, first, to scholars in communication studies and English or writing, and, second, to at least one other discipline or subject area.

Other titles in this series:
Nathan Stormer, *Sign of Pathology: U.S. Medical Rhetoric on Abortion, 1800s–1960s*

Mark Longaker, *Rhetorical Style and Bourgeois Virtue: Capitalism and Civil Society in the British Enlightenment*

Robin E. Jensen, *Infertility: A Rhetorical History*

Steven Mailloux, *Rhetoric's Pragmatism: Essays in Rhetorical Hermeneutics*

M. Elizabeth Weiser, *Museum Rhetoric: Building Civic Identity in National Spaces*

Chris Mays, Nathaniel A. Rivers, and Kellie Sharp-Hoskins, eds., *Kenneth Burke + the Posthuman*

Amy Koerber, *From Hysteria to Hormones: A Rhetorical History*

Elizabeth C. Britt, *Reimagining Advocacy: Rhetorical Education in the Legal Clinic*

Ian E. J. Hill, *Advocating Weapons, War, and Terrorism: Technological and Rhetorical Paradox*

Kelly Pender, *Being at Genetic Risk: Toward a Rhetoric of Care*

James L. Cherney, *Ableist Rhetoric*

Susan Wells, *Robert Burton's Rhetoric: An Anatomy of Early Modern Knowledge*

Ralph Cintron, *Democracy as Fetish*

Maggie M. Werner

STRIPPED

Reading the Erotic Body

THE PENNSYLVANIA STATE UNIVERSITY PRESS
UNIVERSITY PARK, PENNSYLVANIA

Library of Congress Cataloging-in-Publication Data

Names: Werner, Maggie M., 1974– author.
Title: Stripped : reading the erotic body / Maggie M. Werner.
Other titles: RSA series in transdisciplinary rhetoric.
Description: University Park, Pennsylvania : The Pennsylvania State University Press, [2020] | Series: The RSA series in transdisciplinary rhetoric | Includes bibliographical references and index.
Summary: "Explores the bodies, acts, and discourses that constitute embodied erotic rhetoric by foregrounding the material communication practices of performing bodies and proposing complementary frameworks and theories for analyzing them"—Provided by publisher.
Identifiers: LCCN 2020035757 | ISBN 9780271087764 (hardback) | ISBN 9780271087771 (paperback)
Subjects: LCSH: Human body—Erotic aspects. | Burlesque (Theater) | Stripteasers. | Rhetorical criticism. | Feminist theory.
Classification: LCC HQ460 .W47 2020 | DDC 305.4201—dc23
LC record available at https://lccn.loc.gov/2020035757

Copyright © 2020 Maggie M. Werner
All rights reserved
Printed in the United States of America
Published by The Pennsylvania State University Press,
University Park, PA 16802–1003

The Pennsylvania State University Press is a member of the Association of University Presses.

It is the policy of The Pennsylvania State University Press to use acid-free paper. Publications on uncoated stock satisfy the minimum requirements of American National Standard for Information Sciences—Permanence of Paper for Printed Library Material, ANSI Z39.48–1992.

For Mom and Dad.

Mom, I thank you for passing along your feminism.

Dad, I thank you for passing along your appreciative gaze.

Contents

Acknowledgments | ix

Introduction: Embodied Criticism of the Erotic Body | 1

1 Deploying Delivery as Critical Method: Neo-Burlesque's Embodied Rhetoric | 25
2 "You're Bound to Find Out She Don't Love You": Genre and the Erotic Body | 47
3 The Pleasures of Process: Neo-Burlesque's Seductive Rhetoric | 75
4 "I Am a Woman. This Is My Body": Rearticulating Identity in Sex-Work Activism | 99
5 (Anti-)Feminist Monsters: Alterity Rhetorics and the Signifying Body | 127

Conclusion: Embodied Erotic Rhetoric's Acceptance and Rejection | 157

Notes | 167
Bibliography | 183
Index | 197

Acknowledgments

I'm so grateful to so many that I feel my thanks won't do justice to the education you've given me.

First, my most profound thanks go to the performers who met with me, corresponded with me, encouraged me, and performed for me, including all the unnamed strippers in unnamed clubs. Jo Weldon, thank you for being the most influential performer and scholar on all of the topics in this book. Your work has shaped me in more ways than I can even articulate. Thank you for answering *every single question* I ever had, for your patience, kindness, and generosity. Thank you also to Indigo Blue for being the first performer and teacher to take the time to speak with me and teach me about your art.

Thank you to Jennifer Nace for setting my feet upon this research path, for encouraging me to think *with* my body and not just *about* others', for Pilates, for cats, and for friendship.

Thank you to Cadence Whittier for blowing my mind when you talked to me about the role of touch and movement in dance pedagogy. You fundamentally changed how I think and write about the body and embodied knowledge.

Thank you also to Shanghai Pearl, Dame CuchiFrita, Legs Malone, and Lyn Archer for corresponding with me, answering questions, and educating me.

Thank you to all the performers who gave me permission to use your images in this book: Legs Malone, Jo Weldon, Michelle Mynx, Katrina Dohl, Indigo Blue, Waxie Moon (Marc Kenison), Dame CuchiFrita, and Cheeky Lane, and also to the talented photographers—Stacie Joy (so much gratitude for your patience over the years), Olena Sullivan, Chris Blakeley, John Goddard, and Cheeky Lane—for generously sharing your work. I also offer profound thanks to Dustin Wax and the Burlesque Hall of Fame for the use of your materials, permission to research your archives, and Dustin's unwavering support and enthusiasm and to James Habacker of the Slipper Room for permission to use your photos. The Slipper Room was my first (and best) burlesque experience.

Thank you to the Fisher Center for the Study of Gender and Justice and to Hobart and William Smith Colleges for grant funding to support this research.

Thank you to my friends and colleagues who have read and given me serious and much-needed feedback on some part of this beast over the years: Hannah Dickinson, Star Medzerian Vanguri (special thanks for always knowing what my point is), Londie Martin, Ben Ristow, Amy Green, Amanda Wray, and Cheryl Forbes.

Perpetual thanks to Dot Vogt: without your support in all the other areas of my job, I never could have done this.

Thanks to those professionals who have made this work better: anonymous reviewers from *Present Tense* on "The Pleasures of Process"; Debra Hawhee and Lindal Buchanan, for feedback on "Deploying Delivery"; Joshua Gunn, who reviewed this manuscript and gave me crucial feedback; copyeditor Dana Henricks, for fixing my boneheaded errors; Penn State University Press senior designer Regina Starace, for your gorgeous cover; editorial assistant Alex Vose; acquisitions editor Ryan Peterson for *everything* (working with you has been a dream); and series editors Leah Ceccarelli and Michael Bernard-Donals. I so appreciate that you took a chance on an oddball.

Now the personal stuff: Thank you to my Tucson family: Veronica Davidson, Alethea Arellano, Jasmin Virgen, Daniel Virgen Jr., and Viviana Virgen. Love and miss you all, always.

Thank you to my clan: John, Niki, and Angela Werner; Katie, Tod, Justine, and Zane Pearson; and John and Donna Werner.

Thank you to my sister in spirit, Rebecca Brown, for your lifelong love and support.

Thank you most especially to my best friend, closest confidante, greatest supporter, and sister, Beth.

Finally, thank you to my home team: Sampson, Charlie (rest in peace, my soul cat), Mia, Finn, and my partner in life, Penny Hankins. Thank you for supporting me, encouraging me, and loving me. I love you, boo.

Introduction | Embodied Criticism of the Erotic Body

I was just starting my second semester of my first year of college. I had been out of the closet for five months, and I was feeling pretty good about myself, naively thinking that now I could express my sexuality freely instead of jamming it under the mattress like my secret stash of porn when I was a tween. One afternoon, like most other afternoons, I was huddled with a group of new theater friends, catching a smoke outside of Centennial East after one of our classes. A woman walked by. I gave the gaze, the up and down objectifying gaze that I had just learned about in Intro to Women's Studies. I commented on the woman in the short skirt with the long legs to my friends. One rolled her eyes and sighed. The other looked at me with a scowl and said, "God, Maggie! You're just as bad as a man!"

I recoiled.

I don't remember my response, although had I been older with a better education in radical sexual politics, I would have flipped the script and won this battle with an accusation of homophobia. What I do remember, what I remember with my whole body, is the shame I felt underneath whatever sarcastic remark I likely delivered. So much shame that I have spent a lifetime of academic work—as an undergrad, a grad student, a doctoral candidate, a job seeker, a new hire, and finally a tenured professor—explaining my looking. Defending my feminism. Justifying my (objectifying) sexual gaze.

Foundations and Excitations

When I was a young punk—well, actually, a middle-aged punk—in graduate school, I discovered both rhetorical criticism and rhetoric of the body while working on my PhD in rhetoric and composition. I had been studying and writing about queer sexuality and sex-radical feminism since I was an undergraduate, and I had also recently discovered an interest in topless dancing (viewing not performing)—a subject I will return to shortly. The combination of these interests led me to consider bodies as generators of rhetoric. Throughout graduate school, as I increasingly heard the term *rhetoric of the body*, I noticed two things. First, the topic was largely absent from scholarship on rhetorical criticism, and second, the topic was not talked about with regard to sexual behavior or embodiment or action or movement. Rhetoric of the body, at least as I was encountering it, primarily dealt with rhetoric *about* the body, about the discursive structures and contexts that shape the body in language. This lacuna—partially a result of my positioning in a discipline that pairs rhetoric with writing studies—opened up space for me in which to bring together my longtime study of sexuality with my newfound interest in criticism.

When I first began thinking about sexuality critically—and by *sexuality* I mean sexual behaviors and identities of all orientations, not just those queer ones that *sexuality* is often code for—most research was limited to anthropology, psychology, and sociology. The rhetoric of sexuality didn't exist as a field of study. So I sought out spaces containing what Jack Selzer refers to as "material, nonliterate practices and realities"—spaces that foregrounded the material communication of sexed and sexualized bodies to begin figuring out what *sexual rhetoric* can mean.[1] Thus the central questions that have motivated my work for the past thirteen years and that are the central focus of this book are How does one criticize erotic body rhetoric? and How can we theorize embodied rhetoric capaciously to include both discourse about bodies and the body's material symbolic communication as well?

When I began this work as a graduate student, I was preoccupied with defining sexual rhetoric as a subfield of rhetoric of the body, one that centralizes the sexual body as a subject of study that has the potential to rewrite our field's assumptions about logocentric rhetoric, much like disability rhetoric has done. I found myself using the phrase *sexual rhetoric*, without really knowing what that meant. Sexual rhetoric seemed to only exist as a general topic area, rather than as a subfield.

But . . .

The past decade has been good to sexual rhetoric.

Sexing Rhetoric

One publication that has led the way in carving out sexual rhetoric as a subfield of rhetorical studies is Jonathan Alexander and Jacqueline Rhodes's 2015 edited collection *Sexual Rhetorics: Methods, Identities, Publics*. Alexander and

Rhodes—reflecting the theoretical sea change in the intervening years—situate their book specifically in queer studies, rhetorical studies, and gender and sexuality studies. This collection gives form and theory and coherence to a diverse set of multi- and interdisciplinary scholarship on sexuality.

Finally, sexual rhetorics is a thing.

Sexual Rhetorics focuses on discourses of sexuality and methods for interpreting them. The editors define sexual rhetorics as "self-conscious and critical engagement with discourses of sexuality that exposes both their naturalization and their queering, their torqueing to create different or counter-discourses." This engagement "giv[es] voice and agency to multiple and complex sexual experiences."[2] In addition, the authors pursue the related goal of offering ways to engage with these experiences, presenting a set of methods for analyzing sexual rhetorics that arises from rhetorical and communication studies—namely, "case studies, theoretical questioning, ethnographies, and close (and distant) readings of 'texts' that help us think through the rhetorical force of sexuality and the sexual force of rhetoric."[3] The critical work in the book underscores the authors' claim that "any understanding of rhetorical action is necessarily hampered, if not indeed damaged, without robust attention to the sexual."[4] *Sexual Rhetorics* defines this subfield, giving it theoretical and methodological shape and making space for work like my own as both sexual rhetorics and rhetoric of the body continue to grow as vibrant areas of rhetorical studies.

While the body has always played some role in rhetoric, explicit discussions and theorizations of it became increasingly scattered as rhetorical theory split, with the embodied oral tradition going in one direction and rhetoric and writing theory going in another. For scholars in the nascent discipline of speech communication, the body was central. Debra Hawhee's review of the place of "sensuous activity" in one hundred years of the *Quarterly Journal of Speech* finds that "sensation came pre-installed as a relevant area of inquiry" with "bodily processes and movements of expression" being listed as one of the knowledge domains for researchers.[5] In the late twentieth century, however, "epistemic rhetoric and certain versions of postmodern rhetoric ... shunted sensation to the side."[6]

In addition to the importance of the body and movement to early speech researchers, some rhetoricians in the mid-twentieth century began analyzing the body rhetoric seen in the protest actions of the new social movements. However, the body as a knowledge domain or as a theory-making medium was absent in much of this work as many leading voices on body rhetoric characterized it as a passionate persuasive action that operated differently from the logical argument of the new rhetoric, which concerned itself with linguistic activity.[7]

Outside of the waxing and waning interest of rhetoricians, the twentieth century saw the emergence of the interdisciplinary field of performance studies, which drew scholars from diverse fields in both the arts and social sciences in order to analyze the body as a primary transmitter of cultural knowledge, making not just entertainment but communication and theory as well. D. Soyini Madison and Judith Hamera argue that as a "critical dynamic within human behavior and social processes," performance offers "ways of comprehending how human beings fundamentally make culture, affect power, and reinvent their ways of being in the world."[8] As a result, while the field of performance studies is interdisciplinary, scholarship of performance is largely transdisciplinary, exceeding the boundaries of disciplinary meaning making to engage human concerns.[9] Thus performance studies is, as Dwight Conquergood names it, the "borderlands terrain," transcendent of boundaries among social processes, actors, and contexts.[10] In this way, performance studies and rhetorical studies share many of the same concerns, which Conquergood persuasively articulated in 1992 when he reinvigorated rhetorical attention to performance. One of the primary ways that performance studies can (and to my mind *should*) influence rhetorical studies is in analysis of embodied rhetoric, particularly erotic rhetoric, as "pleasure has always been the bedrock of performance studies."[11]

In the past two decades, as interest in performance has grown, rhetoricians and communication scholars have shown a renewed interest in rhetoric and embodiment, retheorizing rhetoric in order to make space for a whole range of cultural practices and sites.[12] This work has raised new sets of questions and methodological concerns for the critical study of rhetorical bodies. The scholarship on rhetoric of the body is wide ranging, drawing on theories of feminism, poststructuralism, and queer theory and enacted on various artifacts: the athletic body, the protesting body, the pregnant body, the disabled body, the diseased body.[13] All of this work serves to broaden the province of rhetoric and of rhetorical criticism and also serves to add to the theoretical and methodological tools of performance.[14] Yet while rhetorical scholars have made a place for the communicating body, studying it is still not without its disciplinary and methodological challenges.

Despite renewed attention to corporeality and performance, many rhetoricians who analyze the body focus primarily on discourse, and this has been reflected in two key ways in the literature: either by subordinating gestural communication to the linguistic or by focusing primarily on the ways that the body is constructed (and variously enabled/disabled, accepted/rejected) via language. The first trend is represented by the study of protest rhetoric in the mid-twentieth century, which tended to treat body rhetoric as distinctly different from traditional rhetoric, and the second by studies of the body in the late twentieth and early twenty-first century, which were primarily focused on difference and inequality in how language constructs the body. Both trends demonstrate rhetoric's tradition as a primarily logocentric discipline in which "material moments of rhetorical action ... have largely remained beyond the reach of rhetoricians, who have traditionally (and understandably) been most attentive to oral and written discourses, narrowly conceived."[15] If the body only concerns us as it is articulated through language, then critics can employ textual methods of criticism, which many studies of rhetoric of the body do. However, relying solely on textual methods can reinforce rhetoric's logocentricity by admitting nontraditional artifacts into the realm of rhetorical study, but analyzing them with methods designed for textual artifacts and neglecting the body's kinesthetic practices and material dimensions. Though widely variable in theoretical and methodological orientations, scholarship on rhetoric of the body tends to emphasize the relationship between the material body and discourse: linguistic practices shape material realities, and material realities exert forces on linguistic practices.[16] Bodies come to "matter" (or not) through discourse; they are materialized, regulated, and controlled through language,[17] yet analysis of linguistic practices isn't always capable of (or useful in) analyzing the ways that bodies communicate through movement, clothing, modification, and adornment—symbolic codes that are central to erotic performance and many other embodied rhetorics. Because analysis of the rhetorical body is often guided by an attention to the relationship between the material and the linguistic, methods of criticizing bodies need to engage in a similar "dialectical tacking," attending to both the discursive and material body, understanding that they are neither the same, nor separate.[18] Thus if critics understand language to be only part of what gives the body rhetorical force, we are presented with both the "formidable challenge" and the "promise" of integrating primarily linguistic critical approaches with material ones.[19]

How *Does* One "Criticize" Bodies?

Current scholarship suggests that rhetoric of the body is produced by both linguistic and material practices, but most criticism has frontloaded the linguistic.

Many critics examine the ways that language constructs understanding of, possibilities for, and reactions to bodies. Such analyses highlight the ways that hegemonic discursive systems can constrain the material body's capabilities to forge arguments. Michael Butterworth demonstrates this with his analysis of Colorado University kicker Katie Hnida, whose presence on a university football team reinforced misogynistic reactions to women in spaces conceived as being for men only. The violent backlash to her playing for the CU team illustrates that "responses to Katie Hnida's transgression point to limitations for body rhetoric[:] ... embodied arguments do not always or necessarily lead to progressive outcomes."[20] Using Hnida's experiences to illustrate the interconnection between discourse and the material body, Butterworth argues, "If we are to think of the body as a vehicle for rhetorical performance, then we must come to terms with the discursive constraints that constitute bodies in public life."[21] Such constraints can be particularly limiting to the communicative potential of bodies, in particular, bodies of difference.[22]

Such bodies are also ones in which the "interconnections of language and material practices" are especially evident,[23] and increasingly, critics are also focusing on the symbolic communication of the body itself. Here analysis moves from a focus on how discourse systems render bodies to reading the body itself—its parts, movements, contours, shades—and its styling—body modifications, clothes, accessories, make-up. For example, a critic focused on these types of material symbolic elements might study fashion runway shows of the past fifteen years in order to understand what makes the bodies of Rihanna's Savage X Fenty line so newsworthy. This line, famous for its inclusion of all body types, skin tones, and genders, showcases humans dressing and moving in ways that don't minimize presence, as runway models have typically done (in order to minimize humanity and maximize the attention to the garment) and has issued a decisive argument about what has long been (mistakenly) valued in the fashion industry. While material bodily communication is often misread, as Butterworth demonstrates, or is unable to dismantle hegemonic discourse systems, it retains symbolic importance. While Rihanna and Savage X Fenty are still constrained by hegemonic racist, sexist, and transphobic discourses, they have posed a significant symbolic (and financial) challenge to them. Thus criticism of the body can illustrate the ways that the material body is embedded in—but not entirely accounted for by—discourse. Concurrent with a growing interest in the material symbolic, scholars have increasingly questioned common assumptions of rhetoric and rhetorical criticism, including the stability of text and context, upon which rhetorical criticism was built. In "cast[ing her] lot with the 'disturbers'" to traditional rhetorical criticism—criticism that was standardized by adherence to particular methodologies and a concern with providing answers—Carole Blair writes:

> From our vantage point in the early twenty-first century, rhetorical criticism of the 1970s and 1980s must appear now to have been rather staid, uniform, and predictable.... [C]ritical works varied little in terms of their general format, tone, and articulated goals. It was to be a brief period of relative uniformity and consensus. No matter which or how many labels one may prefer to describe the source(s) of critical disturbance in the late 1980s and 1990s—poststructuralism, deconstruction, critical theory, postmodernism, anti-racist theory, neo-Freudianism, post-Marxism, sexuality studies, postcolonialism, critical rhetoric, third wave feminism, ideological criticism, cultural studies, etc.—there was disruption in the ranks.... [C]riticism *has* changed noticeably in the last decade as a result of their presence and persistence."[24]

The paradigmatic shift wrought by the discursive turn had the effect, somewhat ironically, of making space for the criticism of material and bodily symbolic communication, whose subjects of study "deman[d]" new "kinds of critical analysis."[25] Thus the analysis of rhetorical artifacts has become more exploratory and inquisitive, demonstrating nuance, messiness, and even confusion, rather than arguments for a particular interpretation. Exploration is encouraged. Criticism is process, rather than product. While the criticism of bodies relies on a retheorizing of rhetorical analysis itself, it also suggests that bodies are always an integral part of rhetorical communication. Through analysis of Kenneth Burke's health and body in relation to his critical work, Debra Hawhee argues that somatic experiences always shape how we think and write and act. Hawhee writes a "body biography" of Burke demonstrating the ways that his body—most obviously when it was ailing—was inseparable from his critical and theoretical work: "Burke's letters show that he grappled with his own aging, ailing body just as much as he did with the body in theory. His letters help document an emerging theory of body-thinking, which later becomes manifest in his cloacal criticism, criticism that focuses on the otherwise repulsive underbelly of humanity: excrement, vomit, pollution."[26] Hawhee's thorough and incisive analysis of the body *in* Burke's work—a transdisciplinary approach that accounts for Burke's transdisciplinary thinking—does not rely on theories that "keep bodies tightly yoked to language."[27]

Building on the work of prior critics of the body, who have prompted retheorizing of the process of criticism, this book suggests that the theories and methods for criticizing the body that I present are productive because they take into account the complexities of embodied rhetoric, which always operates in multiple symbolic codes. Because the body in performance is "the primary site of information, transmission, and transformation,"[28] the book foregrounds specific material communication practices and proposes various complementary frameworks and theories for analyzing them. In particular, the book explores bodies, acts, and discourses of embodied erotic performance rhetoric. Each chapter takes up a different theoretical framework for approaching body criticism; the frameworks are neither distinct nor complete, and it is their partialness that I hope provides an invitation or provocation to scholars of the rhetorical body to work the spaces and contradictions presented by this partialness. In developing critical approaches, I draw on theories both of and adjacent to rhetoric. However, in theorizing them for the study of erotic bodies, I have taken an approach informed by performance studies, which is "sympathetic to the avant-garde, the marginal, the offbeat, the minoritarian, the subversive, the twisted, the queer, people of color, and the formerly colonized."[29] Dustin Bradley Goltz argues that to "approach . . . criticism from a performative frame is to take a step away from essential understandings of what something or someone *is*, and look to how something or someone is *done*."[30] This process-based approach is at the heart of performative methods, and it is vital for analyzing rhetorical bodies. Finally, a performance studies approach "centralizes the body in the heart of the analysis and study of communication."[31] Therefore, the theories and critical approaches presented in each chapter merge insights from performance and rhetorical studies to theorize possibilities for rhetorical criticism that places the corporeal body central in analysis.

The analyses that follow draw variously on rhetorical delivery, genre criticism, postmodern seduction theory, articulation theory, and alterity, in order to develop approaches for interpreting embodied erotic rhetoric and to explore some of the contested arenas of rhetorical action that construct women's sexual bodies such as neo-burlesque performance, commercial topless dancing, sex-worker activism, and feminist "sex wars."[32] These frameworks, while particularly useful to embodied rhetorical performances, are also broadly applicable to a whole range of constitutive rhetorics. I intend for the analyses to demonstrate their generative rather than restrictive aspects, as I am aware that too much attention to method can lead to reductive analyses in which critics find precisely what they were looking for because the method itself suggests that one *will find* certain sets of meaningful symbols making certain sets of arguments.[33] Therefore, readers should understand the analyses here as providing openings to discuss the rhetorical aspects of erotic performance. The findings represent one interpretation by one critic. Less than attempting to make definitive statements about these acts and their contexts, I am interested in expanding the conversations usually had about erotic performance to see them as a particular kind of embodied performance rhetoric.

In addition to the different types of theories and methods used, the analyses in this book also draw on disciplines outside of rhetoric, in particular, sexuality studies, women and gender studies, dance studies, and performance studies. These disciplines and practices are particularly useful for my analyses because they view the body—not language—as primary. Because the body communicates in multiple symbolic realms—it is not merely a textual artifact—analysis of the rhetorical body can be assisted by drawing on the wealth of information on the body that has been done in other fields, in particular, fields that study bodies in action and not only bodies in text. In addition, as a way to be attentive to actual bodies, I also draw on ethnography. Because it is a methodology that is "radically contingent . . . open, flexible, adaptable, and sensitive to situation, circumstance, and nuance,"[34] ethnography enables a researcher to study the body in a way that is open ended and open to different ways of seeing and knowing. In each chapter, I pursue the act of rhetorical criticism—an act with its origin in language—with acts outside of language that are not always perceived as rhetorical, thus I seek to broaden what is included in the rhetorical. Thus my study of erotic bodies depends on perspectives that locate those bodies not only in language but also outside of the linguistic as well. In addition, I let the acts I analyze speak back to, challenge, and revise what counts as a rhetorical approach. That is, I do not just bring a rhetorical perspective to erotic bodies; I also bring the communication styles of those bodies back to rhetoric.

Embodied Erotic and Sexual Rhetorics

Because erotic performances depend on the movement, locations, and adornment of bodies alone and in conversation with other bodies, several of the analyses in this book foreground those features as types of symbolic interaction. Thus I start from the assumptions that the material is part of the province of rhetoric and that the material has symbolic dimensions because rhetorical critics have been arguing for attention to materiality, including bodies, for more than two decades now. Carole Blair argued at the turn of the century, "It seems no longer necessary to argue for the rhetorical character of material objects"; that is even truer now.[35] Therefore, the purpose of the book is to engage with practices of rhetorical body criticism, rather than to defend that pursuit. This book also does not focus on the nonsymbolic materiality that influences rhetorical criticism and theory.[36] There has been compelling work in the past two decades in new materialisms that advances the importance of the material within rhetoric, particularly with regard to feminist new materialism. While I name and engage *the material*, the criticism here is not "materialist" per se, as that term references particular disciplinary subfields and theoretical approaches. Rather, my primary focus is on symbolic practices of the body that are constructed and deployed via codes beyond alphabetic text alone and that are consciously chosen by performers and activists (chapters 1, 2, 3) and on the ways those practices become particularly contentious when they are taken up and interpreted in new—particularly activist—contexts (chapters 4 and 5). Thus even while I focus on objects and bodies, I am specifically analyzing symbolic communication. Sometimes, as in the case of erotic dance, the conscious crafting of the performance rhetoric—choices in costuming, movement, makeup—are my central focus.[37] In the case of neo-burlesque and club stripping, these kinesthetic, sartorial, and cosmetic choices constitute a particular type of material symbolic rhetoric. In my analyses of erotic dance, both the material (which always influences symbolic meaning) and the material symbolic (those symbols chosen for specific communicative purposes) are rhetorically significant.

In addition to focusing on the particularly rhetorical features of the material symbolic codes in public erotic performances, chapters 4 and 5 also consider contexts in which those same material symbolic codes operate to forge identities, which are contested by virtue of being constructed by embodied erotic rhetoric. Thus the subjects under analysis in the book proceed from the highly performative comedic erotic performances of neo-burlesque to the work of club stripping, to the activism of sex workers, to the symbolically aligned SlutWalk protests. That is, the text proceeds from analyses of the erotic body in public performance (chapters 1, 2, 3) to analyses of the erotic body as a cultural symbol. Therefore, taken as a whole, the text engages both material and discursive constructions of erotic bodies in performance. The cultural discourses about erotic performers in chapters 4 and 5 demonstrate that the contexts in which the performances of erotic bodies are not confined to clubs and theaters. In this process, the erotic performer can be stripped of agency. By looking at the rhetoric of sex-work activists deployed through both material and linguistic codes (chapter 4) and feminists' debates about erotic bodies, in which the material symbolic constructs identities as either feminist or not (chapter 5), in addition to the performances themselves, I hope to complicate common (mis)understandings of the public erotic body and its communication practices.[38]

"You Got a Lap Dance... That's 'Data'?": Acts, Artifacts, and the Erotics of Data Collection

Because the chapters deal with various rhetorical acts and artifacts, not all data were collected in the same manner. The work on erotic dance is largely ethnographic, in particular, participant observer, while the chapters that deal with feminist debates about embodied sexual rhetoric represent the analysis of primary online sources of public media. Further, the artifacts were chosen to highlight those areas of embodied sexual rhetorics—cis and trans women's public performances and activism—that are the focus of vigorous feminist debate. The first three chapters all analyze erotic dance, including both neo-burlesque and commercial stripping. Although these two practices have the same historical antecedent and share broad genre characteristics (in particular, the removal of clothing to music), they are distinctly different erotic arts, as chapter 2 will illustrate. Because some definitional work of the two genres is integral to the analysis in those chapters, here I will just offer some broad information about the types of erotic dance, with the understanding that these are generalizations and are not intended to represent all dancers or the genres in which they perform. I also want to further note that terminology is ever changing and also ever contested.

Erotic dancing encompasses a wide range of art forms. As sexuality and dance have long been linked, it is often difficult to pin down what exactly counts as erotic dance, when so many forms of dance operate via sexualized symbolic codes.[39] Dance scholar Judith Hanna explains, "Dance and sex both use the same instrument—namely, the human body—and both involve the language of the body's orientation toward pleasure."[40] Sexualized dance takes certain material symbolic codes and enacts them in an "imaginatively stylize[d]" way on stage."[41] Thus dance performatively communicates experiences of sex and sexuality for audiences, taking codes that are typically private and personal and making them public. Therefore, even in dance forms like ballet that are now considered to be high art, there are long and entrenched associations with taboo communication. However, theatrical dance retains very little of the damaging stigma that affects commercial erotic dancing. Neo-burlesque, which moves along a continuum between the two, avoids much of the stigma of club stripping because of its theatrical stylized nature and because it is removed from the customer-worker transaction that marks a practice as sex work. In the US, where I've done my research, the art of stripping breaks down roughly into the theatrical and the commercial, although these are fluid boundaries. Commercial erotic dancing includes topless and nude dancing in clubs on stages, tables, or in direct contact with a customer. These most often take place in a club, with many dancers performing one at a time to individuals or to groups. Generally, customers tip dancers directly and dancers tip out to clubs a percentage of their total earnings. The degree of contact between customers and dancers is highly variable, depending on municipal ordinances, local mores, and owner preferences. Dancers also have some say over the amount of contact they have with customers.[42] In theatrical erotic dance, including neo-burlesque and cabaret, dancers perform on stages to audiences. Audiences pay for tickets to individual shows and performers typically don't cultivate one-on-one relationships with the audience, although some neo-burlesque shows do allow tipping to individual dancers. Because my own research includes both topless and neo-burlesque, those will be my representatives of each genre (with the ever-present refrain that these boundaries are fluid). In chapter 2, I will spend more time analyzing the dominant symbolic codes—including linguistic, kinesthetic, sartorial, and cosmetic—in each genre.

Despite the fact that my research into stripping was frequently perceived by others as not serious, rigorous, or appropriate, it was with this work that I began to seriously consider a rhetoric of the body that was more than text. In February of 2005, while working on my PhD, I began conducting ethnographic research on topless dancers. The research consisted of participation in the exchange of dances, observation in several clubs, and interviews with dancers. I initially entered a topless club out of curiosity and became a regular customer and a researcher. During the study, these roles were complex, conflated, and confusing. Ethnography, however, is a research method that relies on role conflations if the researcher is to successfully enter any environment as an outsider. Rather than interfere with the data gathering and analysis, I found that by becoming a regular at "the club," that I gained access to information that casual customers generally do not get. Though it was complicated, maintaining the roles of customer, confidante, researcher, and friend proved to be valuable to my research. By being a good customer (*hands at my sides ... unless otherwise directed*) and spending money (*a lot*) on dancers, I managed to give back something to the women who shared their stories with me. For two years, it was a stressful, confusing, and emotionally draining experience, and the "hyphenated space between participant-observer worked hard on me."[43] I used the data I collected from interviews and my experiences as a customer in two graduate research classes. In one of the more boneheaded moves I made in graduate school, I never obtained official IRB clearance for the study. As long as the data were only used in my classes and not published, I didn't need to get full approval. And I didn't. And it languishes still on tiny cassette tapes next to a tiny cassette recorder that stopped working circa 2010. While I can't quote from or directly refer to that data, I mention it now because it was a serious study. Insights that I have gained about club stripping come from that experience and from the wealth of published literature on the subject. Whenever possible, I choose scholarship written by dancers, and I bring my own experiences into the work in this book via narratives of times in the club when I wasn't acting as a researcher.

While still in graduate school and exhausted from the emotional toils of strip-club (*and other kinds of*) addiction, I changed my focus and wrote a dissertation on LGBTQ (although to be honest, there was very little T and Q) social-movement rhetoric. I hated every minute of it but was concerned about the looming job market after being told by more than one member of the field that strippers would look bad to potential employers. Once I was hired and comfortably ensconced in my new academic home where they seemed to support whatever I wanted to do, I took a breath and thought about what I wanted. The research that had been most compelling to me had been on strippers. In an incredibly unlikely twist, one of my early friendships here was with a former peepshow dancer, who happened to be part of the early burlesque revival in Seattle. This friend also just so happens to be good friends with Indigo Blue, headmistress of Seattle's Academy of Burlesque and the founder of both BurlyQ queer cabaret and BurlyCon. Talking to my friend about burlesque got me interested after an initial reluctance to take up this performative stripping. I didn't really get the appeal of neo-burlesque and found the celebration of vintage styles that seemed to me characteristic of the culture off-putting. Further, what I had found so compelling about strip clubs were the one-on-one interactions with dancers and neo-burlesque is a different animal. But with some research, it increasingly seemed like a good option for me. It presented many of the same opportunities to study embodied erotic rhetoric as club stripping, but without the emotional, physical, and financial costs. And so I became a neo-burlesque researcher, traveling as much as I could afford to, and attending as many shows as I could, publishing a couple of articles, presenting at Burly-Con and conferences in my discipline, and corresponding with performers. Thus my research on neo-burlesque has been a combination of live shows, performer interviews, online videos and pictures, and traditional textual sources. Initially, I attempted to only analyze performances I had seen. That proved to be too limiting, however, and so not all of the performers I reference or analyze in this book are ones I have seen. Performances that I have seen in person or that are available online can be found in my notes or bibliography. Live performance is ephemeral, however, and even acts that are performed repeatedly are never the same. What I find intriguing about strip clubs is the high degree of symbolic convergence among narratives of experiences both for customers and for dancers, revealing a "group consciousness, with its implied shared emotions, motives, and meanings."[44] Customers and dancers participate in fantasies that are remarkable for their unremarkability. The fact that the same scripts are repeated *ad nauseum* does nothing to diminish the experience for customers. In fact, it forms part of the appeal. Neo-burlesque acts on the other hand—although the same ones can be performed for years—forge significant parts of their symbolic meanings in the moment, rather than in the repetition. Audience members influence each other, and most performers are highly attuned to those dynamics, which can shape everything from facial expressions to the degree of interaction between audiences and performers. Acts are planned, choreographed, and practiced, but for the most part neo-burlesque has an invisible and permeable fourth wall.

Although my research into neo-burlesque has been nowhere near as intense as my research into stripping—at one point I was regularly going to clubs three to four nights a week—it has completely changed the way I think about what rhetoric of the body can mean and made me rethink some basic ideas within rhetoric, in particular, delivery and audience. As a writer, a writing teacher, and a student of rhetoric and composition, these were concepts that I understood *in theory* but were in fact removed from my actual experiences with writing in which I sat in a room and typed and then someone sat in a different room and read. This act of telepathy, as Stephen King calls it, of a writer transmitting to a reader removed in time and space, is powerful.[45] The metaphor of telepathy, situated in the brains of writers and readers is not applicable to communication with the body, however, because live performance collapses the space between writers and readers. Thus it ties both to rhetoric's history of orality and to rhetoric's present/future with new media texts that similarly revise traditional considerations of reader-writer-text configurations.

Drawing on my research of erotic dance over the past fifteen years, the first three chapters of this book analyze performance directly, and thus the writing is more explicitly personal than in the final two chapters. As a member of the audience and customer, my analyses necessarily engage my role as a participant in the exchange. To that end, particularly in chapter 2, I'm explicitly focused on audience roles in relation to and as themselves, performing bodies. This means that the body under discussion is sometimes my own. Thus my writing bumps up against (and sometimes explicitly enters into) autoethnography. Certainly, the ways that I have collected and processed data have drawn on ethnographic methods, and much of the literature that I have drawn on in my research of neo-burlesque and club stripping is ethnographic or autoethnographic. Observers of erotic performance are almost certainly included in the audience by the act of attending the club or performance and so placed into that role. Participation is a fundamental part of a performance studies' methodology because it is a field in which the "mode of inquiry demands physical sensuous involvement in a performance event. The methodology depends upon personal responsiveness, somatic engagement, and cognitive analysis. Performance studies mandates a methodology of participation."[46] Like sociologist and strip-club researchers Kassia Wosick-Corea and Lauren Joseph, my analysis of strip clubs depends on my "active participation as [a customer] in the club's activities."[47] Also like them, being a woman customer in particular shapes my findings in particular ways. Unlike Wosick-Corea and Joseph, I was never in a club masquerading as a "typical" woman customer. I openly discussed my research and also *was* a typical customer in that I went to strip clubs for many reasons that had nothing to do with scholarship. In this way, my work in chapter 2 has more in common with the autoethnographic scholarship written by dancers than with researchers who are only in the club for their own scholarship. Further, much of the work on stripping in the "post-deviance era" of sociology and anthropology is written by performers themselves.[48] Thus autoethnography is often a fundamental part of the research on erotic performance.

Because of its refusal of objectivity, autoethnography has held a contested place in the social sciences, whose researchers have typically valued a distanced stance. In his frustrating and incredibly snarky critique of autoethnography, Donald Shields uses Ernest Bormann's symbolic convergence theory to demonstrate the ways that autoethnography forecloses on the possibility of critical authority by eschewing authority in the first place: "If one assumes there is no objective truth, then the presentation of the lived experience is only a fiction to be compared to other fictions."[49] Autoethnographers, then, create a symbolic reality in which new work adds to a shared vision of reality and reinforces genre characteristics (the confessional tone, the defensive posture, the generalizing based on one's experience in the name of social justice) thus "merely reflect[ing] the style specific rhetorical vision on which the story is based" and "masquerade[ing] fiction as fact."[50] Inspired by Shield's dismissal, but with a different set of concerns (the aesthetic, rather than epistemic value of autoethnography), Craig Gingrich-Philbrook argues that "however much one applauds autoethnography's artistic and social intentions, those intentions do not in themselves secure artistic results."[51] Pointing out that the "signifier sine qua non of autoethnography is simply italics," Gingrich-Philbrook critiques the ways that autoethnographies often claim artistic value while neglecting artistic visions and desperately wanting "Daddy's approval" as a legitimate and appropriately rigorous method.[52] I've tried to take a cue from Gingrich-Philbrook in this book and have attempted to avoid "justify[ing] the presence of the self in writing to the patriarchal council of self-satisfied social scientists."[53] I agree that it's not worth it. At the same time, I do want to acknowledge that researcher participation is a fundamental part of erotic dance scholarship.

Ethnography and autoethnography are by necessity primary methods of dancer research both in neo-burlesque and club stripping.[54] While one can use a variety of methods to analyze data, a researcher can't observe performance without being either performer or audience member. While my body finds itself in this text in a number of places, the work is not strictly autoethnography, as it isn't myself that I'm analyzing; the self (mostly) serves as illustration of the rhetorical processes that I am observing, rather than as the subject of a systematic analysis of my personal experience that is the aim of autoethnography.[55] What readers will find throughout this book standing in as artifacts of performance and as illustrations are what Carolyn Ellis, Tony Adams, and Arthur Bochner, drawing on Barbara Tedlock,[56] term "narrative ethnography[:] ... stories that incorporate the ethnographer's experiences into the ethnographic descriptions and analysis of others."[57] In narrative ethnography, "the emphasis is on the ethnographic study of others, which is accomplished partly by attending to encounters between the narrator and members of the groups being studied."[58] Because audience members are both observers to shows and participants in them—particularly in erotic performance that engages the audience in intimate and direct ways—there is very little space from which to write that is *not* an intersection of the personal with the analytical. Performance studies' scholars Lynn Miller and Jacqueline Taylor argue that it is this intersection that grants the personal narrative authority, gaining "a measure of authenticity from its very subjectivity: writer/performers draw upon the particularity of their own lives."[59] Therefore, in the chapters in which I analyze performance directly, such encounters both account for my participation and illustrate spaces for erotic performance with which many readers may not be familiar.

The approaches, both to my research and to my analysis, are often what Heather Lee Branstetter describes as "promiscuous," in that they are often "performative, playful, and mischievous."[60] Branstetter argues that analyses of sexual rhetorics benefit from embracing promiscuity by "being so slutty" and "sleeping around with all the other disciplines,"[61] because it enables scholars to "challenge our complacent acceptance of what 'proper' scholarship *feels* like, looks like, acts like." It is "not limited to higher education echo chambers for the purposes of reproduction."[62] Branstetter's theory of promiscuous research is particularly necessary in understanding that the material symbolic codes in this book are often not just transdisciplinary but extradisciplinary as well. They make meaning and communicate outside of the confines of the academy. It is a central thrust of this book that the performers I study are teaching *me*, expanding *my* often-limited understandings of the body.

Things to Remember Not to Forget

Regardless of the theory and critical approach under consideration, regardless of the data sets, studying bodies requires that critics negotiate between the generalizing that criticism requires and the knowledge that people have profoundly different somatic experiences, which can and should unsettle any act of critical analysis. Bodily diversity—including diversity of experience, as well as the discriminatory and often violent attitudes and actions that surround that diversity—makes talk of method almost moot. Thus even within a particular category of embodied rhetoric, generalizing can reinscribe hierarchies in ways that have serious material consequences for people. At the same time, rhetorical analysis of the body can be a powerful tool for social justice, often revealing the difference between debate and discrimination. For example, the analysis of feminist discourse surrounding sex work isn't important because it reveals disagreements about the embodied identities of sex workers. That disagreement is obvious. What is important is that it reveals a rhetoric of existential denial that is particularly brutal for sex workers and even more particularly brutal for trans women who perform sex work, who are erased both as women and as workers. When trans people's bodies are denied existence, we are not witnessing argument; we are witnessing elimination. By engaging in body criticism, we can insist on existence.

Feminism and the Erotic Body

It is an extended claim of this book that analyzing embodied sexual and erotic rhetorics is a feminist project because feminism foregrounds critical analyses of sex and gender in order to challenge inequality by making visible those matrices of patriarchal hegemony that structure humanity. This is not to say that all discussions of the body are *de facto* feminist. They aren't. But feminist analysis of the body also need not engage in the same set of arguments over and over again. Since the late 1970s, feminists have been engaging in "the sex wars," in which we vigorously clash over opposing ideologies about what are appropriate practices and attitudes about sexuality. In the '80s, these battles were commonly fought over S&M and pornography. Today, the same arguments are found regarding neo-burlesque, around social activism that promotes sexual liberation (à la Slut-Walk), and about sex work in particular—namely, whether sexual commerce *exists* as a job or whether it is slavery. In many cases, these opposing ideologies in the sex wars manifest as discourses of oppression versus discourses of liberation. These discourses are so ingrained and so pervasive that they can appear to be the only available conversations to have, yet they are not, and feminist scholars risk talking in circles if these are seen as the only available positions to take with regard to feminism and sexuality. Further, pro-con discourses such as those frequently found in public discourse about feminist sexuality are rarely useful analytical lenses as they restrict the critic's available classification options.

Therefore, it is my hope that analyses in this book disrupt oppressive/empowering as the sole (or even as an enlightening) critical standard for analyzing erotic performance. If critics are invested in the idea of criticism as conversation (vis-à-vis Ott and Dickinson), the oppressive/empowering dyad is practically useless, as it negates the possibility of conversation. Much like the pro-life/pro-choice dyad, *oppressive* and *empowering* are terms that are unanswerable to each other. The ideological disagreement between pro-life—a position resting on a claim of when life begins—and pro-choice—a position invested in the notion of women's bodily autonomy—is one that is "not in stasis; its participants do not agree on the point about which they disagree, and hence two different and incompatible arguments are being mounted."[63] Similarly, discourses that claim that certain sexual practices and attitudes are inherently oppressive make an argument about the connection between individual people's actions and structural inequality, while those that focus on these same practices as empowering focus on the individual's personal enrichment. When placed side by side, it is clear that both of these states can exist simultaneously. Jo Weldon argues, particularly with regard to neo-burlesque, that it is a moot point to try to make close-ended claims about whether burlesque is feminist or not. Some performances and performers are and some are not. Further, *empowering* is a personal emotional feeling. It is difficult to argue that something is *not* empowering, if one feels empowered.[64] Claire Nally explores this dynamic in depth, coming to the conclusion that "the very diversity of performances (straight, queer, 'vintage,' 'fetish') throughout the country, and indeed the world, as well as the complexity of audience demographics and responses, suggest that any simplistic readings of empowerment *or* patriarchal domination should be withheld."[65] Although it doesn't rely on the same oppressive/empowering dynamic, the conflict over sexual commerce—sex work / sex trafficking—has similar barriers that prevent disagreement from proceeding in a rational manner that leads to one position "winning." Like most culture war arguments, these positions have tenacious bonds that resist reasoned argument, demonstrating Crowley's claim that "ideology, fantasy, and emotion are primary motivators of belief and action."[66] The embodied sexual and erotic rhetorics that are the focus of this book rely very little on reason and argument and very much on emotion and suggestion. As a feminist critic, I seek to uncover the ways that bodies act not only as generators of rhetorical belief but also as transmitters of it. Therefore, the question "Is _____ (*neo-burlesque / stripping / sex work / SlutWalk*) feminist?" is not one with which I will engage directly. Instead my focus will be on those symbolic vectors that carry meaning about cis and trans women's sexual and erotic bodies, assuming that to listen to and understand the various ways that such meaning is transmitted is necessary to challenge the dominance of heterocispatriarchal systems of violence.

Because I don't make arguments about whether or not the erotic rhetorics I study are feminist, I have gotten a lot of push back (*a lot*) when I haven't situated my work explicitly within a feminist conversation, so I am going to spend a little bit of time here to address my work's feminist attributes, in order to explicate my standpoint. I identify as a feminist, and I consider my work to be a feminist project because my primary concerns are with cis and trans women's erotic/eroticized/sexualized bodies. I make those bodies and experiences primary in my work because I want to broaden the conversations that rhetoricians have about all women's bodies. For me that means dealing with erotic and sexual bodies in ways that move beyond arguments about how feminist a job as a sex worker or an erotic performance is or can ever be, and that move beyond the impressive/empowering dyad that stymies conversations about women's sexuality. I want to be very clear (and I still expect push back) that these conversations are important and they *should* be had and they *are* being had and they *will* be examined in this book; however, I will often participate in conversations outside of feminism, too. Therefore, while theoretical debates about the relationship between discourse and materiality in relation to the body and about feminist responses to public and commercialized displays of women's sexual bodies inform the analytical work in this manuscript, it is not the intent of the project to take a position in those debates. Rather, I seek to show how rhetorical analysis of erotic performance can broaden the terms of these arguments by moving beyond matter/discourse and oppressive/empowering binaries.

I hope feminists will find much to value in looking at the sites that I analyze here, but the theoretical and critical framings—delivery, genre, seduction, articulation, and alterity—are not in and of themselves feminist, although I hope to be applying them in feminist ways. At the core of this work is the idea that cis and trans women's bodies, in particular, their *sexual* bodies, are simultaneously reviled and desired, exalted and annihilated, made subject and object. And while this statement generalizes about women's bodies, biases against gender, race, and class (among a host of other embodied differences) make it so these tensions affect women in different—often devastatingly different—ways.

Race, Racism, and the Erotic Body

As good feminist work points out, there is not a universal *women's* experience in relation to any issue and particularly with regard to sexual and erotic rhetoric. Neither is there a universal *woman-of-color* experience, except to say that white women's matrix of privileges often result in a centering of white, middle-class cis women as representative of all women's experiences. Therefore, critics of embodied erotic rhetorics should be mindful that race and gender can never be pulled out and set aside. It is always what you're dealing with. That is, conversations of sexual bodies are always also conversations about race and racism. Further, as E. Patrick Johnson argues with regard to blackness in particular, race is in itself a critical lens for analyzing performance, offering "a way to rethink performance theory by forcing it to ground itself in praxis, especially within the context of a white supremacist, patriarchal, capitalist, homophobic society."[67] With regard to the bodies covered in this book, this is especially salient, as "the body is a primary, if not *the* primary, carrier of racial meanings."[68] The twin problematics of whiteness and cultural appropriation have tainted burlesque as an erotic art form in both its classic and neo forms. And for sex workers of color, the dehumanizing effects of racism create an always-available rhetoric enacted in violence against women of color. For black women, the legacy of chattel slavery, Jim Crow, and persistent, unabating racism make the identity of *sex worker* even more precarious, more of an impossibility, than for white women. Asian / Asian American / Pan-Asian women face and fight stereotypes of sexual exoticism, and all women of color share a greater degree of the supposed sexual availability that marks all cis and trans women's bodies. In neo-burlesque, a primarily white performance art, white performers consistently engage in acts of cultural appropriation, despite the fact that this tendency and the damage it causes have been repeatedly discussed by performers of color. Thus for critics of the body, even while the material rhetorics of costuming, cosmetics, and movement do not explicitly signify race, they are always *racialized*.

Entwined with race is gender, and here I specifically mean *who* is included in the category *woman*. Trans women *are* women. This is a point on which I am unwilling to debate, because the idea of debating trans people's existence is repugnant and profoundly antifeminist. However, most of the bodies represented in this book are those of cis women. Although neo-burlesque theoretically welcomes bodily diversity, the genre is still mostly a cis woman's art form.

Most strip clubs are fairly restrictive in terms of bodily diversity, reinforcing a particularly narrow vision of cis-masculine desire. In this vision, women's bodies can and should be modified and sculpted into an exaggerated feminine form. That reshaping doesn't include trans women, however, because clubs also tend to be profoundly transphobic and homophobic spaces, where trans women are seen as threats to cis-male heterosexuality. Therefore, many trans women find themselves unwelcome in strip clubs in the US yet are widely represented in other forms of sex work. Trans women do strip, however, working as cam girls, in some clubs, or as part of other sex work; they are just underrepresented in the venues under analysis in this book.

Race and gender are thus inexorably intertwined within embodied rhetorics. Both are shaped by a combination of material and symbolic codes, and both are dependent on the other. Kelly Happe suggests that rhetorical critics of race benefit from a performative lens because performativity "reorients critical inquiry from the determination of the truth or falsity of claims . . . to an analysis of the effects of discursive practices" materialized in linguistic utterances.[69] Further Happe argues that critiques of race cannot be separated from critiques of sex: "A performative analysis of race benefits from—indeed it requires—an examination of an already-existing bodily attribute—sex—and how the interaction of the two enable race's seemingly endless reinvention and recuperation in the face of spirited and reasonable arguments that it has no place in scientific or political thought. To understand race, I argue, we must understand the somatic conditions of its emergence, conditions which include sexual difference."[70] To Happe's argument, I will add that the linguistic is only one of the symbolic realms through which race and gender are materialized, as the analyses in this book will demonstrate. However, the thrust of Happe's argument is necessary to the subject of embodied sexual and erotic rhetoric, which similarly reveal the interdependence of race and gender in identity performance.

Begin the Begin

Via analyses of various acts and artifacts of embodied sexual and erotic rhetoric, I argue that rhetorical approaches to embodiment would benefit from increased attention to the ways that bodies communicate in symbolic realms other than or alongside the linguistic. Each chapter foregrounds material communication practices of performing bodies and proposes various complementary frameworks and theories for analyzing them. In particular, the analyses focus on the bodies, acts, and discourses of embodied erotic and sexual rhetorics. The sites of analysis include different contested sites of women's public sexuality including neo-burlesque performance, commercial topless dancing, sex-worker activism, and the feminist sex wars. The analyses draw variously on rhetorical delivery, genre criticism, seduction theory, articulation theory, and rhetorics of alterity in order to develop approaches for interpreting embodied rhetoric and to explore some of the cultural practices that construct cis and trans women's sexual bodies. As the analyses demonstrate, the purpose of criticism of the body is not to argue for fixed and closed answers to such questions by narrowing in on an argument for definitive meaning. Rather, criticism reveals the mechanisms through which meaning gets carried and the contexts that lead audiences to a variety of meanings for the communicating bodies they observe.

I start the book by arguing that the rhetorical canon of delivery (one of five traditional parts of the rhetorical art) offers critics of the body a method for analyzing bodily performance. Theorists of delivery, including the classical teachers who first formalized and popularized delivery as a rhetorical concern, have focused on different *topoi* of the canon, which can be used as focal points for critique of performances. The chapter, therefore, details a set of *topoi* particularly useful for systematically analyzing erotic performance: body, space, audience, and genre. I demonstrate the analytical dimensions of these *topoi* via analyses of neo-burlesque performances and artists. In subsequent chapters, I continue to explore the interrelations of these *topoi* through various lenses for analyzing embodied rhetoric. Chapter 2 focuses on the genre *topos* via generic criticism to illustrate the ways that a rhetorical approach to erotic performance reveals genre-specific social actions, and also illustrates the audience interaction *topos*, and the space *topos* as these are key distinctions between the genres of topless dancing and neo-burlesque. Chapter 3 also engages with the audience and genre *topoi* by using analyses of neo-burlesque to illustrate the qualities of seductive rhetoric as a process of symbolic exchange that centralizes pleasure and play and indeterminacy, common features of embodied erotic performance. Although Jean Baudrillard argues that the seductive is not the same as the sexual,[71] seduction's focus on the relationships between speaker and audience and in the delays of gratification that are often the hallmark of embodied erotic rhetoric give it theoretical and methodological significance for performative rhetorics.

Then, moving to the erotic body as cultural symbol, chapters 4 and 5 focus on feminist debates about sex and sexuality and identity, expanding on the identity work embedded in the body *topos*. The analyses also engage the space *topos* because the chapter considers material symbols common to erotic rhetoric in political spaces. Chapter 4 uses the theory and method of articulation to examine the activism of sex workers, in particular, strippers. Sex-worker activists use embodied counter-stories, through their actions as protesters, to reframe their identities in contravention of entrenched understandings of them as victims and criminals. This chapter looks at these larger struggles around sex-worker identity through an analysis of stripper activism in New Orleans in early 2018. Chapter 5 focuses primarily on the audience and body *topoi* by analyzing debates about SlutWalk as an oppressive and demeaning rather than empowering event, one whose rhetoric of sexual freedom, which relies on the embodied and material symbols of erotic performance, is one for privileged white women only. Newer instantiations of SlutWalk, however, draw large numbers of women of color and queer people, challenging not only rape-culture logic but also the critiques of the original SlutWalk by their presence. The arguments and counterarguments around the sexual/sexualized body are typical of the sex wars at large: ones that rely on insider/outsider (identity/alterity) strategies.

By exploring these sites of sexuality, of bodily rhetoric, of public arguments about what can and should be seen and by whom and to whose benefit, rhetoricians, particularly those invested in the material, can have access to communications that are often seen to be outside of the rhetorical. Similarly, not only can erotic performance complicate and enrich the study of rhetoric; a rhetorical approach to the study of erotic performance brings a perspective that requires attention to the interplay among people, practices, and contexts. When the private is made public and the body is the maker of messages, rhetoric's potential to decode a range of human symbolic actions, not just those residing in alphabetic text, can be expanded.

1

Deploying Delivery as Critical Method | Neo-Burlesque's Embodied Rhetoric

In late September 2013, the weather in New York City was mild. But in a cramped theater on Coney Island, where none of the sea air reaches, the bodies and humidity were suffocating.[1] *Despite my discomfort, I was happy to have a good view of the stage from the backless wooden bench that was wrecking my middle-aged body. Slouch, straighten, wiggle. Repeat. Check the time. Check it again. Try to avoid making eye contact. I've found that audiences at neo-burlesque shows, even in New York City, are unfailingly chatty and chipper, so no matter how much I sigh and scowl, I inevitably end up making small talk with the person next to me. This night, hoping to limit that awkwardness, I had strategically placed myself on the aisle. The woman on my unprotected left side was a talkative amateur photographer; we sat companionably despite our differences. Neo-burlesque tends to attract—to make—good-natured audiences. Watching is a communal experience, and good audiences create even better shows, and this was a good audience. We were a good audience.*

Midway through the lineup as the next performer was announced, the woman next to me and I said, "Legs!" in unison: she with camera at the ready; I with a quick slouch, straighten, wiggle. Legs Malone, The Girl with the Thirty-Four-and-a-Half-Inch Inseam, entered the stage—a space that is either bigger than it appears or appears bigger than it is—in a sleeveless black gown with a red feather boa, accompanied by the sounds of mid-century big band. Legs slinked across the stage with an array of classic burlesque moves—shimmying her hips and bumping her pelvis in time to the whomps and bweets of the brass. She held her face in the mask of ecstasy common to classic burlesque, eyes and mouth both partially open and both smiling. Her bare arms directed audience focus, twitching her boa, caressing her shoulder, extending over her head, and lengthening her frame. After a minute of such vamping, Legs turned away from the audience and reached for the zipper on the back of her gown—a move that usually leads to the reveal of the body, the withdrawal of the performer, and the end of a burlesque performance.

Instead, the music, the performer, and the performance changed.

1A–1B | Legs Malone transforms, February 26, 2012. *!BadAss! Burlesque Black & White Party*. Photos by Stacie Joy. Used with permission.

    Legs stopped all reminiscences of classic burlesque and started anew from a thong and pasties, redressing in shiny black fetish wear. Gone were the sartorial and kinesthetic symbols of mid-century erotic dance, as she refashioned herself into another mid-century vision—neo-burlesque icon Bettie Page—all while accompanied by mildly industrial music, the heavy bass line now provided by keyboards and electric bass, instead of trombone and tuba.[2] Legs did not smile now, and her movements, light and quick in the first part, became executed with sharp, heavy precision in the second. There were no words, yet the performance communicated. It communicated to me and to the smiling, cheering audience.[3]

Since 2012, I've researched embodied communication in neo-burlesque, a genre of comedic, erotic, carnivalesque performance. I've attended shows, taken classes, interviewed performers, explored the archives at the Burlesque Hall of Fame, attended festivals, and presented at the international convention BurlyCon. Through these experiences, I've found that as embodied performance, neo-burlesque provides a site of varied symbolic communication, illustrating the ways that theatrical performance "encourage[s] us to observe bodies as rhetorical generators of belief." And while theatrical performance can "teach audiences about the mutability of language *about* bodies,"[4] so too can live performance teach audiences about the language *of* bodies, as I will illustrate in this chapter using rhetorical theories of communicative delivery as a method of body criticism. Delivery is the part (or canon) of rhetoric that concerns the performance of rhetorical messages and thus focuses critical attention on the ways that performative arts like burlesque, which feature the body as spectacle, enrich the study of embodied rhetoric by foregrounding multiple modes of symbolic communication.

Bodily arts demonstrate how rhetoric functions as "a muscle craft (a kinesthetic *dēmiourgos* or *myōtechnē*) of self-fashioning and of self-presentation."[5] Performances like Legs Malone's Bettie Page tribute act illustrate inventive ways that bodies communicate symbolically through cosmetic and sartorial styling and through kinesthetic practices—bodies moving with objects, bodies moving alone, bodies moving with other bodies, bodies not moving or moving in innovative ways. In revising delivery to account for such "rhetorical action" as an important "symbolic form," James Fredal argues that "action constructs meaning not by stringing gestures together but through bodily skill . . . [relying] on the simultaneous coordination of nonverbal, visual, auditory, kinesthetic, tactile, and proprioceptive skills."[6] As a site of such material symbolic forms, neo-burlesque provides an intriguing subject for study of the body, one that illustrates the overlap of rhetoric and performance studies. Because performance "attends to the spatialized dimensions of communication"[7] and neo-burlesque uses material symbols, in particular, movement and costume and space, to communicate with audiences, it is a site in which the rhetorical aspects of performance are apparent. In neo-burlesque, nonlinguistic elements function rhetorically, "open[ing] space for reciprocal dialogue" between rhetoric and performance. Enacting this dialogue requires that "performative and rhetorical vocabularies and perspectives work with and through one another, melding and complementing" each other.[8] While performance offers its own "critical interpretive tool and lens"[9] to the analysis of discourse, so too can rhetoric offer methods of interpretation to performance, thus enriching understanding of what Vershawn Young (inspired by Norman Denzin) calls "Performance Rhetoric," a subfield of both rhetoric and performance studies.[10] Delivery, with its focus on presentation, offers a rhetorical framework for understanding the ways that performing bodies communicate in multiple symbolic codes.[11] Therefore, it offers another way to instantiate the notion of "performance as method."[12]

Theories and training in performance are part of rhetoric's classical origins. Aristotle, though he saw delivery as "equated with the art of acting" and so "somewhat beneath the dignity of philosophical inquiry,"[13] still recognized that performance had the capacity to persuade and instruct when logic alone could not. Classical delivery primarily focused on masculine voice and gesture as persuasive tools, but contemporary feminist rhetoricians have retheorized it to include women's bodies and other bodies neglected in classical rhetoric. Therefore, they have broadened delivery to account for the contextualizing effects of material space and social configuration.[14] This "regendering" of delivery allows it to address "far more than the speaker's manipulation of voice and body on a public platform," viewing "rhetorical performance as the moment when dominant cultural values are enacted and, sometimes, are resisted and revised."[15] Given this attention to the intersections of the material and the linguistic in socially situated acts, a rhetorical approach to delivery functions as a powerful interpretive device for live performance. Neo-burlesque—a type of erotic dance performed primarily by women to audiences largely comprising women and using symbolic codes that are articulated with patriarchal definitions of sexualized femininity including garters, heels, bustiers, and the exposed body as spectacle[16]—illustrates the affordances of delivery for analyzing rhetoric of the body.[17] Delivery offers critics a method for examining the performative interplay of those symbolic codes—which are read variously as either empowering or oppressive by feminist scholars, performers, and fans—providing critical tools to analyze the ways that performances are constructed in terms of body, space, audience, and genre.

Delivery and Rhetorical Bodies

Rhetorical approaches to bodies often focus on the linguistic codes that structure and give meaning to them. This focus is a crucial part of analyzing rhetoric of the body; because bodies come to "matter" (or not) through discourse, they are materialized, regulated, and controlled through language.[18] Yet focusing on linguistic symbols alone risks "dislocating the corporeal body from the voice it produces."[19] Attending only to the linguistic when analyzing bodies risks reinforcing rhetoric's logocentricity by excluding its means of material communication and limiting what rhetoric of the body can include.[20]

Methods of criticism for the body yield complex information about communication when they include an expansive view of the symbolic that places the body's materiality alongside its linguistic practices.[21] Delivery can accomplish this because it foregrounds the "body and all its symbolic resources," accounting for a range of material symbolic actions.[22] While some recent work in rhetoric and new materialism seeks to move beyond the humanist slant that views the material as "subsumed in a rhetoric of language and attendant symbol systems,"[23] my focus on delivery and embodied rhetoric *is* consciously humanistic, invested in uncovering the ways that people use material objects symbolically, rather than in understanding how persuasion manifests in nonhuman networks. This focus is not intended to supplant theories of nonsymbolic materiality; rather it reflects the communicating human bodies that I research. That is, my aim is to highlight nonlinguistic resources of symbolic communication used intentionally by people in performance.

Classical theorists and teachers of rhetoric recognized the power of delivery to engage audiences with dynamic presentations crafted through material means (gestures, clothes, posture) as well as through language. In the first century BC, the Roman philosopher and orator Cicero expanded on Aristotle's work in order to further theorize the speech-making process as composed of five parts—or canons: invention, arrangement, style, memory, and delivery. Delivery, the fifth canon—vulgar but useful in Greek rhetorical theory—was recognized as central to the success of Roman rhetorical performance. Because rhetoric was primarily an oral art, expert command of the voice—*pronuntiatio*—and the body (including its appearance)—*actio*—were crucial for an orator to communicate powerfully and persuasively to an audience.

Thus cultivating skill in delivery was necessary for a range of performers, including orators, actors, and poets, all speakers who sought to move audiences with physical presentations of their language.[24] With its focus on the persuasive manliness of the male citizen subject, however, classical conceptions of delivery "suffe[r] from a number of blind spots," which contemporary rhetorical theory has sought to correct.[25] Feminist rhetoricians Roxanne Mountford and Lindal Buchanan have each broadened delivery's scope considerably beyond the ideal masculinity of the classical rhetor, but the body is still central to the canon as a vehicle for both composing and presenting symbolic messages.

Feminist recoveries of delivery situate the communicating body in space and context, prompting critics to ask who is authorized to speak, where, and in what ways. Mountford argues that delivery "involves space, the body, and the place of both in the social imaginary."[26] Through theorizing "rhetorical space" as a physical as well as conceptual phenomenon, Mountford aligns delivery with the "materiality of rhetorical performance" as in the classical tradition, but she expands the canon by critiquing the ways that space acts on and is acted upon by the gendered body in rhetorical performances.[27] Similarly, as part of her regendering of delivery, Lindal Buchanan provides a model for analyzing how space shapes rhetorical messages in conversation with the rhetor's body, audience, and social forces. Buchanan's regendered delivery not only considers those performances that classical rhetoric would not, but it also provides a lens through which to see the rhetoricity of performances, like neo-burlesque, that are not strictly "rhetoric" but that share "key aspects" with it as "audience-centered social acts."[28] Delivery reflects the social dynamics of situations in which audiences and rhetors cocreate "rhetorical presentations . . . simultaneously as an embodiment of and response to the surrounding social milieu."[29] As a production cocreated with audiences, delivery "enacts invention."[30] Therefore, delivery is not just what affects audiences *after* the creation of a text; delivery also "may mean the beginning of new work and even the motive to produce it," linking rhetorical acts and affecting multiple audiences across time and place.[31] With regard to the embodied rhetoric of neo-burlesque, audiences are directly constitutive of performance; many performers build interaction with audience members into their acts, break the fourth wall, and improvise movements based on audience feedback. Perhaps counterintuitively considering the contested nature of erotic performance, feminist theorizations of delivery can be compellingly applied to neo-burlesque, which are delivered to and shaped by the immediate audiences who view them, the performers who create them, and the social contexts surrounding them.

Erotic dance is enmeshed in a complex of social discourses about women and the sexualized, public display of their bodies. Subsequently, critical attention to neo-burlesque has almost exclusively focused on its sexual and gender politics. Often these conversations, both popular and scholarly, take up the same commonplace: whether women can claim agency and liberation via practices like neo-burlesque that centralize their erotic bodies or if they are harmful manifestations of "raunch culture" in which women willingly "self-objectify" by perpetuating patriarchal oppression.[32] Delivery as a critical methodology offers a way to enrich these conversations, to put erotic performances in the context of these debates, but not to restrict them to an oppressive-empowering dyad that can lead to circular arguments. By focusing on particular common topics (*koinoi topoi*) that feminist theories of delivery highlight—bodies that perform, the spaces they perform in, the ways they perform, the audiences that view them—critics have access to a wider vocabulary that can offer new perspectives to old debates.

Enter Burlesque—An Overture

Despite the fact that bodily arts like burlesque are instructive about communicating with and through the body, rhetoricians have paid little attention to the areas that contemporary burlesque relates most to—eroticism, women's bodies, and humor—focusing instead on burlesque's older legacy as a literary or musical genre containing mockery, caricature, and grotesque imitation, often of high art and serious cultural values. Most contemporary rhetorical scholarship on the burlesque draws on Burke's classification of it as a symbolic poetic category that operates through frames of rejection and focuses on "externals of behavior," which convert manner into mannerism.[33] While Burke identifies the burlesque as a superficial category that we have been "plagued"[34] with, a small number of rhetoricians claim it as a powerful mechanism that "mediat[es] tragedy and comedy."[35] Expanding on Burke's classification of the burlesque as a *frame of rejection*, these scholars theorize it as a category that troubles power and authority.[36] Thus contemporary work on rhetoric and the burlesque acknowledges its tradition as a popular form of low cultural comedy that often mocks those in power, but it neglects the spectacle of women's erotic bodies that has been central to the genre for almost 150 years. In a spectacular reversal, burlesque—always associated with common people—is now invoked by rhetorical scholars in ways that differ dramatically from common understandings of the term.

Since the mid-1800s burlesque has included, and is now almost inseparable from, the display of women's bodies and sexually suggestive humor. In the US, burlesque as a theatrical spectacle became popular in the late 1860s with the arrival of Lydia Thompson and her British Blondes, a London-based troupe who lampooned dramatic stories using popular music, double entendre, and dancing (fig. 2). Women in burlesque broke social mores not only by dancing in front of audiences but also by playing men's roles, which offered occasions to dress, sing, and dance in ways that were taboo for women. These new opportunities for women's bodies on stage allowed performers to develop novel and

2 | Lydia Thompson, 1890. Published by Ohio State University. Jerome Lawrence and Robert E. Lee Theatre Research Institute.

risqué personas that had them wearing pants and acting with blunt confidence by performing masculine heroics.[37] But theatrical burlesque did not last long, and as the art's delivery changed over the next 150 years, so did the genre.

Burlesque has never developed in a neat direction during any time period. Its history is mixed in with other late nineteenth- and early twentieth-century genres of popular variety shows, in particular, vaudeville. In the early twentieth century, vaudeville and burlesque sharply diverged, with vaudeville increasingly becoming the cleaner version of variety acts appealing to middle-class, family-friendly values.[38] In his cultural history of burlesque, Robert Allen disarticulates burlesque from vaudeville, showing how the two forms of variety shows (though "often confused" today) have "underlying principles [that] were as different as night and day." Allen explains: "Whether the impertinent impersonations of masculinity in Thompsonian burlesque, or the overlaying of gender difference on racial otherness in the female minstrels, or the later running battles with municipal authorities over its sexual transgressiveness, burlesque was all the things vaudeville wanted no part of. Burlesque was structured around the body of the burlesque performer, its size and display foregrounding sexual difference and marking it as the body of the low other. Without the performer's body, there was no burlesque."[39]

As burlesque evolved in the twentieth century, focus on performer's bodies and on sexual titillation increased. Women undressing became central, replacing the theatrical narratives of the previous century. This era, commonly considered to be "classic" burlesque, is represented by the work of well-known legends like Gypsy Rose Lee, Sally Rand, and Lili St. Cyr, and also lesser known but significant performers such as Dixie Evans (fig. 3), Toni Elling, Lottie "The Body" Graves, Tempest Storm, Carrie Finnell (she of the "educated bosom"), and Ann Corio to name but a few. During this time, burlesque became synonymous with striptease. The gender inversion that was seen in late nineteenth-century Thompsonian burlesque was largely replaced by a type of "drag" in which women exaggerated femininity and centralized erotic displays. Humor and parody, however, were not lost. Consider the delivery of Dixie Evans's iconic casting-couch routine, in which Evans—the "Marilyn Monroe of Burlesque"—does a striptease in what looks like a movie producer's office. Evans writhes and bounces on the infamous casting couch while spreading her legs in time to the music, vamping for the audience throughout.[40] Her tagline aligns Evans with a Hollywood legend while at the same time staking her claim to her own art form through the adjectival prepositional phrase "of burlesque." The set adds to the symbolic power of the Monroe persona by creating a material rhetorical space that suggests both the reality of Hollywood sexual harassment and her (and by extension Monroe's) shameless participation in the ritual. Thus Evans offers a social critique by seductively mocking what was both serious reality and sex-panicked warning to women about the proper spaces for their bodies and sexuality.

3 | Dixie Evans, "The Marilyn Monroe of Burlesque." Courtesy of the Burlesque Hall of Fame.

Stripping changed again as the twentieth-century entered its sexual revolution. Burlesque with its wink and tease sexuality became less popular, seemingly an artifact of a bygone era. In the latter half of the twentieth century, stripping moved into clubs and developed into a distinct genre, a historical shift that I will analyze in more detail in chapter 2. Stripping had mostly changed from a central focus on tease and glamour, which had characterized classic burlesque until the 1990s, when yet another sea change shifted the cultural landscape of erotic dancing. The revivals of swing dance and rockabilly brought renewed interest in the vintage styles of the mid-twentieth century.[41] Women in these scenes donned looks reminiscent of mid-twentieth century pin-up models updated with a punk-inspired edge (think Bettie Page with ink). Concurrently, some performance artists and strippers were experimenting with acts that brought in humor and also the glamour of classic burlesque. While widespread interest in rockabilly and swing faded, the new burlesque grew and continues to grow with troupes in most major cities, national and international conferences, festivals, and competitions. Although what falls under the label of neo-burlesque varies, the "constant reference to the divine mixture of the sexy and the satirical" is a common feature.[42] Robert Allen's definition of burlesque in the nineteenth century illustrates the ways that the stripping woman has long held a contested place whether on the burlesque stage or on a pole at a club: "Burlesque ... is grounded in the aesthetics of *transgression, inversion, and the grotesque.* The burlesque performer represents a construction of what Peter Stallybrass and Allon White call the "low other": something that is reviled by and excluded from the dominant social order as debased, dirty, and unworthy, but that is simultaneously the object of desire and/or fascination."[43]

Allen's definition holds not only transhistorical relevance for this art form that resists easy definition, but also keys to persistent ways that women's bodies, in particular, women's sexual bodies, are simultaneously reviled and desired, exalted and annihilated, made subject and object. In light of this complex duality, burlesque, even when it is not performed by women or about women and gender specifically, is symbolic of women's sexuality: grotesque, beautiful, frightening, intriguing. Therefore, as a site for rhetorical inquiry, neo-burlesque offers opportunities to uncover and contend with rhetorical constructions of gender and sexuality, to think critically about how bodies communicate, and to illustrate how the fifth canon of delivery—regendered, reimagined, and reembodied—can function analytically to uncover those insights.

Body Language as Symbolic Action

As a critical tool, delivery reveals the interplay of symbolic practices through the common topics of body (including persona), space, audience, and genre, topics that are always interdependent.[44] These *topoi* are flexible and broad.[45] The *topoi* offered here— genre, body, space, and audience—are particularly relevant to performance rhetoric, in particular, erotic performance. Although they are separate concepts, they derive their meanings relationally. While I foreground a different *topos* in each section that follows, analysis of one is always analysis of all.

Genre

As a *topos* of delivery, genre comprises bodies that perform, the spaces in which they perform, and the audiences to whom they perform. While all of delivery's common topics are interdependent, this feature is especially salient with genre because it is produced by relationships. Analysis of genre is particularly important for erotic performance, as different types of stripping (stripping in clubs for money and to audiences primarily composed of men versus the performative striptease of neo-burlesque performed to mixed-sex audiences) share very similar features yet are distinct in terms of their social effects, particularly with regard to the ways that stripping for money is often denigrated more than neo-burlesque, revealing one of the many places where the two genres are classed. Although money is a fairly accurate way to separate these two genres, it only points to one difference. Approaching the distinction from a rhetorical perspective reveals that both stripping and neo-burlesque produce and are produced by the interactions among different audiences, spaces, and bodies. Like discursive genres, performance genres occur in spaces that are "communicative" and "social"; they are constitutive for "participants," offering "mood, attitude, and actional possibilities."[46] Therefore, rhetorical actions should be considered in the social contexts that enable participation in certain genres.[47] If, for example, Legs Malone were to perform in a strip club, audience expectations for her show would change. That is, the same body situated in a different space to a different audience would yield a different genre, particularly with regard to the customer-dancer relationship. In a strip club, performance is ongoing, and individualized interactions dominate. Thus when analyzing embodied performance, the *topos* of genre provides insight into the ways that the other *topoi* come together. Both club stripping and neo-burlesque are genres produced by the interactions of certain bodies, in certain spaces, in front of certain audiences, but the bodies, spaces, audiences, and arrangements of them are distinctly different.

Body/Persona

The body *topos* accounts for the ways that the body is constituted by physical performances classically associated with delivery—movement, clothes, and voice—but also by a constellation of identity features such as race, gender, and ethnicity.[48] Thus the performer's body "inhabits a world of signs."[49] Unlike Laban/Bartenieff movement analysis, used to describe corporeal action, analysis of the body via delivery attends to both discursive and material features. That is, even in a bodily art such as neo-burlesque, delivery exposes the dialectical relationship between materiality and discourse,[50] treating the body, not only as a producer of nonsymbolic movement, but also as a producer of the symbolic action that is central to embodied rhetoric. For example, in neo-burlesque, movement and costume work together to conceal and reveal. These seductive movements focus not on the naked body itself but on the strategic withholding and presenting of it via props or costumes. Thus costuming is part of the actual choreography of a burlesque routine;[51] it isn't just an incidental item hiding the naked body. Therefore, the dress of neo-burlesquers and strippers is different (usually), with neo-burlesquers favoring elaborate costumes, stripping down no further (usually) than to pasties, tassels, and G-string, and frequently using props like fans, gloves, and boas to heighten the drama of the strip. Props and costumes highlight theatricality, and they also construct the rhetorical space for the audience, making it clear that the theater is not a strip club and that expectations for audience participation are different.

The *topos* of the body also includes the construction of identity, realized in neo-burlesque through performer persona. Persona is crafted materially through movement, body types, costumes, spaces, and props and also linguistically through the words of emcees, songs, and stage names. Stage names in particular demonstrate the constant tacking between the material and the linguistic by constructing a symbolic reality that often proceeds from the performer's physical body. Thus naming is a specifically *rhetorical* process in which names "construct social realities" through the creation of personas.[52] For example, "Legs Malone" announces who she is via what she has: her name makes her long legs a spectacle, referencing a "synecdotal sign of the lower body and of female sexuality in general"[53] and suggesting that her legs must deserve the audience's attention and admiration. Further, if the audience gives it, they participate in the creation of her persona, and watching Legs's legs becomes erotic performance in itself. Bodily names like "Legs" also suggest that a performer is materially endowed with the physical gifts to excel in this genre, illustrating the ways that "the body of the persona and performer are put in critical dialogue with each other."[54] This is the case with a number of performers like Jo "Boobs" Weldon (fig. 4) or Mr. Gorgeous or Iva Handfull. Thus names linguistically construct a

4 | Jo "Boobs" Weldon, September 9, 2007. New York Burlesque Festival Main Event. Photo by Stacie Joy. Used with permission.

symbolic reality that audience and performer share for the duration of the performance and often outside of it as well. Names, as "symbolic inscription[s] of meaning,"[55] illustrate how "language and experience interpenetrate and develop together in a fluid, organic, ever-unfolding environment."[56]

Personas also illustrate the ways that the body *topos* connects with audience, space, and genre. Most erotic dancers cultivate personas. Stage names in neo-burlesque, however, have more in common with the tongue-in-cheek names of drag queens and kings than with club strippers. Neo-burlesquers often have more than one name, whether it is a stylized first and last name (Sydni

Deveraux), one that describes the performer's body or identity ("Legs" Malone; Shanghai Pearl), a suggestive, bodily joke (Waxie Moon; Alotta Boutté), or some combination of any of these with a "Miss/Mr." (Lil' Miss Lixx).[57] Although some of the most well-known performers use "real" names (Jo Weldon, Julie Atlas Muz, Angie Pontani), neo-burlesque names are overwhelmingly theatrical and in most cases would not be found in strip clubs, where dancers often go by a one-name pseudonym.[58]

Space

The space *topos*—including material arrangements within spaces—considers the overlapping questions of who is authorized to speak (body), and in what way (genre), and to whom (audience) because performance spaces construct possibilities for performers, performances, and audiences.[59] The body onstage "shapes and relates within and to space."[60] That is, "bodies make manifest abstract spatial experience."[61] Material space affects both what a body can "say" and how audiences will receive it and is an important consideration for analysis of erotic performances. Erotic material can have a negative impact or be perceived to have a negative impact when it is delivered in a space or to an audience for whom it is not intended. Thus location has long affected and still does affect erotic dance, from campaigns in New York City to close burlesque theaters in the late nineteenth and early twentieth centuries,[62] to Rudy Giuliani's 1990s cleanup of Times Square to remove all the sex commerce in favor of the corporate smut that now gluts the area, to local zoning laws that regulate the necessary distance between strip clubs and schools and residential areas. The places and spaces where women may dance and undress for audiences are regulated, zoned, and policed variously across the country, which means that legal and social mores also affect and are affected by the delivery of erotic dance.[63] Such surveillance of public erotic spaces perpetuates a system that classifies dancers as suspect women who sell their "honor by renting [their bodies] for unworthy male interests."[64] However, because neo-burlesque is a genre in which performers rarely show bare nipples or genitals to their mixed-gender or majority women audiences, because the material arrangement of venues doesn't typically encourage one-on-one interaction, and because any audience interactions aren't directly paid for, its performance spaces are less regulated. As a result of this spatial structuring, neo-burlesque has a greater degree of separation between it and the sex work of stripping and consequently less of a stigma for performers and audiences.

Space also directly shapes the kinesthetic and sartorial communication of the body, further constructing specific genre characteristics. The movements of club stripping and neo-burlesque look very similar when they are removed from the club or the theater. Like strippers, neo-burlesquers may undress, undulate, kneel, touch themselves, and shake and pop their booties. Such features, however, need to be carefully considered for their rhetorical functions in different contexts, rather than be assumed to have static meaning.[65] The material arrangements of the space in which such "stripper moves" are performed and the costumes they are performed in enable distinct interactions between audience and performer. Strip clubs often have distinct areas, such as the main floor, VIP sections, and the champagne room. These spaces allow for and encourage direct contact between customer and dancer, but access to them comes at a price: the more interaction a space allows, the more a customer will pay. Assuming that both customer and dancer obey the rules, the agreed-upon and permitted financial transaction between customer and dancer drive these interactions. As opposed to these transactional spaces, venues for neo-burlesque typically have one stage with the audience facing it, because unlike strippers, "a burlesque performer performs to the entire room, not just one person at a time."[66] Seating closer to the stage may be offered at higher VIP prices, but in general, both proximity to and participation with performers are determined not by money but by the performers and the performance space.

Audience Participation/Interaction

The audience *topos* prompts critics to consider the performed text as developing from a dynamic rhetorical situation in which audiences and rhetors cocreate discourse. "Interaction/interactivity," defined as "audience involvement," is one of the *topoi* of digital delivery.[67] Because neo-burlesque and many other embodied performances are similarly interactive, audience—not just who it is, but how it is involved—serves as a critical part of analyzing performed delivery as well. Many performers interact with audiences, break the fourth wall, and improvise movements based on audience feedback.[68] In their "Paradigm for Performance Studies," Ronald Pelias and James VanOosting characterize such interactive performances as ones in which "both performers and audience are seen as coproducers, each contributing to the artistic event."[69] Thus interactive performances intensify the level of audience participation, and "the distinction between performer and audience becomes less distinct. While performers maintain the authority to initiate interaction and to select particular subjects, the audience is invited to create within an established framework. Performer and audience codetermine possible directions for the theatrical event."[70]

Similarly, but speaking of digital rhetorics, James E. Porter notes that the greater the degree of interactivity between audience and rhetor, the lesser the distinction between the two, leading audiences to become "co-producers of content."[71] In neo-burlesque, audience is not just important; audience is definitive of the genre, as definitive as performer and performance. Seasoned performers often stress the importance of audience in teaching young performers how to choreograph successful shows, because ultimately burlesque is an interactive art. Many burlesque classes focus on techniques designed to intrigue, confuse, arouse, and amuse the audiences that attend shows. As journalist and performer, Frankie Tease explains, "The burlesque performer should never leave the audience out of the choreography ... it is a long standing tradition to play to the crowd."[72] Although it does not call for the one-on-one interaction between performer and audience member that other types of erotic dancing do, audience participation in neo-burlesque is still active and complex. Even when participation is not an explicit part of an act, audiences in live performance are always involved: "Not only do the bodies on stage speak and express, but also the bodies of the spectators have some sort of contingent response to these. There may not be a rational understanding of what is occurring on stage, but the visceral experience provides the body a possible way of understanding and participating in the performance."[73] That is, through such "visceral" reactions audience bodies communicate with bodies on stage even when they occur in ways that are not always wholly conscious or able to be described in language. As Rebecca Schneider argues, "Performance *implies always* an audience/performer or ritual participant relationship—a reciprocity."[74] In live performance, feedback is immediate, offering audiences more power to participate in shaping messages. Even if a performance is invented, arranged, and packaged before it is delivered, audiences will react differently to it, constructing a new experience for both performers and other audience members. Thus neo-burlesque is a medium that offers insight into the rhetorical process of audience participation within delivery, insight that is becoming more relevant across multiple genres, including written texts, as digital media closes the distance between writers and readers.

In order for audiences to become coproducers of performances, however, appropriate spectators must be reached. Because neo-burlesque is such a distinctive genre, blending the absurd with the erotic, it can elicit strong negative reactions when it appears in new spaces and to new viewers. Take Trixie Little and The Evil Hate Monkey, formerly a Baltimore-based neo-burlesque team, who appeared on the competitive variety show *America's Got Talent (AGT)* in 2009.[75] The performers—who were well known and celebrated within neo-burlesque circles—were eliminated in the audition round. By delivering their personas through *AGT*, the duo was reaching new audiences in new spaces. The audience, however, had the performance and the performers filtered through *AGT*'s production team who diluted the act, judges who interrupted the act, and the medium of television, which changes the audience experience. As a rule, neo-burlesque does not translate well to screen viewing: performances depend on the intimate and immediate dynamic between audience and performer. Watching neo-burlesque on a TV or a computer screen does not adequately reflect the experience of attending a live show and is, as The Shanghai Pearl notes, "weird." She explains, "It's okay for research, but not for the audience experience. [In live burlesque] you don't know if I'm going to jump on you or make out with you or hump your face or throw [things] at you. . . . You know that's not going to happen [on the Internet]. . . . That's boring."[76] Indeed. And it's not just that watching on a screen is boring (which it often is), performances become "not neo-burlesque" for the viewer who is removed in time and space from the performer and unable to participate directly. In this sense, the television or any screen "flattens" the body by removing the audience factor. The screen changes audience participation so that audiences become viewers; they are no longer part of the show, but spectators to it. In short, appearing on *AGT* necessarily affected Trixie and Monkey's delivery as they lost control of their bodies, performance space, and audience, thus changing their performance genre.

Other neo-burlesque performers have also appeared on *AGT*. In season one, Michelle L'amour made it to the semifinals before being eliminated, but not without some controversy. Judge Brandy Norwood was so offended by L'amour's initial act—a striptease that began with her in a Snow White costume and ended with her in a sparkly red bikini—that she not only pushed her own elimination buzzer but pushed the buzzers of cojudges David Hasselhoff and Piers Morgan as well. Unfortunately for Norwood, Hasselhoff and Morgan both voted to keep L'amour.[77] After the episode aired, *The Chicagoist* reported that viewers on NBCs message boards were offended variously, believing the act to be in bad taste or threatening to children who may have been watching.[78] Like

Trixie and Monkey, L'amour's *AGT* act demonstrates the ways that the *topoi* of delivery shape a performance and its reception.

Analysis of neo-burlesque reveals the affordances of delivery as a critical framework for embodied rhetoric. Because delivery includes a range of material communication practices and contexts, it invites us to imagine symbolic action expansively. The interrelated common topics of body, space, audience, and genre include both linguistic and material symbolic practices. Therefore, delivery as a method attends to the complexities of the body's communication. As Hawhee notes, "Bodies and language . . . are irreducibly distinct and yet parallel and complementary . . . often, if not always, in effect moving together."[79] Because rhetorical theory has so long been "under the spell of discursive construction,"[80] however, it can be difficult to understand or appreciate the body's many ways of communicating outside of linguistic practice. Using delivery to analyze rhetorical bodies can enrich that understanding and appreciation.

From the Mundane to the Spectacular—Bodies in Action

In addition to revealing the interdependence of body, space, and audience in constructing a performance genre, delivery also provides insight into social context; in this case, the varied ways that neo-burlesque operates as a popular cultural practice. Delivery's common topics illustrate why neo-burlesque tends to get claimed as *feminist stripping*. Because neo-burlesque shares features with other forms of stripping but is delivered in different spaces and to different audiences, it is a different genre performing a different social action—namely, production rather than transaction. It is contested by virtue of being a form of erotic dance practiced primarily by women, but this is only one part of its context. Neo-burlesque might well represent the triumph of patriarchy, of women buying into their own sexual oppression in the name of empowerment, of shoring up neo-liberalism by focusing on one's individual desire to be nearly naked in public or to view scantily clad dancing women. The popularity of neo-burlesque might also represent the increasing sexualization of all aspects of Western entertainment and a deterioration of a moral structure that advocates keeping the naked body in private spaces. Such analyses that focus exclusively on the erotic aspects of neo-burlesque, however, risk simplifying the nature of its appeal.

Delivery reveals the ways that neo-burlesque makes the spectacular out of the mundane. Although many top performers have trained in dance and other bodily arts, the bodies of neo-burlesque are not necessarily the specialized bodies of other forms of dance. As a low-cultural popular form, neo-burlesque is as accessible as it is instructive, making it an especially rich site for the study of bodies. Situated at the intersection between the sex work of stripping in clubs and theatrical performance, neo-burlesque's appeal is complex, and understanding it requires attention to what it offers performers and audiences that other types of live performance do not.

Neo-burlesque invites, and it depends upon, response from the audience. Further, and perhaps more critically for my conversation here, burlesque is a type of dance that is potentially open to anyone to perform.[81] Although audiences and producers vary in their body positivity, neo-burlesque tends to have a more diverse selection of body types than other genres of erotic dance. In addition, subgenres like "criptease," boylesque, and plus-sized burlesque present a range of body types and abilities. Thus not only is neo-burlesque audience dependent, but it also lessens the distinction between bodies onstage and those in the audience. Bodies are made spectacular through spectacle, through engaging in particular movements in particular costumes in particular spaces, rather than being chosen for performance because they are already spectacular.

In considering the affordances and limitations of delivery as a method for analyzing embodied rhetoric, it is important to continue to complicate the topics of body, space, audience, and genre. Rhetorical critics should seek to understand not only the interconnectedness of these topics but also how "both context and ideology saturate each."[82] The body in particular, especially in neo-burlesque, is endlessly complicated as a topic of delivery. Despite being accessible in the ways I have described, the bodies of neo-burlesque are predominately able-bodied white cis women. Women of color, however, have a substantial legacy in burlesque. In the classic era, while performers of color were paid significantly less, they still had more opportunities performing as "shake dancers" than they had in "civilian life."[83] Despite this history, or because it is a history that has largely been erased, the bodies of performers of color are differently situated than those of white performers—even when performing in the same space, to the same audiences, in the same genre—because they are "always already subjected to racist spectacle."[84] Sydney Lewis argues that black performers "reinsert erased black female bodies into sexualized narratives," thus "disabling absolute 'abjectification,'" a process that "disrupt[s] the codification of Whiteness" and of "essentialized blackness."[85] Analysis of delivery can concretize the rhetorical operations through which this process happens. By focusing critical attention on the intersections among body, space, audience, and genre, delivery highlights the ways that performers of color insert their bodies into performance spaces that don't always make room for them in order to disrupt the construction of neo-burlesque as a white genre.

Delivery as Critical Method for Embodied Rhetoric

While the ways I have outlined delivery as a critical method here relate most obviously to performance rhetoric, it can be similarly useful for a range of embodied rhetorics and performances via its mediation of the relationship between body and text. Further, analysis of delivery can occur in tandem with other methods for material analysis, like those based on Burke's action/motion polarity (such as Debra Hawhee and Bryan Crable), theories of disability (e.g., Jay Dolmage's *mêtis*), as well as theories of new materialism that look beyond the symbolic realm for sources of persuasion. When the medium of any message is the body, delivery has value for critics, and its common topics are flexible enough to account for a broad range of symbolic actions. Recent disciplinary interest in disability rhetorics, sexual rhetorics, the rhetoric of sport, and protest rhetoric all offer new ways to theorize delivery as an analytical device that directs critical attention to the interrelation among bodies, spaces, and audiences within rhetorical genres.

Many rhetorical approaches to body criticism treat language solely as text, as an artifact of the body separated in time and space from production. Bodies in action can teach us about rhetoric *of* the body itself, what that phrase can mean more broadly and how it can operate through multiple symbolic codes. Bodies suggest how we should study them by being communicative in both linguistic and material modes. The body, as a symbol-using, motion-inducing, acting, responding vehicle for communication, speaks in multiple languages that are neither contained by nor located outside of the linguistic realm. Neo-burlesque, with its fanciful, absurd, and erotically charged performances, demonstrates the many facets of the rhetorical delivery of embodied messages. In theorizing delivery as a rhetoric of action, James Fredal argues that because it encompasses all the "wordless" elements of a rhetorical act that it "remains speechless and unspeakable" marked by "unpredictability ... [and] recalcitrance to being written or theorized."[86] Yet it is this troubled and troubling nature of delivery that makes it a rich analytical lens for embodied rhetoric, which often speaks the unspeakable.

2

"You're Bound to Find Out She Don't Love You" |
Genre and the Erotic Body

September 28, 2013. New York Burlesque Fest. I sit at the B.B. King Blues Club and Grill. I sit in the cheap seats jammed up against the end of a booth parallel to, rather than in front of, the stage. Seven strangers are crammed into the intimate space with me. I crank my body sideways in order to see the stage. Please start, please start, please, please, please start. It's 6:30. The show ends at 11:00. Eleven. I face four and a half hours of avoiding conversation with strangers, not being able to pee, and looking sideways at the stage.

I ruminate. Maybe even pout a little.

My sideways view, though uncomfortable, offers an expansive view. I see the stage, backstage, and the audience. I see the VIPers at the tables facing the stage, see them hug each other, shake hands, nod their heads, self-assured, assured of a full-frontal view. I see vendors with glittering vintage wares—always always glitter—always always vintage. I see a row of youngish hipster types choosing to stand in the back to see the show head on. I see the light board operator, bartender, stage crew; performers backstage darting out and then back. I see the waitstaff dancing with trays of food—in and out and back and forth. My sideways view expands. Always expands, as the venue fills and the minutes drag by. I try to tell myself to enjoy this moment, to enjoy this sideways view.

Time ticks. It's 6:33, and the only way I can avoid talking to the onlookers at my table—all women—diverse in appearance, diverse in social category, giggling with their friends over $15 drinks and $11 sliders—the only way to avoid them is to continue to track the VIPers, the cool kids of burlesque. My default outfit—think Schneider and Fonzie have a lesbian baby—my default outfit of jeans, vest, and Hanes V-neck tagless T looks scummy and out of place with all these shiny, shiny, dresses, porkpie hats, thin ties, polka-dot skirts and white gloves. Who are these people? The researcher in me wonders. The realist in me knows that even with a VIP ticket, I would be as lost down there as up here on my sideways perch. As lost as I am on a wooden bench at Coney Island watching burlesque in a sweating crowd. I realized then, at that moment, at the B.B. King Blues Club and Grill that despite my status as audience *member, the neo-burlesque community remains, and will remain, open to me only from the side. Leaving me with an expansive yet partial view. I don't know the language. I don't know the codes. I look dumb in vintage clothes.*

I can't even pronounce "Swarovski."

According to queer theorist and literary scholar Kathryn Bond Stockton, our trip through life is not a matter of growing up; instead people, especially queer people, grow sideways. To "grow up" implies linearity, a forward motion; vertical progress toward adulthood. Growing sideways on the other hand is lateral, spreading, expanding, waxing; it suggests "that the width of a person's experience or ideas, their motives or their motions, may pertain at any age."[1] Riffing on Stockton's work and inspired by the Saturday Spectacular at New York Burlesque Fest, in this chapter I approach striptease analytically from a sideways view, a view that never only sees front or back, over or under, but all at once. The sideways view is not all encompassing, however. It is always partial, but peripherally one can see what other views tend to miss. Because it is a method that deconstructs the relationships among parts, wholes, and contexts, genre criticism can provide such a view. Although Stockton uses the sideways metaphor as a way to conceptualize growth specifically, the playful, expansive, nonlinearity it signifies is a useful metaphor to describe the always shifting relations among audience, performers, and performances that compose acts of erotic performance rhetoric, which coalesce into distinct genres with noticeably different cultural valuation. Genre criticism can be useful—even imperative—for embodied erotic and sexual rhetorics in which the body can signal in superficially similar ways but yield completely different performances and responses. Joshua Gunn argues that genre criticism can provide a "powerful tool for understanding cultural expressions *if* we attend more assiduously to the centrality of bodily excitation or affect."[2] Such assiduous attention to affect can reveal how two genres of erotic dance, topless and neo-burlesque, which share many characteristics, carry different degrees of stigma for participants and are subject to different levels of surveillance and regulation.[3]

Genre analysis demonstrates some key differences in the ways that relationships are forged with audiences to produce genre-specific affective responses. Neo-burlesque, while a genre *of* the body, does not operate as a "body genre" as theorized by film critic Linda Williams. Williams argues that, in film, body genres create a connection between bodies in the audience and the actors on film as their *primary* goal. It is this affective connection between performer and audience that is a hallmark of the low-culture status of the body genre. Performances on stage can operate similarly, and genre analysis reveals the ways that topless dancing operates as a body genre, while neo-burlesque does not. Therefore, club stripping is more denigrated and regulated than neo-burlesque regardless of the fact that the two share striptease as the central act.

In this chapter, I analyze the material rhetoric of neo-burlesque and topless club stripping, in particular, kinesthetic, sartorial, and cosmetic features. Through the analysis, I show the ways that these features, while often superficially similar, fuse in distinct ways in each genre. Neo-burlesque, seen by many fans and practitioners as feminist stripping, draws mixed-sex, multigendered audiences with women making up a significant part of the fan base. Further, it attracts large queer audiences with its embrace of camp, gender fluidity, and high femme style. As transmasculine neo-burlesque icon Murray Hill joked at the 2013 New York Burlesque Festival, neo-burlesque provides a safe space to objectify women, which begs the question: If the gaze at a neo-burlesque show might be similarly objectifying, what makes it different from a strip club? Two of the primary differences are the composition of the audience and the monetary exchange that drives club stripping. Although these are significant and compelling differences, identifying them leaves questions about the mobilization of performing bodies that genre analysis addresses. A genre perspective compels attention to affect that both complicates and clarifies the differences between the two types of stripping. Throughout the chapter, I illustrate audience affect with narratives of my own experiences doing fieldwork, drawing on the *in situ* field method of performative writing as a way to "to evoke [emotional] dimensions of rhetorical experience."[4] Though *rhetorical field methods* are typically used to critique mundane and everyday forms of rhetorical practice, as opposed to the staged and dramatized erotic performances that are my focus here, the rhetorical criticism of *live* performance demands similar *in situ* methods. Therefore, I strive to demonstrate my embodied experiences as an audience member in these two genres to help clarify my subjective view and to enliven my claims about affect. To that end, the narratives in this piece attempt to work within Della Pollock's framework, which holds that performative writing is *evocative, metonymic, subjective, nervous, citational,* and *consequential.*[5]

Classic Burlesque and Its Descendants: A Primer

Roxy approaches me with a broad smile and an easygoing gait.[6] *I'd been staring at her onstage all night and had finally gathered the courage to tip her, which was both gratifying and horrifying. Tipping had led to this, to her approach, to her "Would you like a dance?" and to my blush and mumble. I had always expected the intimacy of a lap dance to feel contrived, but this time, this first time, it doesn't. It is awkward, and terrifying, and exciting, but it doesn't feel fake. It feels like what it is. "Relax," she instructs. *mumbleblush* "It's my first time getting a dance." She laughs. "I remember my first time. I'll go easy on you." I appreciate it but don't really want her to. I'm not sure where to look—a lap dance problem that my social anxiety will never let me resolve—but she maintains eye contact *clearthroatblush*. Eye contact with anyone—let alone a beautiful nearly naked woman—feels like a fist in my throat; it leaves me breathless, panicked, choked. Reaching through my discomfort, she grabs me behind my knees and slides me forward to the edge of the seat. "I have to get between your legs," she says crouching now and looking up at me. She stands again and leans me back so I'm low in my patterned chair. Legs spread, shoulders back, hands at my sides. Motionless. She continues to look me in the eyes, smiles, removes her shirt, and dances. Breasts brush my lips. Hands stroke my hair.*

I think I love her.

As discussed in chapter 1, burlesque, the antecedent genre to both club stripping and neo-burlesque, has both historical and contemporary significance in the US.[7] Originally comprised of theatrical tableaux and bawdy musical spectacles in the late nineteenth century, burlesque gradually evolved into the more familiar striptease now associated with the mid-twentieth-century classic era. As the twentieth century progressed and sexual expression became more frank and common in a variety of media, burlesque waned in popularity, and the club replaced the theater as the most common space in which stripping occurred. This change in space subsequently changed the genre. Although strip clubs retained the main stage with a dancer stripping before an audience, a new type of performance in which individual customers interact with individual dancers and pay them directly came to dominate the genre, moving striptease closer to other forms of sex work and further from theatrical performance. Thus from a single point of origin, the mostly straight male audience for classic burlesque grew up to be the mostly straight male audience of club stripping. Neo-burlesque, on the other hand, grew sideways, drawing audiences composed of large numbers of cis women, as well as trans, nonbinary, and queer people with a campy amalgamation of vintage style, subversive messages, humor, and gender play that is largely (but not entirely) absent in modern commercial stripping.

In academic literature on stripping in clubs, the classic sociological and psychological perspectives from the mid-twentieth century were deeply invested in the deviance of strippers themselves.[8] *What broken families and broken psyches led these women to such degraded and degrading work?* But at the turn of the twenty-first century, popular and scholarly discourse began striving to destigmatize stripping and to take the work of dancers seriously.[9] The research of former dancers Katherine Frank and Danielle Egan specifically turns the critical gaze to the psyches and psychologies of men who frequent strip clubs, flipping the script on researching motive and motivation from performer to audience. At the same time that academics were changing their approaches, in popular culture stripping was also coming out of the closet. By the mid-2000s, stripper chic was everywhere with weekly TV crime dramas including obligatory strip-club scenes, with rap and rock songs celebrating the hustle of hardworking dancers, and with infomercials hawking the flirty girl fitness pole. *It's only a dollar!*

Concurrent to the popularization of club stripping, neo-burlesque was experiencing resurgence, presenting a grassroots alternative to the increasingly corporate culture of newly popular "Gentleman's Clubs." Although definitions of the genre are widely debated, neo-burlesque is commonly understood to be a contemporary uptake of the classic burlesque of the 1930s. In contemporizing the genre, however, neo-burlesque blends elements of many different traditions with some performers preferring classic striptease in the styles of legends like Toni Elling, Gypsy Rose Lee, Tempest Storm, and Dixie Evans, with other performers drawing on burlesque's older history as a bawdy, parodic form of theatrical spectacle, and with still others exploring avant-garde performance art. Consequently, neo-burlesque offers what performer Perle Noire refers to as "theatre gumbo," blending dance, striptease, carnival acts, and comedy.[10]

The *topoi* of delivery, as discussed in chapter 1, help to clarify the dissimilarities between neo-burlesque and club stripping, with regard to space, monetary structure, and performer/audience interactions. In *The Burlesque Handbook*, Jo Weldon, drawing on her experience in both realms, succinctly describes the differences between audiences in strip clubs and audiences at neo-burlesque shows, focusing on gender and interaction with performers. Weldon writes:

> Certain differences are obvious from the audience's point of view. When a customer goes to a strip joint, he or she (come on, we know it's usually a he) usually goes at any time he pleases (as long as the bar is open, of course). He selects the performer he wants to interact with, and if she is available, he interacts with her for as long as he wants to or can afford to and then leaves. When a customer goes to a burlesque show, he or she goes at the time the show is expected to begin, sits and watches the show, usually doesn't interact with the performers at all, has a drink or two after the show, and leaves.[11]

In this excerpt, Weldon identifies the most apparent points of genre difference, focused mainly on customer experience. Customers of strip clubs decide when the performance happens, who the performer will be, how long it will last, and what fantasy will be constructed. In neo-burlesque, primary control of these same elements shifts to performers and producers. Genre analysis shows how the control and interplay of each of these elements reveal the distinct relational affects between performers and audiences that structure and enable/disable genre-specific acts and also what those acts reveal about cultural acceptance and valuation of erotic performances.

Embodying Genre Criticism

Genre presents both a provocative and a problematic approach to analyzing symbolic communication. Categorizing characteristics is an accessible method for evaluating substantive and stylistic features in the context of certain predictable rhetorical situations. Categorization, however, can return critics to a methodology trap in which critics find only what they are looking to find, making meaning prior to critique and shaping data to fit that meaning.[12] Seeking to retain what is useful about genre, contemporary rhetorical theorists have been complicating genre critique for some time, arguing that it is more than the cataloging of textual features, but a robust method of seeing the dynamic relationships among those features and their subsequent social effects.[13] One of the ways that genre theorists have sought to avoid formulaic criticism is by stressing the role of context in genre analysis, reminding critics to be conscious of the dialectical tacking between creating and maintaining both texts and contexts, as genres are "symbiotically maintained rhetorical ecosystems ... within which communicants enact and reproduce specific situations, actions, relations, and identities."[14] Anis Bawarshi's theory of the genre function, which posits that genres always constitute and are constituted by both texts and contexts in the production of social roles, illustrates why genre criticism is a particularly useful framework for rhetoric of the body. Social roles are constantly being communicated and constituted within embodied rhetoric, not only through what is communicated but also through who is doing the communicating and by what symbolic means. Drawing a distinction between embodied and alphabetic codes, Bawarshi offers a hint of the applicability of genre to embodied rhetoric using the example of the doctor-patient relationship within the context of an office visit. He writes, "We might be tempted to think it is a rhetorically unmediated situation because the doctor-patient relationship is such a sensual, tactile one, but this would be to underestimate the power of genre in shaping and enabling this very physical relationship."[15] Although Bawarshi's concern here is the alphabetic discourse (in particular, the Patient Medical History Form) that structures these "sensual, tactile" relationships, it is not only the written texts that rhetorically mediate this situation. Repetitions of movements, clothing, tools, space, and touch all also structure genre expectations of the doctor's office visit. Because these *things* all carry symbolic as well as material meaning, they are part of embodied rhetorical performances and therefore part of the constructed social identities for both doctors and patients. Therefore, while the Patient Medical History Form is one genre that produces the doctor's office visit, the visit itself is also facilitated by embodied and material rhetoric through the recognizable and recurrent situation and its recognizable and recurrent symbolic features.

Discursive theories of genre like Bawarshi's can be expanded to apply to the body, but they can also shortchange our understanding of the material symbolic as a vehicle for communication and for constituting social identities. Thus part of the work for critics is not only to look for the ways that bodies communicate that are parallel to alphabetic texts but also to look for differences via theories and frameworks that are attentive to the particularities of bodies. For example, in "Maranatha" Joshua Gunn demonstrates an approach to genre criticism that furthers his argument that critics should treat genre as "the signature of an affective apparatus that both presumes and produces bodies-in-feeling."[16] For Gunn, genre "emerges at the point at which the symbolic meets the body; genre, in other words, is form delivered to language, form succumbing to the insistence of languaging."[17] When the symbolic vehicle for the creation of genres is also the body, as it is with erotic dance—body both as symbolic generator and as affective recipient—the type of languaging that critics look for necessarily shifts, but the focus on affect remains crucial. In order to develop his theory that recasts genre as the symbolic form that represents the "body in feeling," Gunn draws on the work of film critic Linda Williams's analysis of body genres in film in order to highlight the neglected role of affect in rhetorical genre criticism. Body genre films centralize bodily sensation:[18] bodies on screen experience something, which is designed to evoke a correlative response in the audience.[19] For example, in pornography people on screen have sex, ostensibly in order to sexually arouse an audience and often acting as a precursor to sexual activity for the spectator. This affective link between performer and audience forms the core of body genre films, in which evoking a particular audience response takes priority over delivering a particular narrative. Williams differentiates the body genres of her investigation, ones marked by "excessive" focus on the feeling body and that enjoy a similar low cultural status—melodrama, horror, pornography—from other genres in which the body is central, such as thrillers, musicals, and comedies. These other genres also "both portray and affect the sensational body," but they enjoy a higher cultural status because they do not create the same mimicry of affect between the body on screen and the body in the audience.[20] The theory of the body genre then offers an embodied critical approach to performance rhetoric by focusing on the dynamism of both texts and contexts via the affective relationships among performers, performances, and audiences. As Gunn demonstrates in his own work, rhetorical analysis of genres is useful because they "provide a metaphorical foothold, stabilizing feeling into meaning for the purposes of thought, reflection, and often prediction."[21] Therefore, although the symbolic forms that represent bodily affect are constantly changing, attention to genre—both the genre function that Bawarshi theorizes as an "overarching concept that can explain the social roles we assign to various discourses and those who enact and are enacted by them"[22] and the "affective approach [that] attends to the feelings evoked by patterned repetitions"[23]—reveals the hierarchy of social value assigned to club stripping and neo-burlesque as related but distinct genres of erotic dance. Each genre constitutes distinct social identities, responds to distinct exigencies, and crafts distinct symbolic representations of and often yields (different) bodily excitations.

Performance as Transaction / Performance as Production

Isabella walks by, chin up. She has just finished dancing to "Porcelain" by Moby on the main stage, managing to barely move—bored, removed, and yet still anchored in the melancholy of that song. The performance undoes me. As she passes, her eyes dart to me just enough to make it clear that she is ignoring me. We're fighting. We've spent months in an uneasy relationship as customer and dancer, interviewer and respondent, friends, and more, and less. I go to tip her on stage 2, and we start fighting over who gossiped about whom and about what in the club. To earn her forgiveness, I ask to take her into the Champagne Room, where we can drink and touch and laugh and argue. Where she will occasionally dance. And pinned in the stare of the unblinking red light from the surveillance camera, we make up. It costs me 300 dollars, but I have desperately missed her. She eventually touches me speaking Spanish that I don't understand in my ear. Knowing her as I do, I am certain that the words mock me, but in my drunken searching in the dark, I let myself believe otherwise. Overcome as always by her. "This is all I want. For you to dance for me." She smiles with eyebrow raised, knowing the lie.

I think I love her.[24]

Genre analysis is always a systematic approach to classification; however, the work of genre theorists from the latter half of the twentieth century on has stressed that any classification is not closed and final and that classification is the beginning and not the end of analysis: if it were the end, there would be little point to the criticism of genres. What this means for critics is that our analytical focus is not on how a particular act or artifact fits into a static and unchanging constellation of features but how acts and artifacts constantly articulate and rearticulate these features in recurrent and "situated actions."[25] Campbell and Jamieson, whose 1978 book *Form and Genre: Shaping Rhetorical Action* made a strong and enduring argument for the dynamism of genre critique, define a genre as "groups of discourses which share substantive, stylistic, and situational characteristics ... unified by a constellation of forms that recurs in each of its members. These forms, *in isolation*, appear in other discourses. What is distinctive about the acts in a genre is the recurrence of the forms *together* in constellation."[26] These features, when "fused" as Campbell and Jamieson call it within recurrent (and therefore predictable) rhetorical situations, reveal particular internal dynamics, and thus genres.[27]

Typified Situations—The Who, to Whom, and What of Topless Dance and Neo-Burlesque

Ima send this one out to the gentleman's clubs.
—Wyclef Jean, "Perfect Gentleman"

Although we likely first recognize genres by their recurrent symbolic forms, I'll begin with the recurrent situations in which these forms coalesce into genres. Each genre under analysis here has a typified situation, which helps us to identify patterns of recurrence of rhetorical action, for "what recurs is not a material situation (a real, objective, factual event) but our construal of a type."[28] Because my critical focus is on types, it is important that I clarify to whom I am referring when I discuss performers and audiences in topless clubs and in neo-burlesque. My focus is on social roles constituted by performing bodies in particular generic situations, not on what we might think of as the real people who perform or view striptease in clubs or in theaters. That is, the same person can be an audience member for a neo-burlesque show and a customer at a strip club. Neo-burlesque performers can work as club strippers and vice versa. Performers can be audiences and customers can be dancers. Inhabiting one role never forecloses on another. So the *who* and *to whom* in each typified situation is a particular type of role.

One of the most apparent differences between neo-burlesque and topless dance is the commercial aspect of strip clubs, which is seen in the transactional relationship between viewer and viewed in clubs: the social roles here are worker and customer. Dancers are doing a job, and earning money is the primary goal of the fantasy interactions that are constructed by their performances.[29] This is not to say that dancers in clubs don't also see themselves as performers or entertainers, or that there is no artistic skill or talent involved. The more skill dancers have, the more money they are capable of making, but in the space of the club, skill is multifaceted. Some dancers excel at pole work or performing other acrobatic feats like handstands and backbends. Some excel as dancers, as rhythmic elegant movers, as shakers. But dancers do not have to possess the bodily capacity to excel in these areas; they can make good money by forging relationships with customers, listening to what and whom they want and performing accordingly.[30] For some, being a good dancer means picking the right song to appeal to the crowd or to a specific customer or customers. And for others, it is all about finding the customers to whom they appeal. Although dancers in clubs do rely on cosmetic and sartorial markers of femininity (makeup, high heels, and costumes that reveal and enhance breasts, hips, and butts), there is more variety in club beauty standards than people often assume. Customers—particularly regulars who are seeking something more complex than a single viewing—have a wide range of tastes that can be accommodated in clubs. This is not to say that clubs are body-positive environments, but as Isabella, a dancer to whom I was an ardent regular, once remarked as she scanned the club, "There is someone for everyone." She herself was one of the oldest dancers in the club, curvier than most, and not a particularly talented dancer, yet I was deeply infatuated with her and she had a long and profitable career because she was good at *being* a stripper. At being fun. At making people laugh and at holding herself with a dark regality. (*"What do you see in her? She is so mean to you."*) There is someone for everyone. Although being conventionally beautiful may be an asset in attracting customers, it does not guarantee profit.[31] Thus dancers who make money are typically the ones who convincingly perform, not only erotic dance moves, but also the persona of the good-time girl who loves her job and has fun doing it. Customers pay for this fantasy and for the company, the closeness, the eroticism, and often the assurances that they are part of what makes the job so damn fun because they are so damn desirable.[32] Therefore, the job, the work of being a topless dancer, is multifaceted, with performance occurring constantly and not only on stage, particularly when it comes to interaction with customers.

Because dancers in clubs are primarily workers, that necessarily means that audiences are customers. They consume. Customers in strip clubs are overwhelmingly, but not exclusively, men. The dominance of class and racial characteristics depends on location, time of day, and day of the week. Customers can roughly be divided into two groups: casual and regular.[33] Casual customers may be in the club for a special occasion, while regulars often visit whenever they can, frequently forming emotional or quasi-emotional bonds with dancers.[34]

Despite the transactional consumer-driven nature of stripping in clubs, and despite the fact that clubs are "designed to elicit an erotic response,"[35] the complex performances are capable of generating an affective response in customers that is often just as or more emotional than it is erotic. This is not to say that regulars *do not* get sexual thrills from strip clubs, but that sex itself is often not the sole or even the primary motivating factor for consuming erotic dance. Katherine Frank writes, "Not one man I interviewed said he went to the clubs specifically for sexual release, even in the form of masturbation at a later time. Most men, and especially the regulars, realized that sexual activity was available in other venues of the industry and were explicit about their knowledge of this fact.... One-time or infrequent visitors were more likely to assume or hope that sexual release would be available in strip clubs."[36]

Regulars attend clubs to play out various fantasies or engage in behaviors not otherwise open to them. Fantasies of romance, or of potent masculinity, or even the actual chance to talk to a woman—particularly a nearly naked woman—without the pressures of dating all motivate regulars.[37] All of these add an emotional element that heightens the affective response that regulars often characterize as addicting. I'll expand on the symbolic resources that construct these performances below by analyzing the genre features of topless and neo-burlesque. Here I want to just classify the audience of strip clubs as customers and to further establish that the linking of one-on-one interactions with layered performances with the direct purchase of services is what generates complex emotional affective responses in customers.[38] And it is the possibility of emotional responses coupled with the erotic or sexual that forms a primary generic difference between club stripping and neo-burlesque.

As I have started to sketch out, performance occurs everywhere in a strip club.[39] Although customers ostensibly go to a strip club to be spectators, they are, in fact, part of the performance. Customers perform for dancers, for each other, for management, for themselves, and dancers do the same. Customers' performances occur in a few key areas: on stage where a dancer performs to whatever audience members are watching, at tables, and in special areas with entrance fees and higher per-dance costs. During stage dances, customers approach the stage and tip (usually small amounts). The amount of interaction you find here varies dramatically. Some customers will use this as an opportunity to dance themselves (*cringe*), to "make it rain" (*that horrifying music video move where a customer showers the dancer with a stack of bills—demonstrating potency both to the dancer and to the rest of the club*), or to solicit a lap dance (*acceptable*). Tipping dancers onstage "blur[s] traditional boundaries between performer and spectator" as the customer becomes a part of the show, paying both to see and to be seen.[40] Thus the stage dance serves both to advertise the dancer to customers and customers to dancers. It also can be a venue for the intimacy that is experienced in other areas of the club to be showcased. A dancer can make a show of the tipping, enlisting the customer into a brief and impromptu erotic performance. Some dancers will choose (if they are offered this option) to only dance on stage, but it is dances off stage where real money is made. Both the lap dance and the table dance typically consist of one dancer dancing for one customer. The degree of contact varies. Some locations prohibit any direct contact, which means that the dancer strips directly in front of the customer or on the table itself.[41] The lap dance usually will include both dancing in front of the customer and on the lap. The lap dance is unique in the club and in the realm of sexual entertainment.[42] It is distinct from other performances in the club and from no-contact table dancing in terms of the physical and emotional possibilities it engenders. Both kinds of tableside performances can include the dancer sitting with or on the customer before or after the dance. Like the stage, tableside performances offer opportunities to upsell to the next level of intimacy, and also to assess whether the customer has and is willing to spend money. Not to be overlooked in these interactions is the chance it provides for dancers to assess whether or not they want to dance more for someone. If a customer is particularly rough, drunk, dirty, handsy, or in any other way poses a risk, they can stay away (*if* they can afford to and *if* the club management does not control whom they dance for). Most dancers I knew at some point exercised their rights to refuse a dance, and the literature on stripping acknowledges this as a power strippers have, although certainly the right can be violated. Despite the variety of performance in the strip club in which dancers and customers together construct fantasy interactions, they all function in a similar way. That is, performers, performances, and audiences coalesce into a genre that serves the purpose of providing a service; what that service *is*, however, is complicated and is controlled by the customer with a particular need and with the dancer who can fulfill it. As I will expand on in the next section, the service aspect fused with the affective responses of customers help construct a body genre in which the viewer and the viewed construct the "body-in-feeling" through the purchase of both emotional and sexualized excesses.[43] It is the function of stripping as a body genre that explains its potent but low cultural value.

Neo-burlesque is situationally different from club stripping in that there are rarely transactional individualized interactions between performer and audience, which alters the affective responses being cultivated by the performance, changing it from the body genre described above to a more narrative genre that features the body.[44] This difference can be seen in all aspects of the performance situation. With regard to performers, while strip clubs tend more to encourage dancer types—goth chick, rocker chick, rap goddess chick—neo-burlesque performers' success often depends on their ability to craft a persona that is distinct, memorable, and recognizable. Neo-burlesque personas, delivered via fanciful names, costumes, and acts, constitute performers as characters, rather than as workers, social identities that are crafted in part through performers' relationships with audiences.

Many of the claims about audience in the literature on neo-burlesque—both popular and scholarly—serve to establish the basic differences between the strip-club customer and the neo-burlesque audience, mainly that women are a fundamental part of the audience for neo-burlesque.[45] It is a difference that is central to defining neo-burlesque as a genre separate from club stripping and from the antecedent genre of classic burlesque. Even for those neo-burlesque shows and performers that are most committed to presenting a classic take on burlesque, audience composition will always yield a different genre from the heyday of midcentury burlesque. Debra Ferreday notes that neo-burlesque's "sense of continuity with the past is constantly disrupted by narratives of difference," in which one of the primary "points of distinction" between classic and neo-burlesque is the gender makeup of the audience.[46] Ferreday also notes that neo-burlesque audiences frequently share the love of vintage styles that many performers display both on and off stage. This love of vintage is one point of connection that makes neo-burlesque audiences and performers part of a shared community. Although strip clubs can also cultivate communities, those communities are discrete and forged around certain places and among certain people. Neo-burlesque on the other hand frequently cultivates a whole lifestyle for performers as well as dedicated fans. Neo-burlesque's cultural community feeds into what Jacki Willson calls a collapse of the distance between audience and performer in neo-burlesque[47] and into what Gerry Harris refers to as the "affective social/sociable contract"[48] between performer and audience, constituting the viewer of neo-burlesque as one part of a vast community, rather than one half of an individualized transaction.

And so, within a context that includes performers and audiences making a community rather than workers and customers making a sale, the striptease performance of neo-burlesque functions to display the talents of the performer and share a particular narrative vision. Although audiences certainly help construct performances because of the interactive elements of live theater, the performer has choreographed the performance ahead of time, often with a particular narrative arc that ties together music and movement and costume. Sometimes this is overt, as in Indigo Blue's "Amazon Damsels in Bondage," in which she dresses in a Wonder Woman costume and dances to the Wonder Woman

TV theme, but the links among the symbolic elements are not always so apparent. I'm thinking here of more neo-classical striptease routines in which the choreographed removal of clothes on a theme is the central feature. One example of this is the routine called "Tiger" by Sydni Deveraux, a.k.a. The Golden Glamazon, in which she does a long, slow striptease to "Night Walk" by Dick D'Agostin & The Swingers. Deveraux's tiger print outfit and her agonizingly slow strip and languid moves pay homage to the jungle cat of the title, but these are subtle gestures. Deveraux doesn't wear a cat mask or play with a giant ball of yarn or engage in any absurdist moves that would certainly be at home in a neo-burlesque show. This is a serious strip. It is sensual and erotic and inviting, and as such, it can certainly cultivate arousal in the audience. But it is not a transaction, and Deveraux, not the audience member, drives the strip. It is as good as it gets. *(And in Deveraux's case, it is quite good.)* While the audience's response—cheering, whistling, and whooping—might enhance the intensity of her movements and create a heightened emotional state in the room, individuals cannot control how much she takes off or how close they can get to her.[49]

Symbolic Features

So far, I have endeavored to show the ways that the genres of neo-burlesque and topless dance are distinct with regards to their situational elements. However, genre analysis also reveals the places where they are most similar, descending as they do from a shared antecedent genre. It is perhaps not surprising then that neo-burlesque and club stripping share the most features in the body movements themselves, part of what I refer to throughout this book as the kinesthetic symbolic, the primary communicative realm for all forms of dance. Like writing and speaking, "dance has purposeful, intentionally rhythmical, and culturally influenced sequences of body movements that are selected in much the same way that a person would choose sequences of verbal language."[50] I have, with difficulty, separated out the common movements; however, it is crucial that readers who have not seen either type of performance understand that all features occur in both. Pole dancing, one of the most recognizable symbols of club stripping, also happens in neo-burlesque. In fact, the best pole routine I have ever seen was by the duo Gravity Plays Favorites and occurred at the B.B. King Blues Club and Grill at the Saturday Spectacular of the 2013 New York Burlesque Festival.[51] Two dancers shared one pole in a blissfully beautiful display of acrobatic core strength

5 | "From earliest antiquity, rhetoricians have been interested in forms" (Campbell and Jamieson, "Form and Genre in Rhetorical Criticism," 20). Gravity Plays Favorites, 2012. Toronto Burlesque Festival. Photo by Olena Sullivan. Used with permission.

(fig. 5). Although it was late in the evening, this part of the show held me rapt as it felt so comfortable and familiar. *(And really, really cool.)*

Despite the fact that movements overlap between the two genres, certain core moves compose the basic vocabularies of each.[52] In *The Burlesque Handbook*, Weldon breaks down the basic, classically inspired movements of glove peels, bumps and grinds, tassel twirling, and fan dancing. Despite the innumerable varieties of neo-burlesque, many performances climax with the dancer clad in bikini bottoms and pasties with tassels, which are then twirled. In my experience, tassel twirling usually leads to an explosion of applause, despite and maybe because of the fact that it is such a common feature of neo-burlesque. It is always exciting to witness the finesse of a good twirl.[53] Tassel twirling is also not limited to women or to people with breasts, many men also make it a part of the act, sometimes as part of a gender-blending performance, but not necessarily. Tassel twirling also can be done via different body parts. Performers who twirl "assels," for example, redirect the audience gaze to the butt. In some cases, this redirection serves as an important resignification. Sydney Lewis argues that for Ginger Snapz, a black performer, "assels relocate that signifier to the seat of black women's sexuality—the butt," refiguring "the decisive signifier of female sexuality."[54] Stripping to pasties or the pasties/tassels combo is the moment of ultimate exposure for most neo-burlesque performances: it is as nude as it gets. Lewis contends that "the history and nature of burlesque dictates that new gimmicks quickly become stock elements of the genre,"[55] and this is true for many of its most recognizable material symbols. Thus tassel twirling, which combines the kinesthetic with the sartorial shifts its symbolic meaning depending on who is doing it and how. The symbolic meaning of this common move has changed over the years from being a stand-in for the nipple that when combined with a tassel focuses the audience's gaze on the bounce and the heft of the breasts, to being a symbol *for* neo-burlesque itself as have many other sartorial elements, in particular, fans, boas, gloves, and their attendant generic movements: fan dances, glove peels, and flashes.

Topless dance also has certain core moves both on and off stage. What defines a lap dance varies by locale and permitted and desired contact,[56] but the core move here consists of grinding and bouncing on or near the lap of the customer.[57] Dancers also slide their bodies down the body of the customer, simulate oral sex, and place the customer's face between their breasts. During onstage performances, "dancers commonly gyrate hips and torso, thrust hips back and forth and rotate them ('bump & grind'), rotate hips into a squat (like a screw), undulate the body or body parts, shimmy breasts, and bend the torso to peek through one's legs."[58] Similar to neo-burlesque without the pasties, in topless dance, stage acts generally reach their peak with the full exposure of the dancer's breasts. In both genres then, the reveal of the breasts marks the point at which the strip is done: maximum nudity has been reached. Also, in both genres the artistry of executing these core moves, along with other elements that heighten the drama (props and story in neo-burlesque, pole work and gymnastics in topless, showmanship in both) is what separates the good from the bad from the average.

Common moves in both genres tend toward the seductive and the sexual. Seductive moves found primarily in neo-burlesque depend on flashes and delaying gratification, in which the delay rather than the reveal becomes the fetishized experience. Sexualized and erotic moves, found mostly in club stripping, mimic the body in sexual acts, from the dancer bouncing her pelvis on a stage or a lap, on her knees mimicking oral sex, or on her knees with her head down and her hips and butt in the air facing the customers. Dances move customers erotically and emotionally because of the "affectively linked associations" with sexual acts that they evoke: "There is the sight of bodies moving in time and space; the sounds of physical movement and breathing, and usually the accompanying music; the smell of the dancers' body odors and perfume; the tactile sense of body parts touching the ground, other body parts, people, or props; the proxemic sense of distance between dancers and between dancers and spectators; and the kinesthetic (feeling of bodily movement and tension) experience or empathy with dancers."[59]

Typically, the moves in club stripping are more sexually overt than neo-burlesque and in some cases can lead to sexual release for a customer;[60] however, both dancer narratives and contemporary ethnographic research reveals that even with the more directly sexualized nature of stripping that sexual release is rarely the primary motive for customers. As compared to neo-burlesque, in which performers play to the crowd, topless dancers play to one customer at a time, and the language of dance in this genre mimics that. Even in low- or no-contact environments, during a lap or table dance the dancer's proximity and attention is focused on the individual who has bought the dance, and the movements that mimic the body during sex cultivate the fantasy of individual attention. That is, through this mimicry the spectator is *positioned as* the body that is performing a sexual act with the dancer.

The body genre of club stripping is constructed through movement but also through the styles seen on the bodies performing those movements. Whereas some clubs' dancers start in gowns, most begin in skimpier clothing as compared to neo-burlesque, in which performers often have elaborate costumes consisting either of dramatic gowns, gloves, boas, and headdresses, character costumes, or of "prop costumes" that make dancers' bodies one with objects. Despite their differences, however, erotic dancing of any genre can generate significant cost, which is an interesting aspect of a performance defined by nudity, one that emphasizes that getting there is most of the fun. While one would expect the often-fantastic costumes of neo-burlesque to cost a lot, stripper clothes are surprisingly pricey. Costumes that consist of three flimsy pieces of fabric can cost $30 to $50. Capes and robes add an additional expense, and shoes—one needs good shoes if one works on one's feet for eight hours—cost $90.00 and up, depending on quality. Stripper shoes, typically a high-heeled, high platform, are arguably the most distinctive stylistic element in this genre. Besides having the benefits that all heels do of lengthening and shaping the leg, the heeled platform also gives dancers the benefit of height. Thus the effect in a club is of women towering over men who spend most of their time sitting. These shoes not only communicate desirability and strength, but they can also become part of the act when dancers bang their shoes on the stage or against each other to punctuate parts of a song. Finally, shoes serve purposes that are more utilitarian: they can hold money and also act as weapons. When one is mostly naked in public, such accoutrements are necessary.

Although there are many variations on neo-burlesque style, vintage dominated for many years. More recently, I have observed that the popularity of vintage is fading, yet it is still emblematic of neo-burlesque. Performers tend to favor highly feminine styles, with heels (usually not stripper heels), gowns, gloves, boas, glitter, Swarovski crystals, painted nails, red lipstick.[61] Many performers make their own costumes,[62] and many performers also maintain some adherence to their styles offstage, making the neo-burlesque look like something that exists not just in performance spaces.

Racing the Racy Body

The most stereotyped styles in neo-burlesque represent the centrist and white femininity that has dominated burlesque from the mid-twentieth century to today. Although performers of all races can be found in the classic vintage get up, increasing numbers are diversifying the genre by spotlighting styles that have been neglected. Because burlesque has an often-problematic relationship to whiteness, the importance of these performances is tremendous. The Brown Girls Burlesque (NYC), the Asian Burlesque Extravaganza (NYC), and the Chocolate City Burlesque and Cabaret (DC) are a few well-known examples that feature performers of color in acts that draw on classic burlesque looks and also bring in histories and styles that are either neglected or appropriated in the larger neo-burlesque world. Because neo-burlesque is a theatrical performance art at heart, the issue of style and race can present a number of problems. That is to say, there is a fine line between honoring people and cultures and exploiting them.

At the Burlesque Hall of Fame in Las Vegas, Nevada, the archive overflows with pictures detailing burlesque's history of promoting the *eros* of women of color in degrading ways, while simultaneously presenting avenues for "class jumping."[63] As described in chapter 1, although women of color in classic burlesque rarely made as much money as their white counterparts, there also were many opportunities to make more money than was otherwise available.[64] However, because burlesque was almost exclusively controlled by white producers, women of color were often billed as "exotics," with parodic and stereotyped performances.[65] This eroticizing of the exotic other still happens in neo-burlesque, along with equally problematic instances of cultural appropriation in which white performers, demonstrating little understanding of the cultures they are borrowing from, build an act around styles and customs and practices of another race or ethnicity. White performers often excuse this as paying homage, yet it usually just underscores white ignorance of racism. This is not to say that performers can never draw on styles that are not part of their personal heritage, but rather that cultural appropriation can be used to reinforce white dominance by exploiting cultures when the people to whom that culture belongs are left out of positions of power in producing and choreographing.

A notorious instance of this in neo-burlesque is Dita Von Teese's Opium Den routine. Von Teese gained widespread notoriety and visibility with her marriage to Marilyn Manson in 2005, popularizing neo-burlesque to an audience it hadn't yet reached and helping to build the swell of interest in vintage styles and in neo-burlesque itself. In 2012, as part of her Strip, Strip, Hooray! show, Von Teese performed her Opium Den routine, in which she—with her signature Bettie Page-esque styling—dressed in an elaborate costume consisting of a Westernized, cinched, glittery dress with a similarly Westernized Chinese Opera headdress, smoking "opium" while stroked to a staged climax.[66] In response, Seattle performer, teacher, and producer The Shanghai Pearl wrote a post titled "'It's Complicated': More on Cultural Appropriation" on her Facebook page, explaining the harm of this and similar acts:

> I was affected negatively by the act and ... I am not alone. I was uncomfortable watching a white woman invoking two dimensional stereotypes of Asian women to convey the message of sex. Opium is also the subject of two vicious wars perpetrated against China and its people. In addition, many of the harmful stereotypes that still exist today stem from this terrible time in China's history. I have spent most of my life defending my three dimensional humanity and sexuality against these stereotypes. It is painful to see those stereotypes casually worn as a costume by someone who has not had those specific experiences.

She then moves from the particular problems with this act to the larger problem in neo-burlesque in which racial and cultural histories are exploited, causing real consequences in terms of the affective responses of audience members.

Individuals who are themselves victim to the stereotyped views that Von Teese casually staged are harmed, and audience members who already hold stereotyped views have them reinforced, in turn causing more harm. As Shanghai notes, Von Teese's legend and status in neo-burlesque matters, as it gives the impression that "the best in the best of burlesque is an outdated orientalist act." Here is a stunning, and yet all too common, exemplar of the way that performance can end up generating negative affective responses, rather than the playful sexiness that it seeks. One of the most common ways this happens is through acts whose style and substance perpetuate harmful stereotypes and demonstrate that the performer failed to imagine the effects on audience members who share that history.

My choosing to detail racism in the style of neo-burlesque is certainly not to say that topless dancers don't also deal with racism and stereotypes of their "exoticism" and sexual availability, but it does play out differently in neo-burlesque and particularly in the arena of style.[67] Neo-burlesque, with its freedom from the sales aspect of club stripping, can also generate positive affective responses in audiences, which is one of the arguments for neo-burlesque's popularity with women, as it presents venues for nearly every body type and ability.[68] Audiences and performers together create an "entire world of performance and community built around women behaving inappropriately for age, size, and gender, and men doing the same."[69] This honoring of diverse bodies is different from the "someone for everyone" energy I ascribe to club stripping, as neo-burlesque offers the communal celebrating of diverse body types. Whether or not it is always realized, *the ideal* of body positivity is central to the genre.

Even though topless dance and neo-burlesque sometimes share material symbolic features, the social actions that these constellations of features accomplish are distinct. In her influential 1984 article "Genre as Social Action," Carolyn Miller argues that genres are "typified rhetorical actions based in recurrent situations."[70] Based on this definition, critics look not only to identify features of discourse but also to the ways recurrent elements and situations fuse to accomplish particular social actions. Identifying the symbolic patterns that make up a genre, what methods and modes of communication and purposes are enabled and discouraged, reveals insight into what social actions are valued in what ways. As I hope this analysis demonstrates, the social actions of topless and neo-burlesque are dissimilar, despite sharing many similar features. These dissimilarities then can "tel[l] us about . . . the character of a culture"[71] in which stripping done in theaters for little to no pay is often protected as free speech and stripping done for money in clubs is subjected to surveillance by cultural critics, moral watchdogs, and the legal system. At the core of these differences is the combination of commercial exchange with the affective experience of audience members. When their bodies are drawn into performances that simulate erotic experience, the genre is shaped into one of sexual exchange, collapsing the distance and distinction between it and prostitution, *whether or not* there is ever contact between dancer and customer. Thus the values that are assigned to different forms of erotic dance have serious material consequences for performers.

For topless dance, indeed for all forms of club stripping, performance is structured by transaction and a number of material and embodied symbolic elements that generate fantasy. Space is one of these elements; like casinos, strip clubs are often timeless. They are always dark; the music is always loud; there is rarely a sense of time passing. Fantasy is also generated by the individual performance acts shared by customers and dancers, particularly for those regulars who pay not only for a lap dance but also for companionship. Dancers and regulars construct these fantasy relationships to varying degrees, but they are usually just talk. Relationships live in the club. Outside that space, contexts change and fantasies fall apart. While some customers get an erotic thrill from their interactions with dancers and others an emotional one, topless dance is about transaction. Performances—their style and substance—both on stage and in hustling customers for dances, are designed to facilitate transaction. In neo-burlesque on the other hand, there is still performed eroticism: costumes and body movements may—but don't tend to—overlap with club stripping. Here performance is a production, a communal production in which audiences participate in vastly different ways from club stripping. All neo-burlesque audiences, in essence, see from the side. Close enough to generate meaning, but not close enough to control performance.

Stripping as Social Action

Coney Island. 2013. The retired white man next to me is at Jo Weldon's Follies Fromage because he "loves the burlesque." Despite the fact that I find making small talk painful, I engage him as that seems the sensible thing for a researcher to do. Before the show and during breaks he tells me about how much he likes burlesque. How it isn't like the strip clubs; he's got no interest in that. How it calls up memories of a different time; how it articulates a past that is meaningful to him, even though he would have still been a child as burlesque passed the *torch to go-go clubs and strip joints, the precursors to the contemporary Gentleman's Club. "Boy, these ladies are great. They all look different. I don't like that Playboy look. Do you know Darlinda Just Darlinda? Aw, she's the best!" I shift on the bench and tell him I don't know her, even as I'm nodding. This is my second burlesque show, my first being the previous night at the Slipper Room on the Lower East Side. "Oh well, let me tell you . . . you are in for a treat." When Darlinda Just Darlinda comes onstage, my new acquaintance cups both hands to his mouth and yells "*DARLINDA! HEY . . . HEY . . . DARLINDA!*" I'm not sure what he expects her to do in response as she is in the middle of a choreographed number, but it seems important to him to signal his fandom. After the show—he and I were planning to ride the train together, because it was after 1:00 a.m., and I was worried about negotiating the hour-long ride back to the West Village and trusting a stranger seemed like a reasonable solution to my anxiety—he said, "Just a sec, I wanna say hi to Darlinda," and he went loping boyishly off, returning a few minutes later to walk with me to the train. "She's the best, isn't she? You ready to go?"*

In the opening of his essay "Genre and Identity: Citizenship in the Age of the Internet and the Age of Global Capitalism," Charles Bazerman uses habitual activities in common places to introduce his argument about the ways that genres produce social identities, which in turn influence the evolution of the genre. The places he lists—dance hall, seminar, church, racetrack—are places that call up an entire visual discourse of associated images. Depending on our religious background, references to church may cause us to envision a firebrand preacher or a white-collared priest; the parishioners may wear big colorful hats or dour black or Lilly Pulitzer. The sermons may be monotone or ebullient or wrathful. How we mentally populate these common places is not important. What is important is that we do. That we can. These features are part of the complex symbolic universe that constructs that social genre "church." Calling up these features shows that we have genre knowledge, and to follow Bazerman's argument, it also shows that when we go to certain places habitually and "do the kinds of things you do there, think the kinds of thoughts you think there, feel the kind of way you feel there, satisfy what you can satisfy there, be the kind of person you can become there," we develop the identity of being of that place.[72]

Within rhetorical and communication studies, the social aspects of genre have been widely explored.[73] Gunn argues that our participation in generic social forms is largely unconscious and that the purpose of rhetorical criticism is to make them conscious by "describing them, in language."[74] Naming the forms fixes them but only momentarily and partially. Thus criticism makes genres recognizable by bringing them out of the "collective mental space of a community or audience" and into a textual space where they reside not only in the minds of the audience but also in a larger public.[75] If a genre is reflective of the mental and social lives of its participants, then genre criticism is indeed an important critical tool for understanding social practices. As Gunn is also careful to point out, those genre features that we identify to show evidence of a genre's existence are only "traces" of this unconscious social life. That is, while shoes, poles, boas, and gloves may help me differentiate among various genres of erotic dance, recognizing them individually doesn't tell me much about the dynamics that help those features to coalesce into a recognizable social form.

Because genre is social and part of identity, it is necessarily embodied. The genre knowledge we construct and apply is part of complex discourse systems of which the linguistic is only a part. Therefore, genre—like delivery—is an embodied critical method whether or not one focuses explicitly on the material symbolic: those codes are always part of genre. For critics of the body, genre offers a theoretical perspective that is attentive to the multiple symbolic realms that body rhetoric employs. In the case of stripping, an eye toward genre can offer a nuanced view of the social, political, and legal hierarchy that exists for public erotic performances. As Bawarshi argues, "Genres do not simply help us define and organize kinds of texts; they also help us define and organize kinds of social actions."[76] Genres offer a way to systematically investigate erotic performance, and as Thomas Laqueur reminds us, "Serious talk about sexuality is ... inevitably about the social order that it both represents and legitimates."[77] Genres connect acts to the social order. By analyzing them, we can better understand the constraints and affordances for actors within those genres. And in doing *that* we can better understand broader social values. In the case of the genres under consideration here, they reveal our ranking of appropriateness with regard to public erotic dancing by women, and the consequences of those rankings, which I will further explore in chapter 4.

In some ways, thinking about topless dancing and neo-burlesque in terms of genre reveals what we already know: these are *different* performances, valued and judged *differently*, but genre analysis stresses how it is the fusion of these features that makes neo-burlesque stripping more okay, more feminist, than other forms of stripping according to some critics, fans, and performers. There is a well-worn punch line that asserts that the difference between the two genres is that topless dancers make money. This punch line is instructive yet partial. It tells us a difference. It doesn't tell us about difference, about the construction of difference. Although this difference makes a distinction between a sales job and a performance art, it closes the door too quickly on issues that remain relevant, particularly for sexual and erotic rhetorics. Focusing only on the end result of pay and not on the constellation of features and actions that are paid for shortchanges both genres by not fully contextualizing the affective responses and hence the social roles that they generate. When we apply Gunn's theory of genre as the names of affects delivered to meaning, we can see that the difference in the cultural value accorded these practices is created not solely by the transaction between customer and dancer but also in the bodily response the performance seeks to elicit, from whom it tries to elicit it, and where it occurs. In the case of these embodied performances, most of the symbolic features are material—kinesthetic, cosmetic, and sartorial—making Gunn's "place where the symbolic meets the body" a meeting between the body as symbolic generator and the body as affective receiver and marking a departure from typical genre studies in rhetoric. However as Gunn notes, within film studies genre has *not* been conceived of in the "relatively flat, text-bound" way in which we often find it in rhetorical studies.[78] Thus for critics of performance rhetoric, in which acts are delivered to many audience members simultaneously, as opposed to the comparatively individual act of reading, film genre theory has much to offer. Further, studies and critical works on erotic dancing tend to frontload one role in the club (the experiences, motivations, and desires of dancers *or* customers), while genre analysis with its sideways view requires that we look at all of these elements together.

In order to understand the distinct social actions of these genres, here I will return to Gunn's affective approach to focus on the "feelings evoked by the patterned repetitions" one finds in the club.[79] Body genres exhibit displays (or dramatizing) of bodily excesses in the structure of particular fantasies. Although film and live performance obviously differ, Williams's suggestion that the low-cultural value for some genres is linked to the audiences' "lack of proper esthetic distance, a sense of over-involvement in sensation and emotion"[80] is directly applicable to the different kinds of audience functions in neo-burlesque and in topless dance. Similar to the body genres of film, club dancing seeks a particular response from the audience: there is a direct connection between the actions of the dancer and the customer. Unlike the body genres Williams analyzes, however, here the affective response that is cultivated by a performance shifts, depending on the viewer. The dancer's performance is crafted customer by customer to evoke a particular feeling, which will encourage a certain fantasy vision.

For some customers that feeling will be arousal generating a sexual fantasy, but for others the affective response cultivated by a performance often yields emotional fantasies of being a friend, boyfriend, or lover.[81]

The body is also the central vehicle for communication in neo-burlesque. Neo-burlesque bodies move, and even sometimes are styled, in ways that share more with other bodies in erotic dance than with most other genres of both live theater and theatrical dance. Yet neo-burlesque performances cultivate a distinct relationship between performer and audience. Neo-burlesque is a highly interactive genre, but even though audiences share in the construction of performances and also in the larger community that exists outside of a particular performance space, audiences don't act as consumers gratifying a fantasy that is tailored to them individually. In theorizing genre constitution in terms of affect, Gunn stresses that the patterned forms that make genres are both "repetitive and addictive" for their participants.[82] This is another feature that highlights the particular body genre aspects of club stripping. Topless dancing relies more on a repetitive performance structure than does neo-burlesque. Although expectations and experiences vary widely within each club, the same patterns of individual and stage dances are performed over and over. In my club, it was dancer on stage 1, then 2, then 3, then the floor. The same pattern over and over. So too with their regulars do dancers perform the same routines, which is one of the reasons customers seek out dancers as temporary companions. The routine is generally predictable because expectations are negotiated. Particular sets of repetitions produce feelings in customers, which they then translate into meaningful involvements, which they then use to organize their experiences. In neo-burlesque on the other hand, repetition of forms exist—glove peels, boas, glitter, tassel twirls—but their purpose is to deliver a particular narrative to the audience, who helps to construct this narrative. Audiences also often share in the forms of the larger neo-burlesque community, but performances are not designed for individuals but for the audience en masse. That is, *audience* as a collective becomes a player in a neo-burlesque show, rather than *audience member*. Because performance is not delivered to one person, fans are less likely to recognize their affective responses as emotional relationships that parallel ones outside of the performance space. Even the most ardent fans of performers are not likely to see themselves as a performer's mate. There is community and camaraderie, but the sense of *being in* relationship is constructed differently. This changes the meaning of the bumping, grinding, stripping body on stage, making neo-burlesque not a "body genre" as Clover defines it, but a genre of the body.

Genre analysis, with particular attention to affective response, clarifies the social hierarchy of erotic dance. Like other body genres, club stripping is more stigmatized because its performances seek to match the actions of the body on screen with the feelings of the body in the audience. Thus it is not so much the stripping body that marks low culture, it is the affective experience of the audience in response *to* that body. This is not to say that neo-burlesque is highbrow art. It is and has always been marked by absurdity and appeals to the grotesque and to the sexual that situate it firmly within popular culture. Further, to some feminist and conservative critics, it causes the same social harms as club stripping. But in terms of degrees of stigma that genre participation carries, the hierarchy of erotic dance places topless below neo-burlesque, although they share many similar characteristics.

Having participated in both genres as an audience member and as a regular, I have always struggled to adequately describe the differences between the two. I have long been aware that my participation in neo-burlesque is much more cursory—what I describe here as sideways—than my participation as a customer in a strip club and that my deep emotional investment in my experiences as a regular were distinct and meaningful. Further, I am still vividly aware of the deep shame I carry with regard to my past as a regular. Feminist shame that I consumed women who had an economic need, sexual shame that I purchased sexualized services and intimacy because it suggests that I am not capable of getting those for free, intellectual shame that time and again I exhibited the same beliefs and behaviors as the men I read about in research studies—lonely, desperate, unsure—men that as a feminist reader I sometimes hate and sometimes pity, bodily shame that I was such a slave to my addictions—women, sex, drugs, booze, cigarettes—back then that I ran myself into debt and nearly killed myself, others, my career with my *poor life choices*. When I have spoken about my time in the clubs, I have claimed that it was research first and that I went native as an ethnographer while there. That is a lie. I chose to research and to write about it after I was addicted to give myself more reason to be there and to lessen my shame. How else could I explain this involvement to my feminist friends, my colleagues, potential employers, my institution, my family? I never feel shame about neo-burlesque. I can and occasionally do feel awkward about it, both when I have to self-identify as an outsider to those in that community and to my academic audience when I write about a subject that is widely perceived as frivolous. Pursuing this genre analysis situated in affect has been a personal as well as a professional project, which I intend the narrative interludes to illuminate. Throughout this analysis, I have used narrative as a way both to position the reader in the situation I am analyzing—a situation better understood through experience—and to own all of the aspects that make me most uncomfortable and intrigued by these two genres. Like many other regulars, I fell stupidly in love with dancers. Every aspect of the genre that I describe here seduced me both emotionally and sexually. As a body genre, there was a link between my body and the performances I sought out. That link persists. This link does not exist between me and neo-burlesque. It does not operate as a body genre to involve me in the same way, and I am not a part of its community. I am only a sideways viewer, always entertained but never in intimate conversation with the bodies onstage.

Roxy never returned. Isabella's gone, permanently 86'd. I have fifteen thousand dollars of credit card debt. I need to stay away from the club, but one more night won't hurt. As I approach the entrance, I rush my favorite doorman with a jumping leg hug, hanging like a monkey for just a second before dropping off so he can hold the door for me. In the foyer, the manager unclips the velvet rope and waves me inside past the crowd lined up to pay the entrance fee. An assistant manager walks by with a serious nod. "How ya doing, Mags?" "I'll be better soon." A bouncer comes up with a grin to show me to my favorite table. "How about tonight?" "Maybe." It's our game. He wants to "convert me." This exchange never feels creepy to me. I enjoy flirting with the giant men who work the club. A waitress hurries over, busses the table, and places a napkin. "Scotch on the rocks and a water?" "And matches and an ashtray. Thanks." As I unload my cell phone, gum, and Camel Lights from my pockets, I wave to a dancer on stage. Another walks by with a smile and a laugh. "How ya doing, Maggie May?" "Hey! I'm okay." Her friend joins her and says, "The Maganator," also with a laugh. I laugh, too. Happy to be here even though I can't afford dances anymore. My girlfriend joins me and orders a Corona. The DJ's voice announces, "Alright gentlemen, coming up topside in her first stage of the evening is the gorgeous Samantha. Get those dollar bills ready. Remember, the better the tip, the better the strip." Samantha takes the stage, active and graceful, with quick hard spins on the pole and fluid dance moves that suggest training. Holy shit! She's beautiful. And she can move. I've never been so instantly hooked. I turn to my girlfriend. "Oh my God. She is so hot. Can I have my credit cards back?" My girlfriend rolls her eyes as I sigh and lean back smiling. "I love her."

3

The Pleasures of Process | Neo-Burlesque's Seductive Rhetoric

On Fridays at the Saint Hotel in New Orleans, Trixie Minx stages Burgundy Burlesque. Accompanied by a live jazz band in a small bar glowing red with the demonic pleathers and fabrics that give the bar its name, performers dance in front of an enormous picture window that faces Canal Street in the French Quarter. Running from 9:00 p.m. to midnight, the performance is a multifaceted production, as both tourists and locals gambol through the Quarter. On April 18, 2018, sipping a Diet Coke, I sat alone at the burgundy bar, feeling worn out by the travel, the research, the body, my body. I'm getting too old for this. On either side of me were couples—on one side a man and woman, older than me, and on the other a man and a woman, younger than me. Here I am, stuck in the middle. At this point in my life, I had stopped drinking. I never really quit, just stopped, and sobriety made the inevitable chitchat almost unbearable. Knowing my tendency to be unintentionally rude with my introversion, I chatted as amicably as I am able, while internally I was screaming, "Bring out the dancing girls!" as emcee Mel Frye had done at my first burlesque show at the Slipper Room.[1] And eventually they came. Shows with live jazz bands are my favorite, and this aspect combined with the glamorous performers, agile and smiling, had me hooked, my enthusiasm slightly muted by a comedian emcee whose humor bordered on the misogynistic. Liking the show, but feeling a bit bored and annoyed by the comedian, I found my attention drifting. Until the next performer took the stage. Halfway through the song, she went upstage to the window and began performing to the passersby, her back to us. Many of them kept walking—just another night in the Quarter—a pair of women broke into riotous giggles and hurried by and then back for pics. The window had become the show, the bar patrons and the street spectators were both viewing and the viewed. The performer, lithe, blonde, beautiful, became the fulcrum of desire between the insiders and outsiders. When she turned to us, we were the audience, performers to the passersby with our gawking, hooting, laughing. With a turn from us, the roles were flipped, creating impromptu street theater. A man walked by the window as she danced to the street. He moved past our view and then walking backwards, mouth agape, shuffled back into the picture. The performer caught the moment, held his attention, pointed and danced to him and for him. Slack-jawed and staring up at the framed woman in the window, his reaction became our focus. The window became a screen; his amusement and desire became our viewing pleasure. Seizing the moment, the comedian ran outside, and with exaggerated gestures, calculated with our viewing in mind, managed to tease the man on the street without our hearing a word.

The dancer whipped the curtains closed and with a turn, a wink, and a slight smile, the number ended.

I was awakened.

Seduction has long represented erotic persuasion, a type of intimate and strategic communication with sex as its ultimate goal.[2] As it is popularly understood, seduction is the erotic conquest of innocents by coquettes and rakes, archetypal seducers whose strategies include flirtation, flattery, and deception to serve selfish needs for attention and sexual gratification. These strategies are designed for a specific "target" whom the seducer desires and who opposes the seducer's goal and must be overcome. Without this source of conflict, there is no need for seduction. The target's resistance provides the exigence that the seducer responds to and is key to defining this version of seductive rhetoric.[3] In this popular view, seduction is purpose driven: strategies are chosen to achieve the goal of sexual satisfaction for the seducer. It is persuasion solely concerned with addressing the exigence of resistance and satisfying the needs of a rhetor, who seeks to manipulate an audience of one. Understood this way, seduction is persuasion based not on the logic of the mind but on the passions of the flesh. Because of this legacy, seduction has a complicated relationship with rhetoric. If we understand it as a means to achieve sexual conquest without concern for the seduced, then seduction represents the worst of persuasion: bending the will of another to serve one's own ends. But seduction's story is not so simple.

Starting with Jean Baudrillard's *Seduction*, postmodern theory has elevated the seductive process, using it as a metaphor to represent symbolic practices that oppose stable meanings and ultimate truths. This postmodern seduction reveals itself not to be about domination and control, but about play and pleasure and process, both about dazzling audiences with dynamic and changing signs and about the celebration of artifice. Recast this way, seduction presents intriguing possibilities for rhetoric and for the criticism of performing bodies. Seeing postmodern seduction not only as a theory but also as a type of strategic rhetoric offers insight into communication practices that do not depend on rationality and logic.[4] In this seductive rhetoric, process—the pleasurable experience of being wooed and wooing—*is* purpose. That is, rather than being concerned with purpose or exigence or result, seductive rhetoric dwells in the "middle part" of communication. Seductive rhetoric, therefore, can describe those processes of symbolic exchange that centralize pleasure and play and indeterminacy and that exist within a range of contemporary rhetorics concerned with the signifying processes used in identification, constitution, and articulation, to name only a few.[5] One site that evinces seductive rhetoric both as a form of erotic persuasion and as a way of creating and disassembling meanings and identities is the performance art of neo-burlesque. As a form of comedic, erotic performance that makes a "public display of sexuality," neo-burlesque showcases features of seduction through its sensual bodily displays and through playing with meaning, often via displays of "excessive femininity of appearance and gesture."[6] As demonstrated in chapter 2, performances are delivered in multiple symbolic codes that often resist and disrupt stable meaning—qualities of a postmodern "Third Sophistic" rhetoric—and illustrate that artifice crafted through seductive rhetorical strategies can move audiences pleasurably, discomposing rhetorical processes in the name of artifice, play, and entertainment.[7] As scholars continue to expand rhetoric's reach into sites of embodied and performance rhetorics and to develop new purposes, the field can benefit from a wider array of theoretical perspectives and methodological options. Seductive rhetoric, which draws its persuasive power from pleasure, provides an alternative critical tool for analyzing rhetoric that operates outside of the realm of rational ends and logical means as rhetorics of the body, particularly those in performance, often do. While rhetoric and communication theorists have established seduction as a mode of communication, applying those theories analytically can seem counter to the basic ideas of seductive communication. Seduction, at least according to Baudrillard, opposes the regularity and rigidity that analysis often implies. However, as I have been demonstrating throughout this book, critical analysis need not foreclose on pleasure and play. Thus theories of seduction provide particular ways to focus on and critique those performances of the body that eschew regularity and rigidity.[8] In using postmodern theories of seduction as a critical framework for erotic performance, I suggest that embodied performance rhetoric benefits from making pleasure a fundamental part of analysis and that erotic and sexual bodies demonstrate the ways that bodies and pleasure are always part of symbolic communication, despite the fact that several theoretical traditions have tried to differentiate the seductive from the sexual in order to ameliorate seduction.

Uncovering Seductive Rhetoric

The literature on seduction, both popular and scholarly, often pursues similar objectives. The first is to validate seduction, showing its value either as a guide to mastering strategies of sexual pursuit and conquest or to show why such a seemingly shallow subject is of intellectual value. The second objective, tied to the first, is to define what seduction *really* is. Even Baudrillard, whose entire project eschews the search for meaning and value, offers an entire book to establish seduction's meanings and value. In that tradition, this chapter pursues similar objectives. In sketching out seduction's rhetorical dimensions, however, I want to avoid writing a master narrative. Instead, I intend to weave together various strands of seduction's diverse history to focus on those features that distinguish seductive rhetoric from other types of rhetoric. That is, while I offer a perspective on seductive rhetoric, I don't propose to offer the truth. In addition, I want to draw a distinction between *seduction* as a process and seductive rhetoric as a process-focused type of symbolic communication with my focus being on the second.

Seduction's popular legacy as a base, bodily, and largely unethical kind of sexual persuasion is one that intellectual work strives to overcome. Representative of popular seduction is Robert Greene's bestselling book *The Art of Seduction*. Greene represents a persuasive and erotically charged view of seduction within popular culture that is ethically challenged and misogynistic. For example, Greene's coquettes and rakes draw on grossly base performances of gender in order to conquer their targets. The rake cannot help but bed as many women as possible—it's a fundamental part of his manliness. The coquette flatters and flirts with little depth. While these are but two of the seven types Greene covers, they stand as prototypical masculine and feminine seducers. Both care only about the conquest and both have a long artistic and literary history, cementing these two as archetypes of seduction. Greene presents a handbook that promises to make its readers masters at sexual conquest. In the handbook's chapter titles, which sum up his system of seduction, he refers to the seducee as a "victim" and shares advice on how to "choos[e] the right victim," how to "create a false sense of security" and how to "use the demonic power of words to sow confusion." It is laughable, but it is also dangerous. While Greene doesn't directly feminize "victims" and he includes masculine and feminine and even androgynous seducer types, clearly the language of victimization, isolation, and confusion will be read and lived differently depending on one's body. While Greene's book is an international bestseller and required reading for self-styled "pick-up artists," the associations he draws between persuasion and seduction are sexist, heterosexist, cissexist, limited, and violent. The book serves as an excellent introduction to why seduction seems antithetical to feminist rhetoric, an antithesis that is furthered by the culture that *The Art of Seduction* fomented.

Greene's *The Art of Seduction* is an important text of the seduction industry that became especially popular in the first decade of the twenty-first century. This self-help industry promised anyone (although it was heavily marketed to men) that they could learn to become sexually irresistible to anyone, anytime, anywhere. Being a seducer was marketed as being a matter not of living up to model standards of masculinity but of learning a system of verbal and bodily signs. Devotees of seduction culture refer to themselves as "pick-up artists" or PUAs. Neil Strauss's 2005 book *The Game* in which he chronicles his experiences in learning PUA techniques led to an explosion in the popularity of seduction with increased media attention, a TV show on VH1 called *The Pick-Up Artist* hosted by the dramatic and foppish "Mystery" (the stage name of Erik von Markovik), and numerous self-help books.[9] While the pick-up genre superficially purports to appeal to both men and women, it is heavily chauvinistic. Writing in *Vice* in 2017, journalist Sarah Ratchford summed up the phenomenon: "Back in the depths of the mid-aughts, women and feminized people got a whole new education on which kinds of behaviours exhibited by cis men could turn out to be dangerous. Whereas before, an extroverted man in a strange outfit or with the ability to perform magic tricks could seem intriguing, those things turned out to often be little more than part of a larger package of bait carefully designed to lure women into bed."[10]

In this excerpt and in my own writing above, PUAs and their seduction seem at best juvenile and at worst dangerous. As Ratchford points out, pick-up artists are not innocuous but are serial harassers and often abusers of women. Thus seduction is not only sold as a strategic game; it is also a man's game, providing tools to help men overcome women's resistance to sex, which they will ultimately enjoy despite any words to the contrary. The strategies used to achieve seduction's purpose of conquest need not be ethical, only effective. In fact, they gain their effectiveness by being unethical. Shoshana Felman argues that the rhetoric of seduction exists "almost exclusively in the deployment of speech acts," which may be summed up by the performative utterance *par excellence*: "I promise."[11] The words "I promise" don't guarantee an action, only the words just spoken. Thus the promise only exists as a "referential illusion."[12] Felman's conception of the rhetoric of seduction then reflects long-standing, never-quite-resolved tensions between rhetoric and dialectic, Truth and artifice, and, as Felman puts it, "The register of knowledge" and the "register of pleasure."[13]

This popular version of seduction as sexual conquest—unethical, steeped in fakery and immorality, concerned only with achieving a goal by any means—closely resembles some notable ancient philosophic critiques of rhetoric. To simplify a complex history, rhetoric was denigrated because it could compel men to believe and to act in ways because they were moved via verbal trickery and artifice. Sophistic rhetoric, with its emphasis on the subjectivity of experience and the impossibility of knowing definitively what is true, was at odds with the "philosophical search for ideals."[14] The Sophist Gorgias, however, argued that language contains the power to confuse listeners about what the reality of their own experience is: "[Language] could interpret experience, and even create its similitude; further, it could conjure up the attitudes and emotions associated with experience in such a way as to deceive listeners, momentarily, into believing they were participating in 'the real thing.'"[15] This gave the skilled user of language powers akin to magic. In his *Encomium of Helen*, Gorgias argues Helen of Troy's case, offering a series of reasons why she is guiltless in the strife over her abduction that led to the Trojan War. Gorgias offers four possible reasons for Helen, the wife of King Menelaus of Sparta, leaving Sparta for Troy with Paris, the ostensible cause of the subsequent war. Gorgias argues that in any of the four possible reasons that Helen is powerless, being a victim to fate, violence, verbal seduction, or love. Of these, Gorgias, himself a master orator, spends the most time on the power of seductive language, which he compares first to witchcraft, comparing its effect on the soul to a magical incantation: "The power of the incantation is wont to beguile it and persuade it alter it and alter it by witchcraft" (10) and then to drugs: "The effect of speech upon the condition of the soul is comparable to the power of drugs over the nature of bodies" (14).[16] By bringing these four different causes together and spending the most time explicating the ways that language's seductive power can render someone powerless, Gorgias "equate[s] without quite conflating necessity, violence, persuasion, and *eros*," thus demonstrating that "persuasion is a form of seduction."[17] Each of these four causes then is equally able to effect a physical change in Helen, suggesting that rhetoric's seductive qualities are embodied. Whether Helen is abducted or persuaded, her body is ultimately subjected to similarly compelling forces.

The Sophistic focus on subjectivity over transcendent truth and the seductive power of language (which was a teachable art that anyone could obtain), positioned the Sophists in contrast with the dominant philosophical thought. For philosophers, most notably Plato, whose writings expand on this theme via the arguments of Socrates, the rhetorician is "the seducer bogged down with the body not the soul."[18] William Kelley illustrates how Plato links rhetoric and seduction in *The Phaedrus* and *The Symposium*: "Seductive rhetoric is comparably insidious for it arises from a philosophical stance endorsing deceit or sham; it loves the body and not the soul, it seeks and creates the ephemeral and not that which endures.... The ratio developing out of both dialogues is this: Love is to seduction as Truth is to rhetoric. Rhetoric is the semblance of wisdom as seduction is the semblance of love."[19]

For Plato, seduction represents the worst of sophistic rhetoric, which has the potential to persuade listeners into acting based not on ethics or logic, but on aesthetics and desire. Thus a Platonic perspective links rhetoric and seduction in the realm of artifice and aesthetics, both dazzling their victims with displays that obfuscate Truth. Unlike dialectic, that tool of the "philosophic will" seeking "to codify, systematize, and control language, to reduce it to *logos*, defined as rational speech" in order to reveal what is "true or probably true," seductive Sophistic rhetoric "resists logic" and "desires to trope."[20] Such negative associations between rhetoric and seduction led to Aristotelian preoccupation with developing an ethical rhetoric, one that operates like dialectic as a rational process of reaching probable truth, and divorcing itself from seduction's preoccupation with artifice, aesthetics, and pleasure.

Since the mid-twentieth century, however, rhetoricians have been expanding the range of both rhetoric and rhetorical study beyond the ends-driven rational discourses of philosophic traditions and reembracing sophistry, which doesn't "confuse language with reality" in the logical pursuit of truth and instead recognizes that language constitutes varied realities and multiple truths.[21] Rather than conceiving of artifice as concealing what is true, a Sophistic orientation to rhetoric recognizes all signs as indeterminate and mutable, a quality that seductive strategies highlight and that Baudrillard theorizes in *Seduction*. Baudrillard lays the groundwork for rethinking seduction's relationship to rhetoric by theorizing it as a game of symbols, not of sex or of deceit. Like Plato, he connects seduction and artifice, but unlike Plato, Baudrillard does not see artifice as concealing any *true* nature of things.[22] For Baudrillard, seduction opposes production whereby production pursues a "means of guaranteeing identity, truth, and presence" through "fix[ing] ... signifieds with ... signifiers." Seduction, on the other hand, leaves "the real ... unrepresented" with its complex systems of shifting signs.[23] While Baudrillard does not claim that seduction and production represent a binary, he does present seduction as an alternative to mechanistic production.[24] In short, seduction offers different modes of communication, knowing, and being.[25] Therefore, seductive strategies are those that encourage multiplicity of meaning and dynamic representations.

Despite these abstract qualities, the rhetorical applications of postmodern seduction are many. Postmodern rhetorical theory (I am thinking in particular here of the work of Sharon Crowley, Victor Vitanza, and Michelle Ballif) has demonstrated the ways that sophistic rhetoric unsettles insistence on agency, mastery, rationality, and pragmatics. Thus the revival of sophistry as demonstrated thoroughly by Ballif makes space for the flexibility and indeterminacy of seductive rhetoric. Yet postmodern theories of seduction can both provide and trouble possibilities for seductive rhetoric. While Baudrillard theorizes seduction as a game of signs that resists the effort to make meaning—a quality neo-burlesque performance frequently demonstrates—he also argues that seduction is opposed to production and is the "opposite of communication."[26] Since rhetoric has traditionally been a productive art, *seductive rhetoric* can seem to be an "oxymoron," much like "'postmodern' and 'rhetoric' [which] have most often in our discipline been taken to cancel each other out."[27] Ballif, however, connects seduction explicitly to postmodern rhetorical theory and opens up the possibility for understanding a seductive rhetoric that is informed by but not constrained by Baudrillard's work. According to Ballif, seduction is a type of "Third Sophistic Rhetoric." It is "the only possible tactic left to us that has any chance of subverting modernism's logic and its will to produce and represent."[28] Therefore, identifying those cultural practices that disrupt stable meaning, centralize play, and focus on the communicative interchange rather than result can reveal how seductive rhetoric functions sophistically.

Although Baudrillard theorizes seduction as "opposed to production" and communication,[29] the seductive rhetoric that I identify in neo-burlesque constitutes both. Further, I locate seductive strategies through rhetorical criticism, a practice that Baudrillard classifies as the "least seductive of discourses" in its search for meaning.[30] Despite these departures from Baudrillard, I approach this analysis not as a way to suggest ultimate meanings or to seek the Truth about neo-burlesque. Analyzing seductive rhetoric requires an approach that

Brian Ott theorizes as an "erotics of reading," a mode of criticism rooted in finding pleasure in text, rather than closing in on final meanings.[31] Ott demonstrates that the critical process need not be the dead-end task of searching for symbolic certainty that Baudrillard imagines. Inspired by Ott's erotics of reading, rather than offering a limited and limiting view of what seductive rhetoric *really is*, my analysis offers possibilities for applying seduction as a critical lens for performative embodied rhetorics. I provide—to borrow Vitanza's term—"provocations" both to seduction theory and to rhetorical criticism by identifying the embodied erotic rhetoric of neo-burlesque as a site of symbolic play that emphasizes open-ended communication, pleasure, and process.[32] Ultimately, what the following analysis of neo-burlesque suggests is that seductive rhetoric emphasizes pleasure and play rather than rationality and determination and is identifiable by its particular means of symbolic action. Therefore, as a critical lens for analyzing rhetorical acts, seduction's focus on process puts the liminal at the fore, representing not motive or result, but action.

Seductive rhetoric provides an orientation to symbolic action, in particular, the shift away from final meaning and ultimate truths, that benefits all manner of rhetorical bodies, not only those engaged in erotic performance. By communicating through multiple symbolic codes, seductive rhetoric takes up the "interconnections of language and material practices" that rhetorics of the body evince.[33] In neo-burlesque those codes are deployed in planned, public, and symbolic performances that make the sensual (and sometimes grotesque) body central to analysis. Neo-burlesque performances and other sites of embodied erotic rhetoric should be understood not for their exceptionalism but for their capacity to illuminate and bring into focus themes of performance, play, coercion, consent, and identity that bring meaning to all bodies in communication.

Focusing on the specific ways that rhetorical bodies deploy seductive strategies helps to illustrate postmodern seduction's oft-theorized relationship to the feminine through analyzing rhetorical practices that foster indeterminacy and fluidity, rather than focusing on the ways that the bodies themselves are sexed and gendered. Postmodern theories of seduction attempt to detach the feminine from women, in order to reconsider what "feminine" and "woman" can mean. Baudrillard disarticulates his conception of the feminine from "woman" as a biological body because he sees seduction as resisting the production of the man/woman binary itself: it is a concept that is "*radically opposed to anatomy as destiny.*"[34] Drawing on Baudrillard, Ballif argues that seduction reveals how "Woman is a rhetorical process" that "question[s] the philosophic concepts of being, truth, and subjectivity" and "challenge[s] ... sexual difference."[35] To simplify Ballif's complex argument, seduction offers an alternative episteme for "Woman," one that is not Other to man.[36] Ballif argues that "Woman as a rhetorical gesture ... question[s] the philosophic concepts of being, truth, and subjectivity."[37] Ballif figures this "Woman" then as one that "embodies the discursive form known as sophistry."[38] Despite the meanings suggested by these names, neither the "feminine" nor "Woman" are "gendered construction[s]" for either Baudrillard or Ballif; nor are they "representational of sex or sexuality" because seduction disrupts the binaries that create man/woman, masculine/feminine.[39] Thus we might understand the feminine in seduction theory as transcendent of ties to biology and social categories that are taken for granted.

While Ballif draws on Baudrillard's *Seduction* to redefine rhetoric by unsettling production-oriented insistence on agency, mastery, rationality, and pragmatics, communication scholars Keith Erickson and Stephanie Thomson take seduction down a more instrumentalist path, theorizing its methodological affordances. They propose that theories of seduction provide a critical lens for interpreting those rhetorical strategies that are at odds with the phallogocentrism underpinning much of the Western rhetorical tradition. Like Baudrillard and Ballif, they tie seductive rhetoric to "the feminine," but unlike postmodern seduction theorists, they articulate seductive rhetoric explicitly with living women's bodies by arguing that seductive rhetoric "claims to establish agency for females" and "seeks to empower women by valorizing a feminine aesthetic and style" that "boldly re-frames the means by which women can exert rhetorical influence—[with] a style less encumbered by logocentrism's censure of aesthetics, charm, allure, and enchantment."[40] They classify seductive strategies—including teasing and withdrawal—as particular types of rhetorical strategies that offer women "a means of rebelling against gender commodification and objectification."[41] While neo-burlesque is performed primarily by women, and thus is a fitting subject for the critical framework that Erickson and Thomson outline—women as nontraditional rhetors communicating outside of logocentric means—my take-up of seductive rhetoric shifts attention away from gender and sex and toward pleasure and process by focusing not on the identity of the rhetors but on the strategies that highlight the "transmogrifications, metamorphoses, and rhetorical tropings" that distinguish seductive rhetoric from other types of rhetoric.[42] Thus rather than claim seduction as feminine *or* woman-centric, I want to move seductive rhetoric away from its typical gendered associations. De-emphasizing gender as an analytical lens, therefore, extends conversations about seduction and neo-burlesque to focus on features that define postmodern notions of feminine seduction, but that resist distilling seductive rhetoric down to the very man/woman binary that it potentially disrupts.

Another way that binaries tend to manifest in conversations about seductive rhetoric is through its relationship to feminism. Seduction and neo-burlesque have been both denigrated as anti-feminist and recovered as feminist. Baudrillard's *Seduction* has raised feminist ire because of his misogynistic statements, indictments of feminism, and his sometimes troubling and limited views of women and gender—particularly for a revolutionary thinker who is often "involved in a common struggle with feminism against the naturalized hegemony of certain patriarchal institutions and the masculinist project of rational mastery."[43] Jane Gallop famously indicted Baudrillard for his "rather rabid attack" on feminism[44] in response to his universalizing dismissals of a seemingly monolithic "feminism" in *Seduction*, a feminism that he claims "efface[s]" the "immense privilege of the feminine," a feminism that "must be incredibly blind to deny the sole force that is equal and superior to all others" (that is, seduction).[45] Gallop and other feminists like Sara Ahmed take issue both with Baudrillard's apparent reliance on the masculinist, positivistic categorization that he seeks to critique as he pits the feminine against feminism—and they also take issue with his criticism of the feminist movement, which he claims fails to see the value of the seductive power of the feminine.[46] Yet other feminist scholars encourage a second look at the concept of seduction as one that challenges "phallocratic masculinity" even when Baudrillard presents himself as an adversary to feminists.[47]

Neo-burlesque, like seduction, has a well-established, yet complicated, relationship to feminism. Often the same material practices of neo-burlesque are used as evidence to support either a pro- or anti-feminist reading of its performances and culture. Like a whole range of other sexualized cultural practices performed primarily by women, neo-burlesque is "haunted by feminism," by "an awareness of feminism," and by the "ever-present" "question of whether burlesque is feminist or not."[48] As with seduction, in neo-burlesque tension exists between the feminine and the feminist, exacerbated by "a widespread, albeit uneasy desire [in fans and performers] to align an attachment to feminine identity performances with a commitment to feminist politics. However, this desire is troubled by an anxiety about whether burlesque is really compatible with feminism."[49] Neo-burlesque centralizes the act of the striptease, is performed primarily by women, and often features highly feminized styles of dress and cosmetics, cultural practices that have been well critiqued by feminist theory as damaging and dangerous to women because they encourage objectification and highlight a patriarchal view of women's sexuality.[50] While many neo-burlesque fans and performers claim the practice as feminist, it is also widely critiqued as oppressive and regressive.[51] Thus both postmodern seduction theory and neo-burlesque have been well critiqued along the lines of feminism and gender. In order to avoid reproducing those arguments here, I hope that identifying and mobilizing seductive strategies in embodied performance can shift focus away from making a judgment about neo-burlesque as feminist or anti-feminist and instead illustrate the material practices of this popular and contested performance art that places women, femininity, and erotics at its core. To put it another way, surfacing strategies that signal seduction doesn't elide feminist critique of seduction or of neo-burlesque; instead it gives rhetorical and feminist critics an expanded vocabulary for critiquing the ways that seductive rhetorics work through the body. Analyzing seductive strategies in rhetorical performance helps reveal expansive definitions of rhetoric and resists making man-woman/oppressive-empowering binaries the terms of rhetorical critique.

The Art of the Tease

As a performance art that centralizes spectacle, neo-burlesque exemplifies rhetorics of display, a "dominant rhetoric of our time" in which meanings are "manifested" by way of the "dynamic between concealing and revealing."[52] Props—most notably the fan and the glove—acrobatics, and choreographed routines attempt to seduce audiences through concealing and revealing parts of the body, a tease that hints at an elusive "more." That "more" is generally withheld, however, and it is the withholding that captivates audiences. Through such tactics, effective stage performances demonstrate seductive strategies when they "stimulate desire and longing, incite the imagination, and aesthetically enthrall" audiences.[53] The performance is a tease but does not pretend to be more than the tease itself. Unlike forms of erotic dance that depend on staging an authentic relationship between dancer and customer, neo-burlesque performers stage a visual display rather than an interaction.[54] Neo-burlesque shares this commitment to spectacle with older burlesque forms. In his history of nineteenth- and early twentieth-century burlesque, Allen writes that all forms of theatrical spectacle "called the very nature of truth into question by exaggerating it. The performer made his living by manipulating his body: he shouted, sang, danced, and gestured. His body was his instrument, his tool, yet the work he did with it was not *productive of anything but pleasure* for those who had paid to watch him show off."[55]

Twenty-first-century neo-burlesque's spectacular qualities similarly cultivate a seductive appeal by "freezing the dramatic narrative's movement toward closure and the (attempted) imposition of final meaning . . . open[ing] up the stage to pleasures other than those generated by words, ideas, and narrative logic."[56] It is performance dedicated to the "charm and illusion of appearances."[57] In short, neo-burlesque is a theatrical and performative genre of erotic dance, displaying seductive rhetorical strategies that focus audience attention on the process—the display and exchange of symbols—of communication. These strategies (in particular, playful sign use and covering and uncovering) illustrate the play, artifice, and appearance found in seductive rhetoric.

Seductive rhetors use these strategies not to achieve a logically determined end as in rational argument but to engage the audience in the process of symbolic exchange for the pleasure of the exchange itself. For example, in striptease, seduction is built around the reveal of the body. In the hands of a talented stripper, the more that the reveal is withheld or challenged, the more the audience is invested not in the naked body but in the process of revealing it. Seductive strategies that build such investment in process are prevalent in neo-burlesque and commonly operate as types of teasing and withdrawal, executed by performers who play with signs—shifting, reversing, multiplying signifiers and signifieds—and who enact variations of covering and uncovering. Strategically, forms of teasing operate by "hold[ing] out potential outcomes."[58] Withdrawal—whether physical or symbolic—temporarily suspends the possibility for outcomes. One type of teasing/withdrawal strategy seen in neo-burlesque engages audiences through the aesthetic appeal of sign play. Personas and props appear, disappear, and change, thus constructing and celebrating artifice and using it to captivate audiences by keeping them from closing in on a particular reality and foreclosing other symbolic possibilities. Covering and uncovering operates similarly. While audiences are teased with nudity, nudity often appears in unexpected ways. Via this strategy, reality is also questioned as erotic expectations are played with and often challenged.

Both commercial stripping and the striptease found in neo-burlesque rely on seductive strategies, but the means of symbol use in each genre have different ends. These differences also illustrate the distinction between traditional, purpose-driven, logocentric rhetoric and process-oriented, third-sophistic seductive rhetoric. In comparing these two genres, Baudrillard's division of producing versus seducing usefully demonstrates a primary distinction between these variations of erotic dance.[59] For Baudrillard, "to produce is to materialize by force what belongs to another order ... production constructs everything in full view."[60] The seduction in strip clubs is based on this materialization, of producing a fantasy of women on display for the customer who pays to see them. Neo-burlesque performers frequently draw on the "pay for display" aspect of club stripping to disarticulate the seductive striptease of neo-burlesque from commercial stripping in clubs, emphasizing that neo-burlesque is not "a sales and service-oriented" job.[61] Commercial stripping is a capitalist enterprise that places the mechanistic values of Baudrillardian production central. It is serious business, and as strip joints have become corporate-owned "gentleman's clubs," they have become even more production oriented. Often customers in strip clubs, in particular, regulars, are seeking authenticity rather than the artifice of seduction. Part of the stripper's work in these relationships is to assure the regular that the relationship is in fact authentic.[62] Thus *artificial authenticity* is a powerful frame of experience in a strip-club environment, making the club a zone of the hyper-real by providing simulacra both of sexual acts and of romantic relationships. Thus commercial stripping is a mode of erotic dance steeped in mechanistic production and transaction in which artifice is the means to a financial end.

In neo-burlesque artifice *is* the end. Neo-burlesque performances are often pleasurable because they play with artifice, but there is never a specific reality that is being mimicked;[63] rather everything is "makeup, theatre, and production" and sex is made into a "total, gestural, sensual, and ritual game, an exalted but ironic invocation."[64] Performances exist as simulation created by seductive strategies that centralize the means of symbolic exchange, rather than its outcome. These "strateg[ies] of appearances" disrupt "systems of power and meaning with the mere turn of the hand."[65] Through the strategy of sign play, performers can appear to draw out the rhetorical process through constantly shifting who they are and what they are communicating. For example, in Miss Indigo Blue's iconic act "Amazon Damsels in Bondage," the Seattle-based performer and headmistress of the Academy of Burlesque presents audiences with a Wonder Woman who is a lesbian stripper (see figs. 6A, 6B, and 6C).[66] Indigo starts the performance dressed as Navy nurse Diana Prince tending to a wounded soldier. A recorded voice-over narrates her story, informing the audience that she has left her boyfriend Lieutenant Steve Trevor "over the Barbara Stanwyck incident" and is now "devoting herself to her patients."[67] With the sound of an explosion and the beginning of the Wonder Woman television theme music, Indigo strips off her nurse's uniform to reveal the iconic Wonder Woman outfit as the voice-over reveals that "late at night after work our mild mannered Sapphic nurse is as beautiful as Aphrodite, wise as Athena, stronger than Hercules, and swifter than Mercury." The performance uses multiple symbolic codes—linguistic, kinesthetic, and sartorial—to stack signs on top of one another: Diana Prince, Barbara Stanwyck, Wonder Woman, Miss Indigo Blue, lesbian desire, bondage, and pasties are revealed in layers as Indigo strips down to end with the uniquely burlesque art of tassel twirling. It is a quintessential neo-burlesque performance blending the absurd and the sexy, not seeking truth but irony, not promising sexual fulfillment, but encouraging—and simultaneously mocking—sexual desire.

Another Seattle neo-burlesque star, Waxie Moon, builds performances around sign play, not so much by *reversing* signs—a Baudrillarian quality of seduction—but by networking them, thereby challenging the binary that the concept of reversibility is built upon. Baudrillard argues that seduction "incarnates reversibility" through "the possibility of play and symbolic involvement."[68] When signs are irreversible, they are locked into meanings. Although

6A–6C | Indigo Blue in "Amazon Damsels in Bondage." Photos 6A and 6B taken on August 19, 2007. Photo 6C taken on December 29, 2007. Burlesque Behind the Pink Door. Seattle, Washington. Photos by Chris Blakeley. Used with permission.

Baudrillard proposes that seduction is what obliterates the idea of oppositional terms and "pushes" them toward each other, the idea of reversibility implies that two concepts exist in opposition, which shores up the binary rather than opening a third space where the terms are united "at the point of maximum energy and charm."[69] Waxie—"the international gender-blending queer lady boylesque performance-art solo stripping sensation"—creates his performance and his persona by multiplying signs and drawing associations between them. Waxie is the stage name of Marc Kenison, a classically trained dancer who graduated from Julliard. Waxie Moon is not a drag queen. Even when he performs in elaborate gowns, high heels, and dramatic makeup, often with the classic burlesque props of gloves and feather boa, he never presents a traditionally feminine character, as he is bald, with impressive facial hair (see fig. 7).

I saw Waxie perform at the Pink Door in Seattle on April 18, 2015.[70] He executed classic burlesque moves like the bump and grind and glove peel with fluid precision. As he stripped to reveal his body, Waxie's networking of signs intensified, delivering the moves of classic burlesque, which draw attention to breasts and pelvis, flawlessly through his masculine body. He did not *shift* signs as Indigo Blue does in "Amazon Damsels"; rather, signs coexisted and articulated new possibilities. Waxie's performance techniques illustrate that the metaphor of networking rather than reversibility might be a more apt description of seductive strategies. As Donna Haraway notes, a "network ideological image suggest[s] the profusion of spaces and identities and the permeability of boundaries in the personal body and in the body politic."[71] Thus as seductive rhetors, performers embody "transgressed boundaries, potent fusions, and dangerous possibilities."[72] With the character of Waxie Moon, "performance is constantly drawing attention to its own artifice, occupying a medial or 'third gender' . . . confounding the usual expectations of gender alignment and speculating on the fluid possibilities of gender outside a traditional patriarchal and/or straight schema."[73] As is evidenced by his tagline, Waxie deploys multiple signs, drawing connections among them that refuse to be locked into meaning. The associative chain of his performance handle—international gender-blending queer lady boylesque performance-art solo stripping sensation—leads finally to the word "sensation," not pinning him down into an identity, but articulating an experience. Waxie Moon illustrates seductive rhetoric that moves beyond the idea of signs' reversibility to their flexibility, multiplicity, and associative relations.

7 | Waxie Moon at the Pink Door, June 23, 2007. Burlesque Behind the Pink Door. Seattle, Washington. Photo by Chris Blakeley. Used with permission.

In addition to playing with signs, neo-burlesque also uses covering and uncovering—the presentation and withholding of signs—as a seductive strategy of teasing and withdrawal, again emphasizing rhetorical process over closure. Neo-burlesque's commitment to the partial nudity of classic burlesque, keeping the nipples and pelvis covered, "remov[es them] from the order of the

8A–8B | Indigo Blue in "Blue Gloves," May 20, 2008. Burlesque Hall of Fame Benefit. Seattle, Washington. Photos by Chris Blakeley. Used with permission.

visible."[74] This performance choice reflects the idea that "nudity veiled by clothing functions as a secret, ambivalent referent. Unveiled, it surfaces as a sign."[75] The glove peel, a signature burlesque move in which the performer dramatizes and prolongs the removal of gloves, often fascinates and enthralls with its presentation of veiled nudity: "Even though all members of the audience are sitting there with naked hands, a well-executed glove peel will drive them wild, proving that the process of the reveal creates the excitement about what is revealed."[76] Performers execute glove peels in endless ways that reference, manipulate, and draw on strategies of covering and uncovering. In "Blue Gloves," Indigo Blue peels off a number of the titular garments, with each glove revealing another underneath (figs. 8A and 8B).[77] She stays dressed for much of the performance and never reveals her hands, which gain the symbolic power usually reserved for breasts and genitalia. Thus in both classic and re-visioned glove peels, the performer makes the hands a secret, and the process, rather than the thing to be revealed, generates seductive appeal.

The concealing/revealing pair, whether it is deployed via gloved hands, pasties-covered nipples, or the peek-a-boo display of a fan dance, is a seductive strategy that is cultivated by many neo-burlesque performers in order to direct audience focus to a particular process or moment in a process. Whatever is emphasized by props and garments through strategic covering becomes a focal point of the act and is used by performers as a "narrative tool" in addition to being a rhetorical strategy.[78] For performers "the controlled act of veiling and unveiling [can be used] to question stigma, to question shame, to question restrictive disempowering roles."[79] In "Untitled with Mask," Dame CuchiFrita, a Brooklyn, New York, performer, dances with her face covered by a mask (figs. 9A, 9B, and 9C).[80] In this act, the final reveal of her face challenges common notions of striptease and of the sexualized body. Cuchi explains, "The norm of the striptease is to build tension to finally reveal what is the most taboo or sexualized part of the body. I chose the other way around." But this act also presents a symbolic address to her cultural heritage through the covering and uncovering of her face: "I grew up in a mostly Muslim country and there's always a discussion of coverage versus nudity to define women's morality. I use my body to either demystify nudity, and therefore the idea of sexiness or the other way around, whereby an individual does not necessarily need to be naked to be seductive and/or sexual." Indeed, "Much of the eroticism of burlesque centres on the tension between clothing and naked flesh,"[81] and "Untitled with Mask" relocates that tension by changing the expected site of coverage. Further, Cuchi's outfit frames her breasts, drawing attention to her naked body in juxtaposition with her face. Burlesque performers, both in classic and neo, use props to both conceal and to frame parts of the body, tactical strategies that draw attention to certain areas by alternating between presenting it and hiding it.[82] The sartorial symbols—lace mask, costume, feather boa—combined with the kinesthetic symbols—framing her covered face with her hands, using the boa to conceal and reveal, unmasking at the end—illustrate the multiple codes through which bodies "speak." This is a seductive speaking that draws audience focus to the performer's execution of embodied erotic rhetoric.

Stripper, neo-burlesque performer, and puppeteer Cheeky Lane also revises typical covering and uncovering strategies as she networks signs to spoof audience expectations around bodily sites of desire. Cheeky's "House" routine, in which she dances in a costume composed of a house with moving parts, refigures seduction in extraordinarily complicated ways. Cheeky's costume house

9A–9C | Dame CuchiFrita in "Untitled with Mask." Photos by John Goddard. Courtesy of The Slipper Room. Used with permission.

10 | Cheeky Lane's House. Photo by Cheeky Lane. Used with permission.

has working doors and windows, located over her breasts, genitalia, and butt (fig. 10). As Cheeky dances, she opens and closes the different sets of windows to reveal black cutouts of couples in sexual contact, which she then *animates* by moving her own body. One window opens and the audience is treated to penetrative sex, another reveals a woman mouth to breast with another woman. When the windows open, we not only see Cheeky's bikini clad body, but we also see couples engaged in sex. The act of watching a dancer reveal her body becomes a voyeuristic act of seeing not just dancing but sex in action. In making her own body an object through which to objectify, not herself but faceless, cartoonish, yet strangely realistic figures, Cheeky unsettles audience expectation. She is both the viewed and the lens for viewing.[83]

Similarly, Legs Malone, "The Girl with the Thirty-Four-and-a-Half-Inch Inseam," showcases seductive strategies of teasing and withdrawal deployed both through sign play and through covering and uncovering in her Bettie Page tribute.[84] She starts the act with a vampy dance in a gown and feather boa, cultivating an image of classic burlesque. Malone then abruptly shifts personas; she strips without ceremony and redresses in fetish wear. The core of the performance is not the stripping, but the dressing. In becoming Bettie, complete with whip cracks at the audience, Malone demonstrates both shifting signs and covering/uncovering as seductive strategies that refocus audience attention and revise their expectations.

Seductive strategies of teasing and withdrawal, such as the sign play and variations of covering/uncovering illustrated here, are at the center of the audience's experience in neo-burlesque. This is not to say that there isn't a point or a purpose to performances, but that seductive rhetoric centralizes means over ends because seduction is an ongoing act. For seduction to accomplish a purpose would signal its end. Part of the appeal of striptease is the ongoing play of the moments of pleasure cultivated between the audience and the performer. Ferreday argues that this "mutually constitutive pleasure of performer and audience" *is* the purpose, the "payoff" in neo-burlesque.[85] As a site to theorize seductive rhetoric, neo-burlesque demonstrates a number of strategies that allow us to see seduction not only through a prism of theoretical femininity detached from women's bodies but also as a process of symbolic exchange with the "capacity . . . to deny things their truth and turn it into a game."[86] Seductive rhetoric then focuses on liminal space between rhetors and audiences where symbols are mutually and temporarily constructed and often destructed as well.

The Pleasures of Process

Neo-burlesque performances illustrate some of the ways that seductive strategies can direct the attention of both rhetors and audiences to the process of symbolic exchange, to the borderlands of communication that exist between— and sometimes separately from—purpose and result. Seductive rhetoric and neo-burlesque share the qualities of artifice, appearance, frivolity, pleasure, and bodies. Performances are rhetorical in that they are "audience-centered social acts," and they are seductive in that they are sites of open-ended symbolic communication in which meanings proliferate in a nonlinear associative nexus.[87] Neo-burlesque performances are purposeful and meaningful, but purpose and meaning exist temporally and temporarily in their act of performance itself. This is seductive rhetoric. Yet it isn't quite what Baudrillard theorizes as seduction because performances constitute meaning-making acts. What seductive strategies and a focus on process can offer to rhetorical criticism of embodied rhetoric, however, is a way to see how the process of constituting can be seductive, and how meaning can be fluid and shifting, keeping criticism from being the dead-end task of seeking predetermined meanings.

Neo-burlesque performers deploy seductive strategies that neither promise nor suggest that they will fulfill audience desire. Performances generally end with a reveal, and then a performer withdraws, which is a critical part of the seductive process that "prolong[s] the *kairotic* moment," thereby fulfilling the showbiz axiom to always leave them wanting more.[88] Like all seductive rhetors, through these strategic processes, performers of neo-burlesque create in audiences "the experience of being captivated," which is "an ecstatic state of wonderment, exhilaration, and joy" born from "the enabling tension between absence and presence, desire and fulfillment, as well as anticipation and closure."[89] It is this cultivation of pleasure in the communicative process that makes for seductive rhetoric.

Much of the conversation about seduction and about neo-burlesque focuses on whether they are oppressive or liberating for women and for feminized cultural and rhetorical practices. Yet seduction has value to rhetorical studies beyond feminized modes of communication, women rhetors, or even the discursive category of woman. Seductive rhetoric "deals not in signified meanings but in the address itself . . . ; it deals not in the said (*le dit*) but in the saying (*le dire*)."[90] Seductive rhetoric can demonstrate a number of postmodern theories that expand rhetoric beyond a purpose-driven logical and rational enterprise. It articulates with Davis's "rhetoric of the *saying*,"[91] informs Ballif's figure of Woman, and illustrates Vitanza's "third sophistic" with its "Play and Possibility."[92] Because of this, seductive rhetoric also offers a theoretical lens for criticizing rhetoric of the body because bodies communicate via a whole range of nonlogocentric symbolic practices that fall within the province of rhetoric but not always comfortably within logocentric rhetorical theory.

In using an embodied practice like neo-burlesque to demonstrate the ways that seductive rhetoric dwells on rhetorical process, rather than on purposes and end results, I hope to show that seductive rhetoric illustrates the breadth of communication. Even though Baudrillard critiques "communication" as the opposite of seduction, we need not understand communication or symbolic exchange as a stable and linear give-and-take between a rational rhetor and audience—that is, as a "territorialization accomplished through the exclusion of the third man or sophistry."[93] Communication need not be bound by the rational project to master signs and make them concrete. Embodied communication, like that seen in neo-burlesque, makes the flexibility and pleasure of symbol use apparent. Further, neo-burlesque performers are "simulators, not philosopher kings"; they are "artisans" endowed with *mêtis*, the cunning that Ballif argues exemplifies postmodern rhetoric[94] and that Dolmage argues is a "distinctly bodily intelligence."[95] Thus performing bodies provide a dynamic and vital site for studying the possibilities of seductive rhetoric because they cannot be contained by *logos*. Bodies are "generative of meaning,"[96] and because they depend so much on the fluid presentation of signs, bodies in neo-burlesque demonstrate the flexibility of meaning. Further, audience is a central feature of neo-burlesque, which crafts pleasure not only for but also with audiences, illustrating the creative force of performers and audiences together.

Seductive strategies offer rhetoric more than alternative means of achieving a predetermined purpose (running for office, garnering support, winning converts to a cause, arguing a case); seductive rhetoric encompasses symbolic exchange that seeks no determined end but rather makes the act of pursuing the purpose, a pursuit that itself becomes a "pleasure-taking performance."[97] As disciplinary interest in rhetorics of the body grows, rhetoricians can develop methods of analysis of embodied and performance rhetorics by looking to cultural practices, like neo-burlesque, where the body is central. Central in form and function. Central in knowledge production. Central in communication. In neo-burlesque, bodies are not just in action, they are in conversation, a seductive nonrational conversation that privileges process, not as manipulation, but as pleasure. As a site of embodied erotic communication, neo-burlesque revises seduction's connection to rhetoric. Seductive rhetoric need not be reduced to immorality but can instead reflect the pleasures of persuasion, offering a critical orientation to a range of communicative practices for which logic and rationality have little persuasive power.

4

"I Am a Woman. This Is My Body" | Rearticulating Identity in Sex-Work Activism

*A flyer distributed by the Sex Workers Outreach Project (SWOP) Seattle advertises an upcoming rally for International Sex Worker Rights Day (March 3) in 2016. The flyer is stark in its design: bright red background—the international color of sex-worker rights—with the black shadow of a hand stamped on it. It isn't the closed fist of protest, but the open hand of hailing, a call for recognition. Across the palm is the social-movement slogan "*NOTHING ABOUT US WITHOUT US,*" in white above the SWOP-Seattle name in red. Above the hand, in white, the poster succinctly sums up the ideology that drives activism by sex workers:*

"Sex workers demand to be included in the creation of policies that directly affect them, to have their rights respected, the right to work in safety, the right to work together and the right to exist."

"Exist," three times bigger than the rest of the demands, dominates the poster, signaling the core demand of the movement and the most precarious right of all.

So far, this book has proposed different lenses for analyzing rhetoric of the body by examining women's erotic performances, in particular, stripping, via the public performances of neo-burlesque and topless dancing in clubs. In previous chapters, I have focused primarily on analyzing the material symbolic communication of those performances, specifically costume and movement. As noted in the introduction to this book, however, approaches to analyzing the body need to be inclusive of *both* linguistic *and* material means of communicating. Therefore, in the next two chapters, I will be analyzing these material symbols in conversation with some key discourses that shape the way women's erotic bodies are read by combining textual and embodied analysis of the erotic body as a cultural symbol, in particular, as a political and politicized one.

The bodies of sex workers—and those profiled as sex workers—are seen by many to exemplify victimhood and criminality, characterizations that sex-work activism both seeks and struggles to counteract by shifting focus away from the sexual acts of bodies and to the material conditions under which those bodies labor. Activists adopted the term *sex work* in the late 1970s to distance their jobs from stigmatized behaviors that are considered sinful, criminal, and misogynistic and reframe their work to align with other forms of service labor. Deploying the term *sex work* is an identity-making activist strategy, which reflects that "sex workers are as defined by their work as they are by their sexuality."[1] Such rhetorical reconstituting of sex-worker identities engages in "transformations of global interpretive frames," a common social-movement strategy in which a new framework "interprets events and experiences in a new key."[2]

Although sex-worker activists have fought to remake their identities to emphasize their humanity and to lessen the stigma of their jobs, institutional policy, policing, and rhetoric constructs sex workers as always embodying criminality. Similarly, certain feminist and social-service analyses argue that sex workers don't exist. There are only prostituted women whose bodies aren't in their own control, who are victims or survivors of abuse and of rape, but who are not—who cannot be—workers. Therefore, as a site of critical analysis of the body, sex-work activism vividly illustrates the challenges of remaking stigmatized identities.

To examine the role of the body in this remaking—what I will refer to as rearticulation—I analyze the 2018 stripper protests in New Orleans, arising from a series of police raids in clubs on Bourbon Street, as a site of sex-work activism that features the body. My analysis frames the protest in the context of the ongoing struggles about sex-worker identity and suggests that stripper-protesters' embodied counterstories bolster efforts to reframe identity, visibly refuting common narratives of victimhood and criminality. According to these narratives, sex-worker bodies are incapable of agency and even existence, but I argue that these same bodies actually serve as powerful generators of counterarguments *to* sex-work antagonists. I use the theory of articulation, which sees all identities as composed of connected—or articulated—elements to identify the ways that dancer-activists unlink and relink ideological commonplaces in order to rearticulate their identities. The analysis demonstrates that articulation can provide a critical approach to body rhetoric. Following Jennifer Slack's assertion that any communication *is* articulation,[3] and my own research into the body's capacity to generate symbolic communication, my analysis shows that articulation engages in the dialectical tacking between discourse and materiality that embodied methods require.[4]

The body is at the center of sex-work activism, as workers struggle to define how they are recognized and understood. Anti–sex work organizations including the police, courts, social-service agencies, and anti–sex trafficking efforts deny sex workers the right to define their identities because of the actions of their bodies. Sex-work activists and scholars argue that the sex-worker's body is over-determined as a victim or a slave because it is a site of commercial exchange of sexual services.[5] As with movements for racial equality, trans rights, and queer rights, the sex-worker's body in appearance and in action is consistently and deliberately misrecognized, thus leaving it out of control of the person who inhabits it. Melissa Harris-Perry, in writing about the entrenched and harmful misrecognition of black women, asserts that misrecognition is characteristic of "marginal and stigmatized groups" who "face fundamental and continuing threats to their opportunity for accurate recognition. . . . Inaccurate recognition is painful not only to the psyche but also to the political self, the citizen self."[6] Sex workers try to counteract this misrecognition primarily through counter-stories[7] that rearticulate their identities in terms of their agency and therefore their humanity. These narratives are deployed through academic research, conferences, community outreach, websites, policy efforts, legal challenges, social-media channels, and protests. Because it mobilizes the subject under debate in dynamic and visible ways, the protesting body is a critical aspect of social activism. The 2018 stripper protests in New Orleans demonstrate the power of the protesting body to rearticulate damaging misrecognition of sex workers that increases harm to them.

The larger struggle for rearticulation by sex-worker activists frames the ongoing political action in New Orleans. Although *sex worker* is not a term that typically signifies strippers—indeed most sex workers use the term politically rather than practically—the actions in New Orleans to link sex trafficking with strippers and strip clubs has resulted in hundreds of dancers becoming sex-work activists. Anti-trafficking forces in New Orleans, as elsewhere, deploy a signifying slide from sex work to sex trafficking. And in some cases, particularly in New Orleans, this has become a signifying slide from stripping to prostitution to sex trafficking. In this analysis, I identify the protesting body as central to arguments that sex workers—in this case strippers—make about their lives and labor: sex work is real work; sex workers have agency; sex workers need protections regarding the conditions of their labor, rather than from the labor itself; sex workers don't need to be saved. Although the movement is routinely discounted and misrecognized, these themes have been demands of sex-worker activists since the emergence of the movement.

To perform this analysis, this chapter takes up the theory and method of articulation as a lens for analyzing rhetoric of the body. Typically a textual analytical method, analysis via articulation allows critics to look at how specific ideological elements make/unmake/remake identities. Because articulation posits that this making and unmaking is always situated in social and political contexts, discourse and materiality are both at work. Thus the analysis in this chapter uses both to broaden my overall investigation of erotic performance by looking at sex-work activism—itself an embodied performance—particularly that done by club strippers.

Articulating Activist Bodies

Social movements provide a rich repository of material for rhetorical study because they so visibly operate at the intersections of the material and the discursive. While these domains are always intersecting (as much of this book argues), within social movements they are especially apparent to participants, bystanders, and scholars. As opposed to identifying the embodied dimensions of alphabetic text or the discursive construction of the body, in social movements even a casual observer can see persuasive bodies and words interacting.

The mid-twentieth century saw the rise of not only the new social movements but also the new rhetoric as well. The revival of interest in rhetoric during a time of immense social upheaval, however, proved to be difficult. The new rhetoric with its focus on discourse, argumentation, and reason, via systematic presentation, seemed to have no place for the tactics of embodied, passionate protest that characterized the new social movements. The body as the central generator of argument, the embrace of emotional strategies, and the stylized presentations all made protest difficult for rhetoricians to categorize.[8] Edward Corbett characterizes body rhetoric as the "kind of persuasive activity that seeks to carry its point by non-rationale, nonsequential, often non-verbal, frequently provocative means."[9] Thus when scholars first began to study "body rhetoric," it was recognized as a persuasive activity but one that was operating in all of the ways that the new rhetoric had distanced itself from. As the following analysis will demonstrate, however, the protesting body, rather than only being a generator of passionate persuasion, also functions as a multicoded symbolic device capable of rearticulating marginalized identities. Here, I suggest that because bodies are so central to activism that any method of social-movement rhetorical criticism should be flexible enough to accommodate the body's multiple ways of communicating. The protesting body as a site of rhetorical communication demonstrates some key ways that thought "happens *as* the body"[10] and that "all rhetoric is embodied."[11]

Articulation as both theory and practice is central to social-movement study and activism because it counteracts the hegemonic tendency to naturalize, legitimate, and entrench social inequities. Articulation as theory posits that any unity, such as identity, is actually composed of smaller elements that are joined together in a particular configuration that is neither static nor guaranteed. Articulation can also be a powerful heuristic for analyses of identities and activism within social movements because it "provides a method for disassembling seemingly unified wholes in order to examine the ideological glue that binds them together."[12] In addition to examining the ways that the elements that make up these "seemingly unified wholes" are thought together and brought together into specific configurations, using articulation as a lens allows critics to see that they may be reconfigured into different wholes. Thus articulation is often a practice of intervention for social movements, which often make strategic identity dis- and rearticulation central to activism.

Social-movement activism, in particular, its embodied actions, consists of varied symbolic acts of communication. Articulation theory offers the rhetorical critic a method of analyzing which elements in these symbolic acts are more strongly linked and why.[13] Identifying why some identity rearticulations (gay marriage) are more successful than others (sex worker) can help activists to mobilize and strategize more successfully. The idea that some links are more difficult to disarticulate can help to explain which framing strategies are successful and why. In addition, because embedded in the very concept of a *movement* is motion, articulation provides an approach that not only recognizes but also prioritizes the idea that meanings shift and change over time. One of the key concepts of articulation theory is that all links are *nonnecessary*. They may be persistent and difficult to disconnect, but no identity is a concrete objective fact. Further, as Ian Angus argues, articulatory practice is not only about the links themselves but also about the *elements* that are "foreground[ed] and selected" in order to make links.[14] Further, Angus claims that these elements are thematized prior to articulation.[15] That is, elements are not randomly brought together to articulate unities. Therefore, for critics employing the method of articulation, the task is to identify not only elements and links but also the ideological work that *produces* the elements to be linked. Another key tool for articulation as a critical method is the concept of antagonisms,[16] which provide a way to identify the oppositional and incompatible ideologies in debates about identity that often undergird social activism. In the case of the sex-worker rights movement, antagonisms provide a way to theorize the relationship between sex-worker discourse and anti-trafficking discourse. The two ideological positions act as antagonisms to each other, as each claims that they are the subordinated position. A key argument of many anti-trafficking organizations is that sex work does not exist apart from sex trafficking. The bodies of sex-worker activists—particularly when their bodies are mobilized in street protest—refute that claim by demonstrating agency and presence.

As it is the work of social movements to change meanings in order to change material circumstances, articulation is a fitting lens through which to understand the political actions of groups seeking material and symbolic change. In short, movement activists are always engaging in processes of articulation—through a series of dis- (taking apart oppressive meanings) and rearticulation (disseminating new meanings in the hope of establishing new systems). As a method of criticism, articulation "motivates scholars to examine, amidst conditions of social complexity, how ideologies and ideological elements are invoked, mobilized, combined, altered, rejected, or ignored."[17] The body itself forms a signifying element (or system of signifying elements) that communicates meaning(s).[18]

Because sex-work activism contains elements of both labor movements and the identity building of the "new social movements" (NSMs) of the 1960s and '70s, it offers a unique look at articulatory strategies across multiple domains. Although sex-work activism's concern with labor makes it more similar to the old social movements with their focus on resources and economics, activists also draw on the identity-framing strategies that are a hallmark of the NSMs. That is, before sex-work activists can achieve their labor goals, they must first be recognized as laborers, recognition that requires unlinking common associations and forging new linkages. The sex-work activist movement is diffuse, composed of a loose network of related organizations and individuals responding to specific exigencies that don't always overlap (i.e., strippers in New Orleans have different issues than street–sex workers in Phoenix), thus rather than a central social-movement organization or identity we see "*forms* of collective action"[19] that are linked by the industry in which they labor and the antagonisms that they counter. And while the labor itself is different depending on the job, one through line is the identity rearticulation contained in the term *sex worker* itself. Therefore, while it is difficult to characterize sex-work activism as *a* social movement, at least as movements have traditionally been analyzed in both sociological and rhetorical studies, sex-work activism functions in a coalitional system in which specific goals and purposes may differ according to local exigencies, but broad challenges to the current order regarding the treatment of sex workers remain the same.

Sex Worker: Anatomy of a Term

Sex-work activism in the United States appeared as a visible movement for prostitute rights concurrent with the rise of gay liberation, feminism, black power, and other new social movements of the mid-twentieth century. While a focus on labor equality dominated social movements prior to this time, the causes of justice expanded in the 1960s as more segments of people were recognizing that labor inequality and class status were not the sole causes of oppression. Situated as it was in the rise of the new social movements, sex-worker activism originally crafted its goals, appeals, and strategies in ways that paralleled other NSMs, but also shared the motivations of the older labor movements. That is, sex-worker activists sought both to improve their working conditions and to destigmatize their identities. The movement, spearheaded by women, sought allegiances with feminism and gay liberation and drew on the ideologies of the sexual revolution.[20] However, despite these allegiances and sometimes overlapping goals, the movement for sex workers' rights has not seen the large-scale social changes of either feminism or gay liberation, both of which moved center-right in the '80s and '90s, drawing on themes of morality, forwarding images of middle-class respectability, and advancing neo-liberal agendas.[21] The sex-worker rights movement is marked by several characteristics that differentiate it from these other movements in a few key ways. The first is that the most visible form of sex work, prostitution, is illegal in most of the US. This makes the movement in some ways parallel to migrant-rights movements in that activists are seeking the right to perform a particular kind of work (decriminalization) and also for protections for that work (regulation).[22] The second is that the labor movement in the US has been seriously eroded over the last thirty years. Thus while sex-worker activists have largely sought to reframe their identities as service workers deserving of the same rights as other service workers, that itself is a weakened position under global capitalism. Despite the potential power of the term *sex work* to rearticulate identities, global neoliberalism normalizes[23] and indeed thrives on precarity, making the identity of any worker always fraught. The last characteristic is that the embodied sexual performances that characterize most sex work are mired in a network of competing discourses about sex and commerce. Because it concerns bodies and sex, sex-work activism "carr[ies] and vector[s] the weight of ideological pressures on bodies and minds," from both within and outside of the movement.[24] As is commonly noted, sex both fascinates and repels, making it subject to myriad taboos and prohibitions that are found in all aspects of society, although they are deployed unequally. In the case of commercial sexuality, those negative ideological pressures multiply. Therefore, sex-work activists face a host of negative and negating discourses, those around the value of work and workers and those around sex and sexuality, creating a unique set of exigencies for activism that doesn't fit strategically or ideologically with parallel movements.

As feminism and gay liberation moved to the political center, both actively distanced themselves from issues relevant to sex workers. Although they share critical moments in their histories, the mainstream gay rights movement has largely written sex workers out of its origin stories, despite the centrality of sex workers who were trans women and gay hustlers in both the Compton's Cafeteria riot (1966) and the Stonewall riots (1969).[25] By the late '70s, with the sexual revolution mostly dead and the conservative backlash of the 1980s on the horizon, sex-worker activists began to focus more on the *work* of sex work as discourses of sexual freedom fell out of vogue and competed with a new conservatism about sex. Via a particularly profound terminology shift, activists began to articulate a new identity for themselves: worker. This shift toward worker rights—away from appeals to liberate the sexual body—is signaled by the widespread adoption of the term *sex work*, popularized by prostitute and activist Carol Leigh, "The Scarlet Harlot," in 1978. For Leigh and other activists, adopting this term was "the beginning of a movement [that] acknowledges the work we do rather than defines us by our status."[26] While the move to prioritize the work of sex work has been more successful outside of the US, particularly in European countries with strong labor unions, it has allowed for some important changes, most notably the creation of a political identity around which an entire politics of sex work has coalesced.[27] Although opponents to sex work disavow this political identity, it has gained traction, largely replacing the term *prostitution* in academic and news writing, and has helped to reshape many popular discourses about sexual commerce through highlighting elements of labor, advocacy, and agency and deemphasizing elements of immorality, criminality, and victimhood. Yet the staunchest opponents to sex work, who still hold the most power to shape law, policy, and public understanding, deny that the *work* of sex work exists, illustrating the ways that articulated identities composed of different elements often exist as antagonisms.

Although the terms *sex work* and *sex worker* have been widely adopted in both public and academic discourses, used in news media and social media, by activists and bystanders, by academics, and in the health professions, they are consciously *not* used by people who oppose sex work. The opposition to the movement is composed of various constituencies that don't necessarily align in other ideological ways. Primary opposition comes from religious conservatives, law enforcement, certain social service agencies and NGOs, legislators, and some feminist groups. Both *sex work* and *sex worker* serve as a means of political organizing that unites both legal and illegal as well as higher and lower value jobs (such as escort versus street–sex worker) by taking the focus off sexual acts and putting it on the job. Under such expansive terms there is room for porn actors, street–sex workers, escorts, cam girls and boys, strippers, professional dominatrices, dungeon masters and mistresses, and massage parlor workers, to name only a few. These are vastly different jobs in nearly every way, but all are capable of being classified as sex work. Thus these spacious terms serve one important goal of social movement organizing by building coalition among disparate constituencies. The term *sex work* also (although this is debated by the movement's opponents) distinguishes between enslavement—persons who have been trafficked and forced into working in the sex industry—and chosen sex work. In discussing and critiquing the conflation of sex work with sex trafficking, it is important to note that for activism on the issue the point is that not all sex workers are trafficked, not that sex trafficking doesn't exist on a grotesque and damaging scale. Conflating the two can further harm victims of sex trafficking by turning attention away from their specific needs and to a population who finds they are not in need of help. Conflation also tends to obscure other types of trafficking including "domestic work, agricultural labor, manufacturing and the service industries, [which] affects men as well as women and children."[28] Human trafficking in domestic work is prominent in the US but rarely does it get discussed, which makes it more difficult to respond to and conceals the crimes of those wealthy people who purchase humans. The National Trafficking Hotline reports that "worldwide, experts believe there are more situations of labor trafficking than of sex trafficking." Yet "there is much wider awareness of sex trafficking in the United States than of labor trafficking."[29] In addition, the element of choice itself in the articulated identity of sex worker is a complicated one. First, journalist Melissa Gira Grant argues that insisting on proving that choice exists places a burden on sex workers that we do not expect with regard to other jobs: "Sex workers, more than any other, are expected to justify their labor as a choice, as if the choice to engage in a form of labor is what makes that labor legitimate. An even more insidious double standard is that sex workers must prove they have made an *empowered* choice, as if empowerment is some intangible state attained through self-perfection and not through a continuous and collective negotiation of power."[30]

Second, it is important to note that the idea of choice is fairly moot in a capitalist society organized around a vastly unequal distribution of resources. Thus the terms *chosen* and *choice* should not be understood as elements that are unconstrained by material realities. All sex work exists "on a spectrum ranging from limited choice to full choice."[31] That is, for impoverished people, the idea of choice can mean little. While one may choose to do sex work rather than work at a lower-wage job with more time restrictions, this choice is not a free one. It is one, like all economic choices, that is dictated by material realities.[32]

As a social-movement strategy, deploying the term *sex work* widely and consistently for more than thirty years has served to build coalition among various types of sex workers and create an identity for organizing. While activists like Sylvia Rivera in New York City and Margo St. James in San Francisco were organizing in support of prostitute rights in the seventies before the term *sex work* was popularized, the effect of those efforts were positive yet limited. So strong is the articulation between *prostitute* and *criminal* that the concept of prostitute rights tends to restrict participation and coalition. Thus historically activists have not been able to rearticulate the identity of *prostitute* partially because the word is "loaded with stigma and shame"[33] and partially because the signification of that term is narrow. While early activists created the frameworks that subsequent workers would build upon, the rearticulation of identity via the term *sex work* helped to reframe the issue to align with other constituencies in addition to prostitutes. The Global Network of Sex Work Projects (NSWP) argues that the adoption and dissemination of the term was part of the international response to HIV/AIDS by sex workers, one that "moved global understandings of sex work toward a labour framework which provides solutions to many of the problems faced by sex workers."[34] Thus the term shifts to *sex work / sex worker* are a key component of a social-movement frame that was transformed to "mobilize potential adherents and constituents, to garner bystander support, and to demobilize antagonists."[35]

The term *sex work* presents lexical complexity that illustrates both its potential and its problems as an organizing term.[36] Critics who use articulation as a framework don't typically focus on the grammatical constraints and affordances of discursive formations; however, the grammar of a construction is one element that constitutes a unity and can provide one path of understanding as to why dis- and rearticulations fail or succeed by providing insight into what happens semantically when ideological elements are linked discursively. In *sex work*, the semantic power of the modifier is central. At the grammatical level *sex* is a noun adjunct—a noun modifying another noun. Because the activity *sex* signified by the noun adjunct carries so many associations, in some ways the construction *prioritizes* the sex. In its use here, *sex* as a noun represents an activity that is embedded in a nexus of conflicting values. Thus it signifies differently from a superficially similar articulation like *factory work*. While the modifier *sex* defines *work*, it is a word that itself carries stigma and in the case of *sex work* transfers that stigma onto the *work*. In essence, *sex* overpowers and—as we will see in antagonistic discourses—often negates the *work*.

The second complexity of the term *sex work* is that it can blur important political differences among different jobs in the sex trades, differences that construct inequalities because privilege and precarity are meted out unequally along classed, gendered, and racialized lines. For example, with regard to prostitution, while people who work as legal escorts perform their work indoors, are protected by law, and can earn high rates, people who sell sex on the street—primarily poor trans women, cis women, and gay hustlers—are performing illegal work, outdoors, and generally for less pay than legal escorts. In this second group, *sex work*, like prostitution, gets associated with criminality; that element persists and transfers onto legal sex work and can blur the particular needs of different populations, adding to the burden already carried by the most precarious workers. Thus while *sex work* is inclusive, and the numbers brought by inclusivity can be of great value to a political and social movement, inclusivity can also obscure the many legal and social and personal privileges granted to higher-status workers. Therefore, the term *sex work*, like the work itself, is deployed unequally,[37] and street–sex workers, in particular, women of color, in most particular, trans women of color, bear the brunt of the personal and institutional violence leveled against all sex workers.

Sex work implies agency and subsequently rearticulates identity to make political alignments with labor movements by way of the transformed social-movement frame: prostitute rights to sex-worker rights. The concept of agency is crucial to distinguish from choice, because choice is an argument that is often used in popular capitalist discourse to discredit labor activists with a "love it or leave it" rhetoric (i.e., if you don't like the conditions under which you work, you have the choice to quit). Yet agency is always "contingent on a matrix of material and social conditions."[38] The agency implied by *sex work* is a "constrained agency," in which the agentive possibilities engendered by the rearticulated identity of *sex worker* meet the "regulatory power of authority."[39] Agency is constrained in both material and discursive ways.

Opponents to the concept and the term *sex work* use lexical markers to remove agency from the phrase and therefore from the identity itself. When *sex work* is used by its opponents, it often carries its own modifier, as in *so-called sex work*, or is surrounded by quotation marks to disavow ownership of the term and create distance. The typical argument against the construction of *sex work* and *sex worker* is that they do not exist because they cannot exist. For sex-work antagonists, freely chosen sex work is a fiction: one cannot choose to be a slave. Therefore, all sex workers have been to one degree or another trafficked, either explicitly (kidnapped, isolated, threatened, abused) or implicitly (poverty, racism, sexism) forced into the labor. In this line of argument, *sex work* is a contradiction in terms, referring to a class of people who do not exist engaged in an activity that does not exist. For opponents, the term *sex work* does not represent a grassroots' activist effort to rearticulate marginalized identities in order to achieve a global frame transformation; it represents a top-down marketing campaign by the men who control and profit from the sex industry.

An open letter to the Associated Press from the Coalition Against Trafficking in Women (CATW), an NGO dedicated to ending human trafficking, and their allies demonstrates this rejection of *sex worker / sex work*. I chose the CATW letter and to quote at length from it to represent both opposition to the phrase *sex work* and the core of the debate between anti-trafficking/anti-prostitution activists and sex-work activists.[40]

> We strongly oppose the terms "sex work" and "sex worker" and urge the AP to use alternative vocabulary as proposed below. These terms were

invented by the sex industry and its supporters in order to legitimize prostitution as a legal and acceptable form of work and conceal its harm to those exploited in the commercial sex trade....

The chasm between the meaning of the word "work" and the lived reality of the average prostituted or trafficked person is too vast to be ignored. The term "sex worker" wrongly suggests that the person in prostitution is the primary actor in the multi-billion dollar sex trade. This renders invisible and unaccountable its true beneficiaries—the traffickers, pimps, procurers, brothel and strip club owners, and the buyers of sex. These exploiters prey on vulnerable individuals marginalized by poverty, homelessness, racial and gender discrimination and histories of sexual abuse....

Instead of "sex work," we suggest "sex industry," "sex trade," or "prostitution." In lieu of "sex worker" or "prostitute," we recommend "person in prostitution" or "prostituted person" or "commercially sexually exploited person."[41]

Several important themes surface in this letter, which explain the opposition's rejection of the rearticulated identity of *sex worker*.[42] These themes produce the elements that sex-work antagonists link to create the identity of the "prostituted" or "trafficked" person. The first theme is prostitution. Although "strip club owners" are mentioned, the only job that is focused on is prostitution: "These terms were invented by the sex industry and its supporters in order to legitimize prostitution." This statement serves a few important purposes in disavowing the sex-worker identity. The theme of prostitution both counteracts the expansiveness offered by *sex work* and narrows it back to focus on a mostly illegal job with entrenched negative associations. The second theme that emerges is social status and gender. The CATW letter ties *sex worker* not to the people who perform the labor but with the "traffickers, pimps, procurers, brothel and strip club owners, and the buyers of sex"; these people are labeled as *beneficiaries*, making it clear that CATW rejects the notion that actual workers benefit from their own labor. The letter defines the workers unequivocally as "vulnerable individuals marginalized by poverty, homelessness, racial and gender discrimination and histories of sexual abuse." This classification adds weight to the overall argument of the letter that sex work can't be chosen, because the women doing it are already in social positions with little choice. Because these classifications fit with popular visions of sex workers as people entrenched in poverty, it carries significant ideological weight and makes for a tenacious articulation: a link that is difficult to unlink. The last theme that is stressed is ownership of the term *sex worker*. Building on the classifications of theme two, the letter ties *sex work* to the *beneficiaries*, giving power to them and shaping *sex worker* as an identity that further disenfranchises the women doing the work by assigning its creation to the beneficiaries. Although there is a clear distinction given between the workers and the beneficiaries, the letter doesn't explicitly gender these roles. Yet given that women still purchase sexual services in much lower numbers than men, and that CATW classifies prostitution as violence against women (according to its website), gender emerges as a salient subtheme that undergirds the others. Thus by opening with the claim that *sex work* and *sex worker* were invented not by the women laborers themselves but by the men who profit from them, CATW rejects the rearticulated identity on what is perhaps the term's strongest grounds: its genesis. CATW makes a clever rhetorical move here: by saying that *sex work* was invented by "the sex industry and its supporters," but by not defining who is included in that, CATW can't be accused of actually lying about the expression's past because the woman who is credited with coining it was certainly part of the sex industry. The widely quoted and commonly accepted narrative of *sex work*'s origin is that Carol Leigh (who has written about the term's creation herself in her book, *Unrepentant Whore*, and in the essay "Inventing Sex Work") used it in her one-woman play and helped to rally other sex workers around it. This ownership is important to the term's rhetorical power: it is its use *by* sex-work activists that has helped to popularize the phrase and remake identities, politics, and law for the sex trades.[43] But because the CATW letter implies that sex workers have no choice and no power, it implies a different history. Because the letter sets up a clear distinction between workers and beneficiaries and because it does not address the accepted origin story of the term, it implies that men in control of the industry, not the workers, created it. Therefore, CATW underscores its argument that sex-worker agency is a fiction by removing the power to self-identify.

Another argument CATW makes about agency is that "the term 'sex worker' wrongly suggests that the person in prostitution is the primary actor in the multi-billion dollar sex trade." In this statement, a sex worker is clearly not in the same position as other types of workers, who are not typically assumed to control the industry in which they labor. The letter does nothing to further warrant this claim by explaining why it suggests that this is true. It's hard to imagine parallel situations in which *worker* is read as indistinguishable from *the primary actor* in a given industry. The argument does not move beyond this one claim to expand and explain why the term suggests that the worker is the one person in control of the industry (suggested by the definite article *the*), a warranting that is critical. Instead, the claim is followed by the statement that *sex worker* "renders invisible and unaccountable its true beneficiaries." I would assert that this is always a characteristic of the word *worker* when it is used by labor activists who want to focus on the people who perform a particular job rather than on the owners who profit from that job. Thus in many ways the arguments for and against the use of the term are built on the same assumptions of where focus is shifted, yet they differ in terms of why that shift has been done and who benefits from it. The argument against the term *sex work* from the perspective of CATW and similar groups can be summed up in the following statement from Autumn Burris, a signatory to the letter, who identifies not as a worker but as a *survivor*: "There is no such thing as 'sex work.' It is really damaging to a survivor and all survivors worldwide to use this terminology. You are implying that there is something about it that is regular work. If you keep the harms and damage of prostitution right up front, what you come out with is that it's not a job. 'Sex work' has nothing to do with work. It has everything to do with harm."[44] Therefore, if sex work and sex workers cannot exist, sex-worker activists also cannot exist. To their opponents, the embodied experiences of women identified as survivors negate the discourse activists have fought to adopt and disseminate. Instead, for sex-work antagonists, the activist efforts that I will analyze next amount to industry lobbying, designed to increase profits by increasing harm to women's bodies.[45] Currently, any sex-work activism is influenced by similar antagonisms as we find in the CATW letter. These antagonisms deny the existence of sex workers by collapsing all sex workers into prostitutes and all prostitutes into trafficked people. Therefore, sex-work activism has to reestablish the identities that its opponents erase; the activism becomes an issue of fighting not only for labor protections but also for workers' existence.

The Sex-Worker Activist Emerges

Although *sex work* has gained traction as a term, its power to rearticulate identity is consistently challenged via antagonistic discourses and laws, and the modern movement for sex-worker rights returns repeatedly to the same battle for identity that Leigh and other activists were waging with its adoption forty years ago. Despite the popularity of the term *sex work*, the actual work of sex work is still devalued, criminalized, and shunned and the workers themselves are largely treated as victims and criminals. As the phrase *sex work* has gained in popularity over the last twenty years, so too have discourses that collapse sex work into human trafficking, which counteracts efforts to organize for labor rights. Rather than being anti–sex worker or anti-prostitute, opponents to sex work organize under the umbrella of anti-trafficking, making the identity politics for sex-worker activists additionally fraught as they negotiate a double bind, arguing for their own agency by fighting anti-trafficking discourse, while at the same time promoting their own anti-trafficking agendas. To negotiate this bind, sociologist Crystal Jackson argues that sex-worker activists deploy rights-based "framing"—a social-movement strategy of rearticulation, which works on multiple levels to counteract their opponents' antagonisms.[46] Jackson identifies sex-worker "counterstories" as a strategy that enables activists to weave "themes of their own self-determination and agency into rights-based frames."[47] The rights-based frame then benefits from humanizing strategies of which other social movements have made use, but it also specifically addresses a core antagonism of the anti-trafficking movement, which holds that sex work is the same as sex trafficking, and therefore all sex workers are either victims or complicit in their own and others' exploitation and abuse. As Jackson notes, counterstories function to give "voice" to the actual workers who often fall out of anti-trafficking discourse. When sex workers repeatedly rearticulate their identities as "not victims" (although people who are *victimized* by the system), it helps to strengthen the distinction between chosen and coerced sex work. The emotionality of trafficking victims' stories, however, complicates the logical argumentation that rights-based framing usually depends upon: "As sex worker rights activists react to being framed as victims-in-need-of-saving by police and social services, they struggle to figure out how to be heard over evocative antiprostitution discourse and mainstream anti–sex trafficking advocacy and legislation."[48] Building on Jackson's research, the following analysis of embodied articulation suggests that by foregrounding the denied identity of sex workers as living people, embodied counterstories add an affective dimension to sex-worker activism that bolsters its persuasive power. Much of the anti-trafficking discourse eliminates the distinction between victims who exist and suffer and workers doing a job. Therefore, the body carries enormous signifying power in terms of demonstrating agency. In debates about sex work, the protesting body is particularly important as a symbol for sex-worker activists whose bodies become counterstories to trafficking victims, functioning as "signifying agents actively engaged in the production and maintenance of meaning for constituents, antagonists, and bystanders or observers . . . deeply embroiled . . . in what has been referred to [by Stuart Hall] as 'the politics of signification.'"[49]

Because the sex-work movement is part labor movement, part rights-based movement, politics of signification are embedded in all forms of activism. Similar to LGBTQ social-movement activism, one aspect of the struggle is countering persistent misrecognition of identities by reframing them. The mainstream LGBTQ movement accomplished this by embracing narratives of love, family, consumerism, and patriotism. That is, its constituents were able to become recognizable as human, as citizens, and as similar to everyone else. Collapsing the difference between straight lives and queer lives aided in the attainment of two big social-movement successes: open military service and marriage equality.[50] For sex-worker activists, however, rearticulation of stigmatized identities cannot be achieved in the same way, due, in part, to the criminalization of prostitution. Further, the rhetorics of erasure that popularize the idea that sex work does not exist, only human trafficking does, also challenge projects of political rearticulation. Repeated claims that sex workers "'[d]on't exist' articulates an attack on ontology, on beingness, because beingness cannot be secured."[51] This negation doubly binds trans people who are sex workers, as a primary attack they face is erasure of their trans identities. Thus anti–sex work rhetoric has profoundly different material effects on the bodies of sex workers. Not all sex workers live this struggle for recognition in the same way because of the hierarchies of value assigned to different forms of work, hierarchies that are sedimented by class, race, and gender categories.

In addition to fighting the politics of erasure, *sex worker* also presents a unique set of challenges to people in the legal sex trades, because the term is widely recognized as signaling *prostitute*. If the illegal work of prostitution becomes articulated with legal sex work, such as stripping, it can bring social and political pressure to close clubs and therefore threatens dancers' jobs. Yet strippers have a long history of organizing in response to threats to their jobs that is a vibrant part of the history of US sex-worker activism. In 1954, long before the splitting of erotic dance into neo-burlesque and club stripping (among other forms), burlesque performer Jennie Lee, "The Bazoom Girl," formed the Exotic Dancers League (EDL), an organization dedicated specifically to the labor concerns of exotic dancers (figs. 11 and 12).[52] Although burlesque dancers were already technically represented by the American Guild of

11 | EDL event. York Club, May 1965. Photo includes Ann O'Brian, Beverly Styles, Lita Paul, Linda Lucern, Diane Lewis, Christy Anderson, Honey Boo Tenz, Patty Varga, AIKO, Jennie Lee, and Tanayo. Courtesy of the Burlesque Hall of Fame.

Variety Artists, bias against their work led to marginalization within the organization. The early activism of the EDL used the same strategies as other labor organizations—work stoppages, organized boycotts, demands to owners, legal support for their members—and the EDL "emerged as a viable organization with industry clout and respect."[53] As burlesque declined in popularity and stripping moved into clubs, the EDL transformed into a social organization, which preserved the history of midcentury burlesque and eventually, through the efforts of Lee's friend, Dixie Evans, became the Burlesque Hall of Fame.

Responding to a different set of exigencies, but the same core issue of gross inequalities in their work environments, San Francisco stripper-activists Johanna Breyer and Dawn Presser formed the Exotic Dancers Alliance (EDA) in 1993. Dancers were paying increasingly high fees to the clubs in which they danced, had little control over decision making, worked in unsafe environments, and suffered widespread sexual harassment. The EDA hoped that unionizing dancers

12 | EDL protest against the *Los Angeles Times*. Courtesy of the Burlesque Hall of Fame.

would improve working conditions for all. During the 1990s, the EDA had several successes, including securing a ruling from the California Labor Commission that dancers *are not* independent contractors—a status that is used to relieve clubs of responsibility to their workers; helping dancers to retrieve back pay they were awarded in a successful class action lawsuit against the O'Farrell

Theatre, whose stage fees robbed dancers of wages; increasing oversight of the safety of the buildings they worked in; and forming coalitions with other local labor and feminist groups.[54] Not all strippers in San Francisco, however, supported the union, arguing that the independent contractor status gives dancers more options and more flexibility. Opponents to the EDA who still sought better working conditions formed several alternative coalitions, including the Independent Dancers Alliance (IDA), Strippers to Retire in Prosperity (STRIP), and the Strippers' Society of San Francisco (SSSF).[55] Thus stripper activists wrestle with the same issues that permeate other service sectors in the US: to unionize or not to unionize. Despite the fact that these disparate groups were not united, San Francisco in the 1990s was a site of significant sex-worker activism led by dancers or former dancers seeking to treat sex work like any other work. Although the strippers' groups formed in opposition to the EDA were not following a labor model of activism and promoting unionization because they were more focused on individual-earning potential, they were still concerned with basic issues of work protections. That is, regardless of the aim of the activism itself, the fact that activism around these workplaces existed underscored the argument that sex work is real work.

This spate of stripper activism in San Francisco in the 1990s, including the famous unionization of dancers at the Lusty Lady peep show,[56] continued over the next several decades, mostly in the form of lawsuits concerned with the same set of issues: sexual harassment and assault by management and customers, draconian fee structures, OSHA violations in clubs, and at the core of all of these: the independent-contractor assignation that EDA successfully challenged in San Francisco. As was true in San Francisco in the '90s, dancers are still often divided on the issue of independent-contractor status. Many feel that the status gives them flexibility, while others argue that it is an inaccurate label that allows for exploitation. Independent contractors are legally self-employed, which means that clubs are not their employers and have no responsibility for them. But as stripper activists have repeatedly stressed, clubs exert an enormous degree of control over dancers and act as employers, whether they claim that status or not. Clubs can require that dancers work a certain number of hours, work specific shifts, wear certain outfits, dance to certain music, dance in certain areas, turn over a portion of tips to the house, and even tip out to other employees of the club. With so much control of a dancer's labor and wages going to the club, the independent-contractor status makes little sense. It puts dancers in a double bind in which they are called "independent" but really are not. Because clubs vary in their exploitation of dancers, however, not enough strippers support the push for the employee status that is required for unionization. Dancers in clubs also work alongside their competition, and many dancers seek anonymity and privacy, both factors that further challenge mass organizing and class action.[57] Thus much of the sex-work activism of dancers is targeted and individual. The collective action that typically defines social movement and labor activism, however, still surfaces in specific cases and places.

Bourbon Street, Not Sesame Street: Embodied Counterstory as Rearticulation Strategy

In New Orleans, activism around the sex work performed by strippers has been on the rise since 2016 when Act 395, or "the age ban," passed the Louisiana state legislature. The ban raised the legal age to work as a dancer from eighteen to twenty-one. Act 395 passed easily, fueled by assertions from its backers, primarily the powerful anti–sex work Covenant House (an organization started by serial sex offender Bruce Ritter). Three dancers who were fired in the wake of the ban sued the Louisiana Office of Alcohol and Tobacco Control (ATC).[58] In March 2017, District Judge Carl Barbier issued an injunction that temporarily prohibited the law from being enforced. The state appealed, and just before the case was due to begin in the Fifth US Circuit Court of Appeals, there was another explosion of activism around stripping in New Orleans.[59] Over a period of ten days in January 2018, in a joint operation between Louisiana Alcohol and Tobacco Control (ATC) and the New Orleans Police Department (NOPD), agents and officers raided strip clubs in the French Quarter after months of undercover operations aimed at exposing illegal activities. The raids corresponded with ongoing efforts to reduce the presence of the sex industry in the French Quarter in favor of more family-friendly entertainment. In the fall of 2017, a NOLA.com/*Times Picayune* series titled "The Track" reported that their year-long investigation had revealed that "sex trafficking has taken hold of Bourbon Street."[60] Citing this series and its claims, city council member Stacy Head introduced a proposal to limit the number of clubs in the French Quarter. Despite the repeated use of the phrase "human trafficking," activists argue that the paper's investigation actually failed to produce concrete evidence of the strip-club sex trafficking that was used to advertise the story and shock locals into supporting actions to dramatically curb the adult industry in New Orleans.[61]

The article "The Track" and subsequent statements by former police superintendent Michael Harrison used anti-trafficking rhetoric similar to that of CATW that collapses sex work into human trafficking. Melissa Gira Grant writes, "The paper's series referred interchangeably to stripping, selling sex, and trafficking, and concluded, vaguely and without data to support it, that victim advocates and law enforcement told them that French Quarter strip clubs were a 'trafficking opportunity.' This phrase—'trafficking opportunity'—has no meaning. Any business in which labor exploitation is possible (which is a lot of businesses) could likewise be described as a 'trafficking opportunity.'"[62]

The result of linking sex work, in this case stripping, with human trafficking is powerful, not only for the identity building that is performed (erasing the existence of sex workers) but also in the material consequences that result from it. Superintendent Harrison insisted that human trafficking—the purported reason for the raids—is happening and that arrests for it would be forthcoming.[63] However, in the weeks following the raids, there were no arrests for human trafficking or underage prostitution directly related to the clubs. But by raising the alarm about trafficking and underage prostitution—two crimes defined by coercion—the mainstream press in NOLA, the city government, and the police force, were able to in essence criminalize the legal profession of stripping.

Club closings after the raids resulted in hundreds of strippers being out of work. On February 1, dancers held an "Unemployment March" on Bourbon Street, chanting slogans like "Let us dance," carrying signs critiquing the purported links between sex work and human trafficking, calling out the authorities, and asserting their humanity, with onlookers draped over the balconies above. The protesters wore flannels and slogan t-shirts, jeans, and tank tops. People wore boots with fishnets or fetish gear or sparkly bikini tops or all of the above. A protester in a shiny shirt held a bright-pink platform heel aloft alongside a protest sign. The signs in the march showcased the major themes of sex-work organizing. Some signs addressed the government, in particular, Mayor Mitch Landrieu, and civic participation via tax payment: "Mitch & shitty hall R-NOLA's biggest pimps!" "Mitch's Cheap Political Shot (against his own citizens) is more lewd than my (God given) Pubic Hair (You're not Guiliani, NOLA's not NYC)," "We Pay Taxes and Pimps Don't," "I Pay Taxes Let Me Dance," and "My Neck My Back My Body Still Pays Tax." Others addressed sex-work antagonists directly with pleas to "Stop Saving Me!!" and with bodily humor, tinged with anger: "Human Trafficking MY ASS." Some engaged in identity articulation through focusing on sex workers as humans and sex workers as workers: "Strippers Rights are Human Rights," and "Solidarity with Service Workers." And finally, several signs identified the particular local context that affects NOLA strippers: "Boobs for Beads = YES, Boobs for Money = NO (the O's in both "boobs" have nipples drawn in, making boobs out of the "boobs") and a popular one "Bourbon Street, Not Sesame Street." AZ, a stripper protester, summed up these themes with a declaration of personhood: "You think I'm being trafficked. You think I have a pimp. You think I don't have a voice for myself. But I can speak up. I am a woman. This is my body. And I feel *fine* about it."[64] Here AZ asserts her authority and bodily autonomy, two things that her opponents proclaim she does not possess. Not only does she reference her body and her ownership of it, but she is also doing so while standing in a protest march identifying herself both as a stripper and as a protester, defying the stigmatized identity that the discourse of the raids has put upon her. Her physical presence then creates the rhetorical presence that Chaïm Perelman claims gives argumentative weight to a particular element, an affective result of protest.[65] In AZ's case, that element is her body, and she is using it to rearticulate her identity as a worker, as a woman, and as an activist, rather than as a slave, a victim, and a criminal.

In addition to their presence, the bodies of the NOLA protesters display a multicoded rhetoric—the kinesthetic, the sartorial, and the cosmetic—realms of the body that communicate symbolically via material means. During the march, some dancers wore their work clothes and danced in the middle of Bourbon Street. These displays of embodied erotic rhetoric, usually performed for money in the clubs, here serve to raise awareness and assert agency. The movements, clothes, and makeup mark them as strippers, and the addition of signs underscores that identity but also makes them identifiably activists. Images from the march show the bodies of activists who are also dancers, sex workers who are also people. Those dancers who are performing in the streets draw attention to the hypocrisy of the governments of New Orleans and Louisiana, which have long profited from tourist traffic to strip clubs on Bourbon and from NOLA's ethos—of which sex work and sex workers are a large part. In the context of the protests, NOLA's strippers rearticulate the bodies that are at the core of the raids, invoked simultaneously by authorities and the NOLA mainstream press as victims and as criminals. In addition to taking the stripping body out of the club and putting it in the streets, the act of protest takes the very individual work of the stripper and makes it part of a group. This is seen in the hundreds of dancers on the streets marching side by side. Within the club, the bodies of strippers are usually solitary, dancing by themselves in a series of individual performances. On the streets, we see their bodies as parts of a collective, a collective composed of dancers and their supporters. On the streets, the dancer body "becomes a site of resistance."[66]

In addition to marches in the streets, protesters in New Orleans have engaged in other forms of direct action and political activism. On January 31, 2018, the day before the Unemployment March, protesters interrupted a press conference that was intended to update the public about progress of construction on Bourbon Street in advance of Mardi Gras. Protesters chanted, "Sex work is real work," and "Worker's rights are women's rights," drowning out the city and tourist officials hoping to promote a new Bourbon Street, one that protesters and critics argue is evidence of its long-planned "Disneyfication."[67] In a rally after the interrupted press conference, which Mayor Mitch Landrieu was scheduled to be at but ultimately didn't attend, several protesters spoke out against remodeling Bourbon Street, arguing that strip clubs are part of its unique identity. Protesters have continuously stressed that New Orleans's sex-positive environment makes working in French Quarter clubs a safer and more affirming experience than working other places and that the raids and subsequent closing make dancers less safe by leaving them without income, a situation that increases the likelihood of exploitation, prostitution, and drug dealing. Lyn Archer, development director for the Bourbon Alliance for Responsible Entertainers (BARE) and a stripper on Bourbon Street, summarizes this argument: "Stripping gives young women true flexibility, freedom and financial solvency. It allows us to become independent, support a family, establish community and engage in civic life. Strippers are people. Whether or not you value our contributions, without jobs like this, my coworkers and I will face more difficult, dangerous lives. Where legal work disappears, illegal economies inevitably appear, entrenching cycles of poverty and crime, causing the 'net harm' that people who don't acknowledge or understand us claim they can prevent."[68]

The activism and coalition seen on Bourbon Street lend embodied weight to Archer's pleas, as the impassioned responses and steady opposition to raids counteract the images of drug-addled victims and criminals of the official narratives about why the raids occurred. As always, the activism of sex workers in New Orleans is a battle over identity and agency.

Personal narratives have played a strategic role in articulating identity in the current New Orleans activism. In addition to the economic devastation the closures bring to dancers and other club workers, activists in New Orleans have spoken passionately about the abuses of power by the police during the undercover investigation and the raids. While police and government officials have repeatedly argued that illegal activity in the clubs: drug dealing and usage, prostitution, including underage prostitution, and sex trafficking were the reasons for the undercover stings and raids, the targets of those raids have accused the New Orleans police and ATC of sexual misconduct and other abuses of power. Thus what emerges from the Bourbon Street narratives are counterstories to official (what critical race theorists call *stock*) stories of victimhood and criminality. Stock stories are powerful tools for disseminating and reifying hegemonic ideologies because they "feign neutrality ... [and] are often repeated until canonized or normalized ... stories that counter these standardized tellings are deemed biased, self-interested, and ultimately not credible."[69] Conventional stories about stripper experiences appear in a few well-used formats highlighting victimhood and criminality that deprive dancers of agency and render competing narratives—usually those that arise from dancers' own experiences—unimaginable and therefore nonexistent. In Louisiana, as in most places, the two versions work in tandem. One dominant story used by the rescue industry—organizations dedicated to getting women out of sex work—describes the strip club as a zone controlled by pimps and traffickers, a characterization that is used regardless of whether or not illegal activity occurs in a club. A series of articulations give this stock story its intelligibility. Because anti-trafficking rhetoric makes chosen sex work impossible, thereby making the sex worker a fiction, all who perform any job in the sex trades are prostitutes, and all prostitutes are those who are acted upon, not those who act. Further, strip clubs with their lack of labor protections and independent-contractor system *are* a site in which trafficking victims—not all of whom perform sexual labor—can be left with little to no access for help. Therefore, despite the fact that strippers exchange sexualized performances rather than sex for money, their ideological—and sometimes material—proximity to prostitution makes them subject to the same stock stories as prostitutes. In another stock story, this one favored by law enforcement, strippers—again through their proximity to prostitution—are always criminals, always less than full citizens. Despite the fact that stripping is legal, its sexualized nature, particularly that of lap dancing, often persuades bystanders that it is prostitution and therefore is always immoral/unethical/violent. These stock stories about strippers, like other tools of ideological domination work on two levels: their circulation renders competing narratives as unimaginable because the stories themselves render subjects incapable of telling those stories. Both counterstory and counterstory teller are delegitimized at once.

Although they may not always be recognized, the use of counterstories by marginalized groups has the potential "to expose, analyze, and challenge stock stories."[70] In the case of the NOLA protests, counterstory operates not only as a narrative form but also as a rhetorical one, specifically as an embodied rhetorical form through the physical presence of the protesters and their appeals to agency. Through sharing the benefits of dancing on Bourbon Street and emphasizing it as a chosen and even desired profession, dancer-activists disarticulate stripping from trafficking. Further, they *rearticulate* the violence of the stock story with their antagonists, arguing that strippers are victimized by violence, but that it comes from the efforts used against them and their jobs. Bringing attention to harm expansion in this way has been one of the recurring themes in the NOLA strippers' counterstories. In addition to the economic devastation wrought by the raids, dancers are also speaking out about abuses by the police during the undercover investigations and subsequent raids. Some dancers have accused undercover agents of taking pictures of them on their personal cell phones, using abusive language, and forcing them to change clothes with only male officers present.[71] One dancer, Elizabeth, clearly attributes her own violation to the police: "As soon as I was 18, I started working in the Quarter. The first time I ever felt violated was when [the police] came into our club. They were taking pictures of us in our lingerie, forcefully. When I told them my rights, asked them to delete the photo, and asked to see the warrant, they put me in handcuffs and threatened me with arrest."[72] Elizabeth not only attributes violence and predation to the NOPD and ATC officers but also asserts agency over who sees her body and under what conditions, an agency that is routinely discounted under the assumption that sex workers have forfeited their rights to bodily autonomy. Because the age ban is now intertwined with the raids, Elizabeth's choice to add the age she started dancing (18) and that she *first* felt violated during the raids bolsters strippers' claims that the age ban robs them of legal and profitable work that helps them better themselves and support their families. This and her invocation of her rights are assertions of her agency as a dancer, counterstories to standard victimization narratives. However, as the police state in the US repeatedly makes clear, an assertion of rights is far from the recognition of rights. An anonymous dancer reported to BARE that during the raids "[the police] laughed and said, 'You lost your right to decency when you became a stripper.' I looked at him and was like, 'Every person has the right to decency.'"⁷³ Like Elizabeth's words above, here BARE, on behalf of this and all dancers, shares a counterstory in which the officers are disparaging the dancers to reverse one of the most common stock narratives about dancing: that it is inherently demeaning work. The officer character here criminalizes all strippers, not only those accused of criminal activities, not only those in the Bourbon Street Raids, but all strippers. Thus he serves an important synecdochal function. He represents law enforcement, the legal system, and all those who denigrate and harass dancers in the name of harm reduction.

Sex Workers Exist

Zero trafficking victims were found in the raids. The New Orleans City Planning Commission's own 2016 report found no instances of "secondary negative effects" as a result of the clubs.⁷⁴ Still, in order to reopen, the clubs on Bourbon had to agree to increased and random surveillance and a host of other measures that imply that trafficking was indeed happening. On March 22, 2018 the NOLA City Council narrowly voted to reject a cap on the number of strip clubs on Bourbon Street, yielding a victory for the NOLA strippers. Considering the popularity of anti-trafficking discourse, BARE and other sex-worker rights' groups are likely to face many battles about their labor and identities. The conflation of sex work and sex trafficking continues to increase. The Fight Online Sex Trafficking Act (FOSTA) and the Stop Enabling Sex Traffickers Act (SESTA) are strongly opposed by sex-worker advocacy groups, who argue that the criminalizing of all activity related to sex work online makes sex workers less safe by leaving them with no way to network with each other and screen potential clients. The bipartisan support of FOSTA/SESTA brings together Democrats, Republicans, feminists, Trump, religious groups, social-service agencies, celebrities, and social-justice advocates in the name of harm reduction, with few bothering to actually speak to those sex workers who claim agency for themselves and for their right to be workers. Sex-worker advocacy groups also fight sex trafficking, but they do it without eliminating the existence of an entire group of humans who are literally shouting in the streets that they exist.

Ultimately, despite the defeat of the cap on the number of clubs on Bourbon, public support for the strippers' claims, lack of evidence of trafficking, the history of the French Quarter, and the damage to the lives of working-class people, the legacy of the NOLA raids is likely to be one moment in the march toward a gentrified Bourbon Street, which city planning commissioners and developers hope to remodel in the style of Disney's immaculate parody. A simulacrum of a simulacrum. Strippers—dancer activists—are deploying their bodies on Bourbon in what may be a futile attempt to retain the character of New Orleans as it is being rapidly eroded. Although the Battle for Bourbon was won, overall the situation in the US is dire with regard to sex work, as stock stories of human trafficking continue to dominate sex workers' own narratives of agency. Whether or not they are heard or willfully ignored, sex-worker activists are demonstrating a powerful embodied rhetoric. Their bodies tell counterstories about their bodies, about activists who are waging a battle not only for their jobs but also for their existence.

5

(Anti-)Feminist Monsters | Alterity Rhetorics and the Signifying Body

Scene: A college. A classroom. A class.
  I speak.
  "Alright . . . so . . . uh . . . we're at the point in the semester where we're going to be shifting our energy toward your Long Analysis essays. To prep for that, we're going to be reading published rhetorical analyses and theory. So for Thursday, read Hill's 'SlutWalk as Perifeminist Response to Rape Logic.' It's on Canvas. I haven't done this one before, but I thought that because SlutWalk is an artifact that you'll be familiar with, it'll be easier to understand than some of the older pieces of criticism that we've read."
  Silence.
  The students speak back.
  "What's SlutWalk?"
  "SlutWalk? I haven't heard of that."
  "Yeah . . . I don't know."
  "Oh, like Amber Rose?"
  "Oh, yeah! Amber Rose SlutWalk?"
  "Ohhh, okay. Yeah I've heard of that."
  Silence.
  I speak.
  "What? No . . . wait . . . Who . . . who's Amber Rose?"
  End scene.

Identity construction as a recursive process of making both individuals and collectives is central to the study of rhetoric of the body.[1] As I argue in chapter 1, identity is one aspect of the *topos* of the body, within the canon of delivery. While identity's shadow side—alterity or "otherness"—has not received as much critical attention in scholarship of the rhetorical body, it shares a similar rhetorical function with identity. That is, alterity can function as a strategy to define insiders and outsiders and to call attention to inequalities based on those positions. Like identity, alterity is produced by the body and its material symbolic resources as well as embedded in discursive networks. As this analysis demonstrates, alterity as a theoretical framework provides critics resources to see how physical bodies produce discourses and vice versa, and how those bodies and their identities are contested. Rhetorics of alterity operate via the mechanism of *disidentification* that José Muñoz theorizes as a political strategy that enables "minoritarian subjects" a way to "activate their own senses of self."[2] Often, these strategies include material symbolic resources that mark a particular identity as "other." Thus rhetorics of alterity not only outline the discursive and material borders between us and them, but they also call attention to the ways that the *we* is marginalized, silenced, oppressed, ignored by the *them*.

Jeffrey Nealon has carefully argued that alterity has a politics. Using alterity to interrogate and problematize identity politics and its "failures of sameness," Nealon writes, "If *identity politics* is an attempt to thematize the other in terms of its similarities with the self, I am interested here in constructing an ethical *alterity politics* that considers identity as beholden and responsive first and foremost to the other."[3] Nealon's uptake of the politics of alterity "refus[es] to thematize difference in terms of the possibility or impossibility of sameness."[4] Here, I build upon Nealon's work to examine the ways that debates about sexuality among micro-cohorts of feminists prioritize difference with other women as a means of securing a feminist identity and refusing that identity to others. In particular, I focus on the alterity rhetorics central to erotic performance. Therefore, an extended claim in this chapter will place alterity alongside the other theories and frameworks in this book. As a particular lens for analyzing embodied rhetorics, alterity is deeply embedded in sexual rhetorics, which operate in (and often against) a system of disciplining/normalizing discourses and material practices.

In chapter 4, I noted the ways that the material symbols of stripper-protesters in New Orleans take on various meanings as they are used to articulate the conjoined identities of stripper/worker/protester. In this chapter, I analyze the debates about SlutWalk because similar material symbols form the core of parallel debate about identity and who can/cannot claim it based on sexual and erotic practices and performances. As a site of embodied performance rhetoric that makes use of many of the same material symbols as neo-burlesque and club stripping, SlutWalk and its parallel international movements claim to use such material symbols in performances of protest to challenge persistent rape mythology that behavior, dress, movement, and adornment encourage rape. SlutWalk's use of sexualized attire is purportedly an attack on this rape myth, a challenge to "rape logic's conflation of clothes with consent."[5] SlutWalk's anti-victim blaming rhetoric is one that is often sex-worker inclusive, as they are people whose erotic labor is frequently seen to justify rape. Indeed, Melinda Chateauvert explicitly includes SlutWalk in her history of sex-worker organizing in the US.[6] Further, political marches and rallies, especially ones that make use of costume, are instantiations of performance rhetoric: both detractors and supporters of SlutWalk note its theatrical and carnivalesque elements.[7] Finally, many feminist critics of SlutWalk include it in the same symbolic universe as club stripping and neo-burlesque, a universe they argue is void of structural critique of patriarchy and complicit with a culture of "raunch"[8] in which women strengthen the conditions of their own oppression through adopting labels like "bitch" and "slut," proclaiming their sexual freedom, and embracing the very clothes and cosmetics that earlier generations of feminists had tied to women's sexual slavery under patriarchy. Thus SlutWalk is adjacent to the erotic performances that are my focus throughout this book. SlutWalk contains "carnivalesque performances"[9] in which bodies "mobiliz[e] against a specific instance of sexist oppression" via a "politicized use of clothes" in order to "challeng[e] the pervasive ideology of sexual violence."[10] As several scholars have noted, it is Slut-Walk's use of symbolic resources, in particular, the word *slut* and the choice by some protesters to dress in clothes coded as slutty (i.e., heels and tight/revealing apparel)—that becomes the sole focus of its critics, leaving SlutWalk's stated challenge to rape culture via the policing of women's dress and sexual behavior largely ignored. Feminist cultural sociologist Kaitlynn Mendes's research on SlutWalk reveals that despite its rather diverse and aspirational goals, SlutWalk has been widely read as nothing more than privileged young white girls parading their licentiousness in public. Writing of the feminist struggles around Slut-Walk in Delhi, Rituparna Borah and Subhalakshmi Nandi argue, "With the use of *appropriate* symbols, semantics and messages, some arguments could have been made for a woman's right to move around freely, to pursue her desires and to make her choices."[11] To its feminist critics, however, SlutWalk is a mess of inappropriate symbols and offensive embodied performance steeped in racism and patriarchal oppression.

Both the excitement and the furor around SlutWalk have died down significantly since it sprang up early in the second decade of the twenty-first century. In the US, SlutWalk is now linked with Amber Rose, a model, former stripper, and self-identified "feminist monster,"[12] whose Amber Rose SlutWalk has become the epicenter of movement activity in the US. Other marches have rebranded, many to distance themselves from blistering critiques from black feminists citing SlutWalk's racism and tone-deaf ignorance of women of color's particular struggles with sexual violence and oppression. Rose, on the other hand, "has taken [the] grass roots idea" of SlutWalk and "branded it" with her own identity, including an "official Amber Rose SlutWalk press conference, complete with a logo banner, [and] an official SlutWalk after-party."[13] Under Rose's leadership, SlutWalk has stayed active in LA, having a march every year between 2015 and 2018, the same time frame in which marches and events elsewhere died out.[14] She not only kept the movement active, but she also steered it toward being explicitly inclusive of trans women, sex workers, and women and queer people of color. Thus although she didn't start it, Rose is a major reason why SlutWalk is still relevant to talk about and why the movement finds a place in this book. Like SlutWalk itself, Rose is a complicated and often controversial feminist figure. As a former stripper and as a woman of color who is also outspoken both about her body and about the vitriol she faces for being a sexual woman who isn't ashamed to claim that identity, Rose is the ideal figurehead to take on SlutWalk. One need only look at Kanye West's widely cited comment about Rose—that he had to "take 30 showers" after being with Rose before he could get with Kim Kardashian—to appreciate the ways that Rose is marked as dirty and slutty and less than. She is dismissed as vapid, opportunistic, narcissistic, uneducated, and a bad mother.[15] Yet her politics have become more nuanced as the years have progressed. The Amber Rose SlutWalk is no longer her personal clap back against critics, as structural analyses of sexism now appear alongside rhetorics of the choice to be slutty. In short—in this moment—Rose and her brand of SlutWalk represent the uneasy resting place that the feminist sex wars—ideological debates among feminists about sexual identity, behavior, and politics—now find themselves. Neither resolved, nor ablaze.

Debates about bodily expression, labeling, and feminist identity in SlutWalk divide women through a process of sexual stratification created in part through rhetorics of alterity that construct and emphasize differences, allegiances, and power imbalances. The SlutWalk controversy, then, is a contemporary battle in the larger arena of the feminist sex wars,[16] which reveal the strategic deployment of rhetorics of alterity in defining who does and who does not possess feminist sexuality. Rather than recognizing adjacent but differing factions as micro-cohorts—"activists who become politicized during a single generation, but because of differences in timing, social context, and community come to adopt identities and ideologies different from other movement activists"[17]— each side claims to be a truer representation of feminist identity, *incompatible* with the politics of the other. Rhetorics of alterity obscure those values that are shared between differing ideological positions and stress incompatibility among micro-cohorts.

Although *the sex wars* is typically used to refer to a particular set of debates in a particular time period (summarized below), I consider ongoing debates about sexual practice and feminist identity—primarily cis and trans women's— in the context of patriarchy all to be part of the same sex wars,[18] staking out parallel positions and deploying similar alterity rhetorics. In the history of the wars, which spans more than thirty years, feminists have debated a range of topics about sexuality, most visibly about the effects of practices such as pornography and sex work, but also about individual behaviors, such as the lesbian dildo debates of the late 1980s and early '90s, butch-femme identities, and S/M participation. More recently, feminist debates about SlutWalk engage with different concerns via parallel arguments. Contemporary battles in the wars focus primarily on sex work and human trafficking, how to dismantle rape culture, and whether or not there is anything feminist about the "raunch culture" that Ariel Levy so roundly critiques in her popular 2005 book *Female Chauvinist Pigs: Women and the Rise of Raunch Culture*. What all of these battles share across the years, however, is women's sexual and erotic bodies defined and excluded by a set of rhetorical strategies that define *us* and *them* and structure the power relations between the two.

As with neo-burlesque and club stripping, SlutWalk is a contentious site of public embodied performance, which incites vigorous debate about the signifying power of cis and trans women's sexual bodies. Although its moment in the spotlight has passed according to media coverage (or lack thereof) of its events,[19] SlutWalk offers important insights for critics of erotic body rhetorics. First, it highlights a number of feminist debates about women's sexualized bodies that dominate all sites of erotic performance—namely, the question of how to read material and discursive signifiers that to some signal patriarchal oppression and to others signal femme sexual empowerment. Second, it highlights the ways that race is an especially powerful signifier in bodily rhetorics that often gets silenced or co-opted. Finally, it shows how alterity is a powerful rhetorical strategy and one that is useful for critics of the body, which is often enmeshed in contentious identity politics.

Alterity as Strategy

Alterity as a rhetorical strategy includes defining both who *is* "the other" and *responses to* the other. Rhetorics of alterity often construct polarized identities, but they also rely on taking control of those polarities for persuasive, activist purposes. Contemporary debates about sex work, neo-burlesque, and SlutWalk continue decades-old arguments about feminist sexuality, which illustrate that the feminist sex wars are still very active, located not in a single historical moment but in the sexual politics of feminism itself. The representations of feminist sexual identity constructed via these wars reveal the strategic deployment of rhetorics of alterity both as an identity-making and identity-denying strategy.

The fact that identity creates alter-identity (the other) is a function of language. To put it simply, one can't define some people without excluding others, or to crudely paraphrase Ferdinand de Saussure: the very practice of signifying is based on differences.[20] That is, for me to *be* any particular identity necessarily means that there are people who *are not* this particular identity. The relationship between *me* and *not me* or in the case of collectives like the feminist movement, the relation between *us* and *them* is always a political one. As political theorist William Connolly argues, "Identity requires difference in order to be, and it converts difference into otherness in order to secure its own self-certainty." Connolly further argues that maintaining identity often requires converting otherness into "evil."[21] Rhetorics of alterity construct the evil other in one of two key ways: (1) *they* (those who are not the same as *us*) are opposed to *us* by nature of their differences and they will do us harm, and (2) *they* (those who are not the same as *us*) construct *us* as an evil other out to do *them* harm.

In a Burkean model, it is the human condition of separateness that creates alterity and that is the basis for rhetoric.[22] That is, identification via rhetoric offers a sort of antidote to alterity. While Burke doesn't explicitly theorize alterity, the idea that rhetoric can linguistically minimize the differences between *us* and *them* positions alterity as a problem to be solved by, not one that is constructed by, discourse. Diane Davis, while explicitly not working in the realm of criticism that I take up here, theorizes alterity not as something that can be ameliorated by rhetoric, but as the condition that presents us with all occasions for rhetoric. To simplify her very complex argument, the fact of the other calls for communication with the other—not necessarily to close the gap, but just because there is no reason to communicate without alterity.

If alterity and identity are not opposed but codependent, then *rhetorics* of alterity and *rhetorics* of identity are similarly so. For my purposes here, I conceive of articulating identity and articulating alterity as parallel processes that are necessary for rhetorical communication but need not be ontologically stable, separate conditions of being. In a roundabout way then, alterity always returns us to identity and vice versa. Thus if identity is a crucial aspect of criticizing body rhetorics, alterity is too. As I've stressed throughout this book, bodies communicate in multiple symbolic realms, tacking between linguistic and material signifiers to make and share meaning. Analysis of body rhetorics often brings critics into intimate conversation with rhetors and their audiences because bodies have immediate presence when we encounter them in rhetorical situations. The critic of the body can't detach rhetor from rhetorical performance. Rhetoric of the body is always engaged in multicoded signifying[23] in the immediate presence of an audience, and those signifying practices construct both identity and alterity.

Because *alterity* is so connected with a particular philosophic tradition, it is important to note that the rhetoric of alterity that I am sketching here differs fundamentally from Levinas's conception of *the other*, one who cannot be represented in language. According to Diane Davis, for Levinas the other "figures an interruption in identification," but as Davis effectively highlights, even in Levinas, interactions with the Other are rhetorical in nature through the process of interrupting rather than constructing meaning.[24] In response to Levinas's theories of ethics and otherness, Davis argues that we reconsider the foundational assumptions of rhetoric by focusing less on making meaning and more on the preconditions that enable rhetoric to exist. In particular, she proposes that we rethink rhetoric, starting from the basic assumption that rational subjects use rhetoric to persuade an audience through symbolic interactions. Instead, Davis's theoretical and philosophical project establishes our "responsibility" as language-using creatures to respond to the other as the basis for rhetoric. Thus alterity belongs to philosophies and theories of ethics and rhetoric, but it also is realized in political and material ways. While treatises on alterity are usually driven by the idea of the subject's need to respond to the other, I suggest that alterity can also be a useful lens for understanding how subjects respond to *being* other/ed. I agree with Davis that rhetoric operates in nonhermeneutical ways; my goal here, however, is to identify some ways that alterity is constructed in and used strategically through rhetoric, making alterity a critical tool for analysis of bodily rhetorics. Rhetoric, including material and embodied rhetorics, gives form to our *perceptions* of and structures our relations to, those who are not us.

In social movements, participants make strategic use of alterity similar to the ways that they make strategic use of identity.[25] Dana Anderson argues that identity functions as a "kind of persuasive strategy" that "matters less as something that one 'is' and more as something that one *does* in language."[26] Activists have always depended on language to determine and communicate who is *us* and who is *them*. People form social movements precisely because they are "other." Some activists and movements treat this otherness as a problem and seek to assimilate. Another social-movement stance is to attempt to use the condition of otherness as a way to build an "alter-identity" that is opposed to the mainstream and pursues rights on its own terms, sometimes even attempting to leverage a fundamental shift in the values that define *us* and *them*. To simplify, if rhetorical identity strategies focus on defining who *we* are in social movements, alterity strategies define who *we* are by defining who is *not us*. Because there is a political agency that social movements have created around the lack of political power, however, alterity is not just something that one strives to overcome but something that can offer political legitimacy to rights-seeking subjects. For example, Jeffery Nealon analyzes the ways that the White Angry Man (or WAM) has increasingly defined himself as a subaltern subject, despite privileges that he holds. The alterity rhetorics of white angry men are persuasive recruiting tools because they exploit the feature of identity politics that "offers solace to virtually any subject position, as long as it claims to be a minority oppressed by the weighty and influential norm."[27] When the WAM constantly claims his "otherness" to show how his needs are culturally shunted, he draws on rhetorics of alterity.

Defining otherness strategically is a complex and recursive process, and in the analyses of sex-war discourses that follow, I will focus on two ways that it works, recognizing that they are neither separate nor independent from each other or from identity strategies. In one cluster of alterity strategies, a group highlights its own "otherness" or subaltern position as a way of claiming agency to argue for treatment that is more just. Another set of strategies converts that otherness into identity and uses rhetorics of alterity to define who is *other* to the other.

The discourse of SlutWalk is a vivid example of rhetorics of alterity as the movement engenders the type of discourse that frontloads alterity/identity rhetorics, which declare otherness based on a fundamental disagreement about meaning. In SlutWalk this disagreement is centered on the march's purpose. Proponents see it responding to an exigence of rampant and self-perpetuating rape culture, while critics see it as self-indulgent spectacle. Mendes's analysis of media coverage and critique of SlutWalk demonstrates that "while most critiques of the movement seemed to centre on the idea that the march is about promoting female promiscuity and reclaiming the word 'slut,' discourses that defended it focused on how SlutWalk combats rape culture, victim blaming, and shaming."[28] This fundamental disagreement highlights rhetorics of alterity that demonstrate the rhetorical utility of otherness.

The Sex Wars, Then and Now

Because the origins of the sex wars help to provide context for current debates about cis and trans women's erotic bodies and for the other erotic performances that are the subject of this book, before turning to SlutWalk, I will step back to look at alterity rhetorics in the original sex wars. Looking back at the wars' origins shows the persistence of alterity rhetorics in debates about feminist sexuality, especially bodily practices and signifiers. The phrase *the sex wars*, also called *the feminist sex wars*, *the porn wars*, and *the S/M wars*, generally refers to the ideological debates of the late 1970s and early '80s when feminists were debating sexual identity, particularly as it related to behavior.[29] As Jo Reger notes, the sex wars "serve as one source of generational disidentification" among feminists, which is also seen in the SlutWalk controversy.[30] Publications as well as reflections on the wars demonstrate the ways that the discourse allows feminists to disidentify with each other and lay claim to the identity of feminist. Artifacts from the wars distill the factions into two main antagonisms: radical feminists versus pro-sex feminists. These binary representations of feminist sexual identity reveal the strategic deployment of rhetorics of alterity. Each faction rhetorically constructs the other as composed of inauthentic feminists, and also claims the oppressed position as their means of rhetorical power. That is, each side claims to be the true representation of feminist sexuality while simultaneously claiming that they are oppressed by the position of the other. Elisa Glick argues, however, that both positions share much in common: while "radical feminists see 'female sexuality' as repressed by 'the patriarchy,' the pro-sexuality movement sees repression as produced by heterosexism and 'sex negativity.'" Therefore, "both pro-sex and radical feminists reproduce the ideology of personal emancipation ... by making the liberation of sex a fundamental feminist goal."[31] Thus the discourse of the sex wars highlights how rhetorical strategies of identity and alterity are created and maintained through social systems of varying degrees of power and tenacity.

In the early 1980s, feminist critiques of patriarchal sexuality, in particular, pornography, came to dominate the movement.[32] The rhetorics of dominance or structural feminist theory frontloaded critiques of violence against women at the hands of men and quickly replaced the focus on women's liberation that first ignited the second wave. Inspired by this shift in feminist discourse about sexuality, Barnard College hosted *The Scholar and the Feminist IX* conference titled "Towards a Politics of Sexuality" in April of 1982. The conference aimed "to address women's sexual pleasure, choice, and autonomy, acknowledging that sexuality is simultaneously a domain of restriction, repression, and danger, as well as a domain of exploration, pleasure, and agency."[33] This description, along with the planned speakers and panel topics, incited structural feminists to protest because it suggested that feminist sexuality was more nuanced than dominance rhetorics made space for. Conference organizers articulated women's sexuality with "restriction, repression, and danger"—traditional domains for feminist politics and scholarship—but they also forged a new connection for feminist sexuality by adding the elements of "exploration, pleasure, and agency." Further, they start from the assumption that women's sexuality is one of "pleasure, choice, and autonomy," key words that counter dominance feminist rhetorics. The conference immediately drew a barrage of criticism for its framing of feminist sexuality. Women Against Pornography (WAP), Women Against Violence Against Women, and the New York Radical Feminists, "denounce[d]" the conference organizers for "inviting proponents of 'anti-feminist' sexuality to participate."[34] The administration of Barnard College confiscated planning materials and the Helena Rubinstein Foundation withdrew its financial support. Conference opponents picketed, and the feminist magazine *off our backs* published the names of participants in a women's S/M play party that was unaffiliated with the event as a calculated move to link the conference with sexual activities that many radical feminists argued were dangerous and repressive.

It's not surprising that the Barnard Conference drew such a heated response. The mainstream (read: white, straight, cis, middle-class) women's movement had been built on a particular ideological stance toward sexuality and patriarchy. Now some were suggesting that there might be more than one ideological orientation toward feminist sexuality available. In essence, the proposed conference embraced feminism's alter-identity and still called itself *feminism*, refusing to accept that women's sexuality can be defined solely with regard to patriarchal violence and introducing the idea of *feminisms* as a way to embrace plurality. Many of the sex-radical feminists who were in support of the conference were arguing for the liberation of feminist sexuality, including pornography, sadomasochism, role-playing, and sex toys, as valid and valued expressions of sexuality. Sex-radical feminist Susie Bright, part of the founding team of the lesbian porn magazine *On Our Backs*—a direct swipe at *off our backs* that demonstrates the oppositional rhetorics of the wars—criticized the turn that mainstream feminist sex theory had "reduced itself to [by] purging anything aggressive, vicarious, and non-oval-shaped from its erotic vocabulary [and by] mouth[ing] sexist clichés about 'the nature of men and women' that could have come out of a fundamentalist pulpit."[35] Lesbians, who had been shunned by many factions in the mainstream women's movement, played an active role in the wars, which became a site for valorizing the sexuality that had been a "menace" in the early days of the women's movement. Many lesbian-feminists supported dominance critiques of patriarchal sexuality and argued that lesbianism was the ultimate feminist sexuality because it was by its very nature different from patriarchal sex. Thus the wars became an important site for defining lesbian sexuality and legitimizing it within the movement.

Writing in 1991, feminist-activist and lesbian Gillian Hanscombe denies the identity of *feminist* to women, like Bright, who partake in the "antifeminist" market of the sex industry as consumers or purveyors, because its "stated values do not attempt to challenge patriarchy and do not promote egalitarianism between women."[36] Here, Hanscombe articulates not only a lesbian identity but a feminist one as well, which she assumes can only challenge the patriarchy by remaining outside of the sex industry. The focus on "egalitarianism" contains a critique against the sexual and erotic practices of S/M, butch-femme, and role-playing, which were common sites of debate among lesbian feminists. Since Hanscombe takes it for granted that this is the only way for feminism to operate, she focuses on persuading lesbians to understand these truths: "Some of us who have been watching ... rather silently, now need to stand up and be counted and to say clearly what we think decent lesbian sex is really about: decent meaning satisfying; and decent also meaning ethically defensible. Decent lesbian sex, first of all, can't be traded; and decent lesbian relationships can't be successfully commercially packaged."[37] Hanscombe composes several strategic forms of lesbian-feminist sexual identity via alterity rhetorics in this passage. First, she claims the status of silent observer, indicating that the lesbian-feminism that she advocates has been marginalized. The lesbian-feminist is othered by the patriarchy because it, not she, is culturally dominant. Second, Hanscombe claims to know what "decent lesbian sex is *really about*" indicating that there *is* a reality that can only be accessed through her values. With this move, Hanscombe casts the sex-radical lesbian-feminist as the alter-identity: she cannot exist because one *cannot be* a feminist and embrace phallocentric practices like pornography, S/M, and sex work.[38] Finally, she simultaneously defines what "decent" means for all lesbians and what "ethics" means as well. Such language sets her position up as that which is moral and right. Thus she defines both feminist and anti-feminist identities via analysis of specific sexual practices. Therefore, how bodies behave defines their politics and their identities. Throughout this passage, Hanscombe makes the dual functions of rhetorics of alterity clear. She persuasively makes her position other, and equally persuasively, she makes it central.

A counter articulation of lesbian-feminist sexual identity is expressed in the essay "Thinking Sex: Notes for a Radical Theory of Sexuality" by sex-radical lesbian writer and S/M practitioner Gayle S. Rubin. Rubin, writing in 1984 during the height of the wars, criticizes radical and dominance feminists for engaging in a moralistic war, arguing that feminist discourse has damned almost any variation of sexuality as anti-feminist. She notes that for traditional lesbian feminists (like Hanscombe), "monogamous lesbianism that occurs within long-term, intimate relationships and which does not involve playing with polarized roles, has replaced married, procreative heterosexuality at the top of the value hierarchy."[39] To rearticulate feminism to make a place for lesbians like herself, Rubin advocates for "'pro-sex' feminism . . . spearheaded by lesbians whose sexuality does not conform to movement standards of purity (primarily lesbian sadomasochists and butch/femme dykes), by unapologetic heterosexuals, and by women who adhere to classic radical feminism."[40] By reclaiming sexual liberation as a "classic" goal of feminism, Rubin has rearticulated feminism into a standpoint that allows for a vast variety of sexual expression and urges other women to do the same. Sex radicals like Rubin claim that feminist sexuality is fluid. It doesn't require women to believe or act in prescribed ways. Not surprisingly, Rubin uses the same alterity rhetorics as Hanscombe: she positions herself as the powerless other and simultaneously claims her feminist identity as more valid than that of "antisex feminists." Similar to Hanscombe, she uses the specific sexual practices and expressions of women to define them as feminist. That is, the body's actions specifically lead to the identity. While they disagreed over what constitutes feminist sexuality, both groups of feminists in the late twentieth-century wars strategically deployed rhetorics of alterity via the sexual and erotic body in order to construct a specific feminist identity both for themselves and for their opponents. The lines of argument that have chained out over three decades of the feminist sex wars since the Barnard Conference and its aftermath focus on various areas of public and private sexual behaviors and how those fit or do not fit within a feminist identity.

The sex wars of the '80s and '90s provided the opportune moment for the inclusion of lesbian feminists who had previously been seen as a PR nightmare for the early feminist movement, which strenuously sought distance from lesbianism in order to legitimize itself. Despite this expanded inclusivity in the feminist movement, published writing from the wars is dominated by white women, who sometimes invoke women of color's experiences to bolster an argument without actually including their voices. In one of the few published artifacts about the wars by a woman of color, Cherríe Moraga responds to Fran Moira for her coverage of the Barnard Conference. Moira had criticized the "Speak-out on Politically Incorrect Sex," that happened during, but not as part of, the conference, identifying Moraga as an attendee. Moraga calls out Moira for choosing to "collapse a 'politically incorrect speak-out' [about sexuality] into an across-the-board endorsement of s/m, while citing Kitchen Table: Women of Color Press throughout, not to have inquired of The Press what was our actual relationship to the event as a whole."[41] Moraga's article is an important intervention in the discourses of the sex wars. She writes, "The way the movement is breaking down around sex makes me feel that women of color are being played between two white (sector's) hands. And, I don't like it."[42] Interventions like Moraga's illustrate the ontological instability of the dichotomies created by alterity rhetorics in the wars and also call attention to the assumptions by white feminists that they can speak universally about women without paying attention to the arguments and somatic experiences of women of color, a critique that resurfaces (albeit in different ways) in the SlutWalk controversy.

At the core of debates about SlutWalk is a question that is common to all feminist sex wars: What is anti-feminist sexuality? Because this central question is one about what is *not feminist*, rather than what is, it is a site of rhetorics of alterity, which are common tools used to define who *we* are *not*. At issue with regard to SlutWalk is what the movement communicates about women's sexual practices and women's sexuality and race. Does it, as organizers and supporters hope, speak out against slut shaming, a victim-blaming tactic that holds women's sexuality against them and encourages rape and sexual violence? Or does it, as its detractors claim, reinforce hegemonic patriarchal views about women as essentially sexually available by way of natural promiscuity, by way of purchase, or by way of force? And finally, are the goals of SlutWalk compatible with the goals of feminists of color? Can SlutWalk as it was envisioned accommodate feminists of color or are the somatic and cultural sexual experiences of white women and women of color too different?

Like the original wars, artifacts of the contemporary feminist sex wars are instantiations of rhetorics of alterity used to structure feminist and nonfeminist identity and likewise, feminist and nonfeminist sexuality. Analysis of these artifacts suggests that strategic deployments of alterity act as a type of rhetorical agency that can enact a persuasive ethos in the making of feminist sexual identity. That is, definitions of self and other based on sexuality and attitudes about sexuality create categories that act not only as definitions but also as strategies that attempt to garner support for a particular perspective. Ultimately, because both sides ostensibly share a commitment to the identity of feminist, alterity gains power as a rhetorical tool. While rhetorics of alterity function to construct feminist sexuality in both discursive and material ways in a number of contested domains, not all of which are in coalition (that is, sex-work activists fighting for labor protections are fighting a very different battle than sex-positive feminists marching in SlutWalks), the rhetorics serve a similar identity-making strategy. I focus here on debates about SlutWalk because the controversy it caused in feminist circles had an effect not seen in the original sex wars by frontloading the critiques of women of color as a central issue in feminist sexuality.

SlutWalk's Multicoded (Uniracial?) Rhetoric

The original Toronto SlutWalk defined itself as "a worldwide movement against victim-blaming, survivor-shaming, and rape culture."[43] In 2011 SlutWalk formed as a protest march organized in response to Toronto police officer Michael Sanguinetti's remark that "women should avoid dressing like sluts in order not to be victimized." Although it is not a requirement, some marchers enact what dressing like sluts looks like through material symbolic means, such as wearing items like fishnet hose, heels, fetish wear, lingerie, or going topless, carrying signs like "Still not asking for it." While the SlutWalk movement has a variety of planks in its platform that are distinctly feminist—such as the idea that sexual violence is not caused by the way a woman is dressed and that the act of victim blaming and ignoring the actions of rapists shores up rape culture—these goals are not generally recognized by opponents.[44] Conversely, proponents of SlutWalk in both popular and scholarly literature focus on the challenge to rape culture as SlutWalk's main contribution to contemporary feminism. However, it is the performance of slut identity, via the material symbolic, in particular, the dress and cosmetics of the protesters, that critics focus on. In addition to its purported challenge to rape culture, SlutWalk is also a type of what's come to be known as *sex-positive feminism* in which women claim ownership over expressions of sexuality that have traditionally been coded as patriarchal and oppressive. Sex-positive feminism focuses on the ideas that women have the right to express their sexuality in any way they choose—provided no one is victimized—and that there is empowerment in the act of choosing. To simplify the sex-positive feminist message: being pressured to wear garters and makeup is oppressive. Choosing to wear them is empowering. Because it draws on these contested versions of women's sexuality that have been under debate for thirty years, almost as quickly as it appeared SlutWalk drew criticism from many feminists who questioned the celebration of sluttiness as an effective and ethical political move to end abuse and sexual violence and harassment. To its critics, the choices of SlutWalkers victimize all women.

Scholars have categorized the SlutWalk backlash into one of several strands. What unites the various oppositions to SlutWalks (including conservatives, the mainstream media, and structural and radical feminists) is that they emphasize and reject its body spectacle and reclamation of the word *slut*. SlutWalk's stated goals to challenge and end rape culture, victim blaming, and sexual violence is consistently obscured by the co-goals of sexual freedom and liberation. Thus SlutWalk points to a clash of ideologies with regard to its messaging: the articulation of victim blaming with slut shaming, the promotion of sexual liberation, the reclamation of the word *slut*, and the revealing (or absent) clothing were too controversial to mobilize many feminists to join the cause, with the most vociferous objections coming from structural and radical feminists and feminists of color.

The symbols of SlutWalk are clearly at odds with structural feminism's critique of patriarchal sexual violence and (as Hanscombe would argue) its position "in among the market forces." For structural and radical feminists, *slut* is not a word to reclaim, and dressing in slutty clothes only feeds into patriarchal myths about women's sexuality. In a widely cited piece by Gail Dines and Wendy

Murphy, the authors note SlutWalk's positive goals to protest the idea that women encourage sexual violence when they dress or act in a certain way, but the authors' main critique is of the reclamation of *slut*:

> The organisers claim that celebrating the word "slut," and promoting sluttishness in general, will help women achieve full autonomy over their sexuality. But the focus on "reclaiming" the word slut fails to address the real issue. . . . The word is so saturated with the ideology that female sexual energy deserves punishment that trying to change its meaning is a waste of precious feminist resources. . . . [Young women] have been told over and over that in order to be valued . . . they must look and act like sluts, while not being labeled slut because the label has dire consequences including being blamed for rape, depression, anxiety, eating disorders, and self-mutilation. . . . Women need to take to the streets—but not for the right to be called "slut." Women should be fighting for liberation from culturally imposed myths about their sexuality that encourage gendered violence.[45]

Dines and Murphy's appeals to the "real issue" and what women "need to" do and "should be fighting" for, along with their claim that resignifying *slut* is a "waste of precious feminist resources" reflect the general feminist opposition to SlutWalk, although the authors' tone suggests that they would welcome allegiance with SlutWalkers in a different context. Interestingly, the authors' claims about the word *slut* are the same reasons that SlutWalks give for marching under that term: to contest its use as a label with "dire consequences" for women. Further, one of SlutWalk's main goals is indeed "fighting for liberation from culturally imposed myths about . . . sexuality that encourage gendered violence." Dines and Murphy's piece then illustrates the ways that pro– and anti–slut walkers share some core values but differ in terms of the symbolic resources used to articulate those values.

Many feminists of color have voiced similar concerns about slut symbolism, but specifically with regard to their embodied experiences of sexual violence and the ignorance of SlutWalk's white leadership in planning an event without consideration of how the word *slut* signifies differently for women of color. As Cherríe Moraga noted with regard to the Barnard Conference, women of color's voices tend to be ignored or co-opted to speak in the service of white women's agendas. Indeed, published arguments by women of color on either side of the early sex wars are rare, but women of color have always been deeply affected by, invested in, and part of these debates. In the contemporary sex wars, while published arguments about feminist sexuality still favor the voices of white women, digital and social media has given women of color new forums in which to speak. In fact, "a growing community of Black women . . . use the web to protest and build social networks that extend far beyond their computer screens" providing a space where women with voices that are routinely silenced can "disrup[t] hegemonic understandings of violence against women and racial minorities."[46] As in all variations of the sex wars, however, the most widely cited arguments against SlutWalk do not represent all feminists of color.[47] In particular, the revival of SlutWalk by Amber Rose has changed its meaning through who she has specifically targeted with its message, starting with her friends and fans. With less focus on privileged white cis college women and more on people of color, trans/nonbinary/gender noncomforming people, and sex workers, journalist Zeba Blay argues that Rose's SlutWalk "changes the game" for women of color:

> [W]hat made Rose's event so important, was that it wasn't a SlutWalk organized by white women speaking for *all* women. It was organized by a woman of color and marketed to her mostly non-white fanbase. The event was crucially inclusive of women from all backgrounds, but Rose was also speaking to and for women who share similar experiences. She was speaking to and for women like her best friend Blac Chynna—black women who have been active participants in a hip-hop culture that has capitalized on their sexuality while simultaneously shaming them for owning it.[48]

The Instagram account @slutwalk_la shows a diverse array of SlutWalkers and supporters. In one picture posted on June 7, 2018, two black women pose with signs reading "WE'RE TAKING SLUT BACK" and "MY PUSSY MY CHOICE." A post from May 3, 2018, has a mustached young person of color with leopard print cat ears, fanny pack, and polka-dot shorts holding a sign proclaiming, "IF YOU BELIEVE IN EQUALITY YOU ARE A FEMINIST." Thus despite Rose's (current) economic privilege, her message and her march has resonated forcefully with young, black, queer, cis, and trans women of color, an audience that changes the literal embodiment (and therefore the message) of the movement dramatically by moving away from the white cis college women who started SlutWalk.

Before Rose became the central figurehead for SlutWalk, some of the most damning (and compelling) critiques of it came from feminists of color who argued that the young white women playing dress up were demonstrating ignorance of the ways that embodying "slutty" clothes and identifying as such has different histories, contexts, and consequences for women of color. In the months following the original SlutWalk protest in 2011, a range of criticisms articulated SlutWalk with hegemonic whiteness and patriarchal violence.[49] In a blog post titled "Slut Walk: A Stroll Through White Supremacy," journalist Aura Bogado constructs an argument against SlutWalk's protest performances that demonstrates two key components of alterity rhetorics, deployed here through themes that contrast *collusion* with *coalition*.[50] Bogado establishes one of the persuasive functions of alterity rhetorics by constructing a set of arguments that stake out boundaries between the *us* of her post (women of color) and the *them* (SlutWalk organizers) by demonstrating the subaltern position of women of color. In a note that precedes the actual post, Bogado shares that she published the piece on her own blog after it was rejected by the *Guardian* and *HuffPost*, adding weight to her argument that both within the SlutWalk movement itself and in the feminist debates about it "white women have constructed a conversation that women of color can't seem to participate in," a sentiment that echoes Moraga's critique of the earlier sex wars. Bogado uses alterity strategies to show the dominance of white women in SlutWalk's leadership, "which has systematically silenced the voices of women of color." Bogado argues that this dominance is in collusion with patriarchal violence on several levels, all of which serve to shore up SlutWalk as a white-supremacist movement. Bogado carries the theme of collusion through several levels in the blog. The first concerns collusion with police. Bogado quotes the SlutWalk website, which includes the following line: "SlutWalk 'want[s] Toronto Police Services to take serious steps to regain [their] trust'"; Bogado responds, "Our communities . . . never trusted the police to begin with." SlutWalk is not only in collusion with police, however. Bogado argues that it is also not in *coalition* with groups already working specifically to address "systemic [police] violence . . . directed against women in communities of color," an organizing choice that "dismiss[es] the work that our communities have done to make sense out of the disproportionate accumulation of violence that we face." By arguing that SlutWalk is in collusion with the police rather than in coalition with communities of color already working to end violence, Bogada shores up her argument about white supremacy. SlutWalk, through the mechanism of white privilege, is empowered to create a spontaneous, instantly recognizable movement that doesn't depend upon the coalition that is so central to marginalized communities. Embedded in this argument about collusion is a lesson about alterity: not only is SlutWalk in collusion with forces that use violence to control people of color, but also by refusing coalition, it refuses contact with the other altogether, something that only people of privilege have the power to do.

In addition to showing the othering effects of SlutWalk's collusion-over-coalition strategy, Bogado also brings up another theme about SlutWalk's white imperialism (my term): that of reclamation as a *failed* alterity strategy. For me, a white woman who came of age in the 1990s, who wrote *bitch* on my body and listened to Bikini Kill while smoking cloves and writing angry poetry, it is hard to look back and objectively assess reclamation of terms as an empowerment strategy, which Bogada does here. The use of hate terms—*bitch, dyke, faggot*, and now *slut*—by the people whom those terms were directed at was a common sign of alterity politics in action at the end of the twentieth century. Their argument was simple and attractive to young people: if I use this term for myself, you can't use it against me. Hate term reclamation also offered a sense of power to use forbidden language to mark one's embodied identity. Using slurs to identify is a model rhetorical strategy of alterity because it makes the sign of abject otherness the source of agency: it builds identity in otherness. For some scholars and activists, the evidence is compelling that "despite public criticism of using the 'profane' to spur social justice, the current data suggests that slurs, such as *slut*, are an ideal vehicle for sparking social change."[51] Bogado and many feminist activists like her disagree. Bogado writes:

> There is no indication that SlutWalk will even strip the word "slut" from its hateful meaning.... Words are powerful—the connection between speech and thought is a strong one, and cannot be marched away to automatically give words new meaning. If I can't trust SlutWalk's white leadership to even reach out to women of color, how am I to trust that "reclaiming" the word will somehow benefit women? The answer is, I can't. In fact, "reclaiming" is defined as taking something back that was yours to begin with, and the word "slut" was never ours to begin with, so it would be impossible to reclaim it.[52]

Here Bogado questions the logic of rhetorics of alterity that claim to find power in the language of the oppressor class. She reminds her readers that entrenched systemic racism and violence can't be changed through adopting the perspective of the people who oppress them, which she does by emphasizing that the word *slut* was "never ours." In short, she uses one alterity strategy to dismantle another.

Finally, Bogado ends with a paragraph that explicitly argues that SlutWalk's organizers and supporters have used their privilege to silence women of color, again both identifying the boundaries between identities and the dominance of whiteness. She writes that SlutWalk proves that "liberal white women are perfectly comfortable *parading* their privilege, *absorbing* every speck of airtime *celebrating* their audacity, and *ignoring* women of color.... SlutWalk has ... effectively *silenced* the voices of women of color and re-centered the conversation to consist of a topic by, of, and for white women only" (emphasis added). In this final salvo, with language that shows the social power of white women to move and behave however they please—they parade, they absorb, they celebrate, they ignore, they center, they silence—Bogado makes the dual functions of rhetorics of alterity clear. She persuasively makes her position other, and equally persuasively, makes it central.

Bogado's themes appear in other arguments by feminists of color against SlutWalk. Although not all of them explicitly articulate SlutWalk with white supremacy, many use similar rhetorics of alterity to show that SlutWalk has created divisions between us and them that serve to reinforce whiteness as central and feminists of color as marginal. In the blog post "SlutWalks v. Ho Strolls," Brittany C. Cooper, writing under her blogger name "Crunktastic," argues that reclamation of *slut* is a rhetorical strategy that is doomed to failure, because it doesn't speak to women of color whose sexuality is subject to different surveillance and violence than white women. Cooper explains her reaction to SlutWalk's mission statement, which explains the movement's desire to end slut shaming by reclaiming the word *slut*: "As I read the mission statement, I was struck by the righteous indignation these women had over being called slut. While that indignation is absolutely warranted, it also feels on a visceral level as though it comes from women who are in fact not used to being fully defined by negative sexual referents."[53] Here, discourses of alterity are used to highlight the privilege of the white women who started SlutWalk, who have a space not available to women of color from which to mount their movement for reclamation, or as Cooper puts it, their "protests of privileged white girls." In this statement, Cooper uses rhetorics of alterity to highlight the sexual oppression of black women as something markedly different from that of the white women of SlutWalk, and in doing so she creates an identity for SlutWalk as Bogado does, but while Bogado constructs SlutWalk organizers as white supremacists, Cooper focuses on ignorance more than violence: *they* are privileged white girls, a decidedly different damnation. Cooper's purpose is to identify the ways that SlutWalk simply does not speak to her as a black woman, and therefore is exclusionary and misdirected. She writes that "slut" is "off-limits to me" because it "is a word used to shame white women who do not conform to morally conservative norms about chaste sexuality, the term very much reflects white women's specific struggles around sexuality and abuse." That is, although black women are called *slut*, it doesn't serve the same disciplining function because "black female sexuality has always been understood from without to be deviant, hyper, and excessive." Thus as Cooper sees it, SlutWalk is a white women's movement dealing with white women's sexuality. For both Bogado and Cooper, it is the presence of white women and symbolic communication about rape based on their experiences that forecloses on the possibility of black women's involvement. In these two responses, two of the differing yet related functions of rhetorics of alterity are evident. Bogado highlights *us* versus *them* to draw attention to the violence done to people of color at the hands of whites. By colluding with police, refusing coalition, and deploying a strategy doomed to failure, SlutWalk reinforces the subaltern position of women of color. Cooper on the other hand, uses rhetorics of alterity to draw distinctions between the *us* and the *them*, as she repeatedly returns to the different contexts and histories for white women's sexuality and for women of color's sexuality. While she clearly draws attention to the cultural dominance of these "white women of privilege," throughout her article, she also shows the ways that rhetorics of alterity, when used to call attention to one's own oppression and otherness, simultaneously build identity. Here we can see the agency granting moves of speaking from the position of the other. Cooper identifies that the *we* of SlutWalk does not include her, nor does it include black women like her, but in their otherness, they have their own *we* that, as she argues, "necessitates different strategies."

Five months after the original SlutWalk protests, the Black Women's Blueprint (BWB), a social-justice organization "committed to amplifying the voices of women of African descent in all their diversity" published an open letter to SlutWalk on their website. Like other critiques, BWB highlights the subaltern status of black women specifically with regard to how their sexuality has been constructed, such that reclamation of *slut* is not something they have the privilege to do. Unlike Cooper who disidentifies with the SlutWalk mission on the grounds that the shame of *slut* is endemic to white women's sexuality, BWB argues that *slut* is emblematic of racist appropriation of black women's sexuality, so much so that their organization can never associate with a movement that claims to find power in that term. But the result is the same for BWB as for Cooper: SlutWalk—a movement built creating a symbolic universe that ignores the way that those symbols communicate differently for women based on their class, race, gender identity, physical ability, and age—leaves "no space" for women of color. Like Cooper, who uses the spatial metaphor "off limits" to highlight conditions of alterity, BWB defines SlutWalk as a movement with "no space" for black women and girls because its fundamental mission of reclamation is flawed and ignorant of the ways that black women's sexual bodies have been constructed by "slavery . . . Jim Crow kidnappings, rape and lynchings, [and] gender misrepresentations." Sexuality, particularly for black women is one clear indicator of the limits and violence of "Western social thought [that] associates Blackness with an imagined uncivilized, wild sexuality and uses this association as one lynchpin of racial difference."[54] SlutWalk's brand of empowered feminist sexuality without shame ignores black women's particular history, a history BWB argues is replete with "narratives of sexual surveillance" and an "institutionalized ideology about [black women's] bodies as sexualized objects of property, as spectacles of sexuality and deviant sexual desire." In short, BWB argues that black women's alterity, particularly with regard to sexuality, leaves SlutWalk closed to them. BWB's use of spatial metaphors link SlutWalk to the structural effects of racism that segregate through law, custom, and violence and make black women's sexuality something that SlutWalk cannot possibly represent.

Because I claimed at the outset that rhetorics of alterity are deployed on both sides in the feminist sex wars, I want to conclude this section by showing them at work for those women of color who march, speak, and blog in support of SlutWalk. I offer these artifacts as examples of the variety of feminists of color's responses to SlutWalk. Women of color, who at the time of its emergence supported SlutWalk, are the forebearers of the Amber Rose SlutWalk, locating the movement's importance in the material reality of black women's sexual experience. The Global Women's Strike (GWS), a grassroots labor justice movement, seeks economic justice for the two-thirds of the world's work done by women and girls that is not paid. GWS's response to BWB titled "Women of Colour Respond to Black Women's Blueprint Attack on Slutwalk" was published in advance of GWS joining the SlutWalk London march in 2012. GWS takes issue with the claims that *slut* is not a concern for women of color, writing that "women of colour are among the most likely to be put down as 'sluts,' which is why we rejoice at SlutWalk embracing the word 'slut' to remove the stigma; if we're all identified as sluts, that's the end of the insult which can divide us."[55] Here GWS makes two important countermoves. The first is to draw on the "particular history" that BWB claims leaves no space for women of color in Slut Walk, and reposition it as a reason why SlutWalk does speak to them and also provides a motive for joining. The second is that they express their support for SlutWalk's reclamation strategy with the claim that women mass identifying as sluts will "end" both the insult of the term and the "division" it creates, although GWS isn't specific about who is divided currently by the word. More interesting is the way that GWS rearticulates the issue into one of economic privilege. They take issue with "mainstream feminists" both white and of color who "think they are above this because their higher income and lifestyle lifts them above the rest of us." GWS reminds its readers that "some people of colour have been let in to the 1% against the 99%," implying that women who speak against SlutWalk of any color have economic privilege that protects them from street harassment. This is an important reclamation move in its own right. SlutWalk was started by college women and enjoyed much of its original popularity from college students. Long before Amber Rose would make it more of a working people's movement (ironically, by branding and marketing it), GWS argues that Slut-Walk is critical for those women who have the least economic privilege. Further, GWS informs readers that "Black Women's Rape Action Project was invited to talk about anti-rape and anti-poverty organising by Black, immigrant and refugee women" as a response to arguments like BWB's and Bogada's that SlutWalk never builds coalition with other groups working against rape and sexual violence. GWS takes the position of the other and claims that it is SlutWalk who is actually concerned with and in coalition with the subaltern.

GWS is certainly not the only organization of women of color supporting SlutWalk, nor is their response particularly unique. As AlterNet writer Andrea Plaid points out, SlutWalk "became some litmus test around women of color and being down with the 'WoC agenda'" a term she uses "facetiously" and a phenomenon she "wasn't feeling."[56] Plaid questions the use of the *we*'s and the *us*'s by feminists of color who argue that "'women of color' don't see the use of the march because 'it doesn't speak' to 'us' categorically" despite the writings of women of color in support of SlutWalk like "Morgane Richardson, Harsha Walia and Creatrix Tiara [who] have spoken their truths on why they joined the protests in their respective countries." Plaid also provides an analysis of the ways that *slut* is a slur relevant to black women. By placing her "woman-of-color self" in support of SlutWalk, Plaid draws attention to the instability of identity politics, which is one of the functions of alterity rhetorics.

Alterity rhetorics challenge the identity politics promoted by SlutWalk in which an imagined *we* of the privileged white leaders actually includes all women. But this is a failure not just of SlutWalk but of identity politics in general, which, as Jeffrey Nealon argues, is "a project ... doomed to fail because every specific identity ... fails to be complete, [and] falls short of some kind of plentitude. The specific 'I' that lacks wholeness is symptomatic of a generalized 'we' that lacks wholeness, and vice versa."[57] Yet as the SlutWalk wars demonstrate, it is through the challenges to identity politics that alterity rhetorics *forge* identities.

Race, Gender, and the Erotic Body

As a theoretical framework, alterity is an important lens for analyzing body rhetorics, because rhetorics of the body are frequently also rhetorics of identity. Who we are is intimately intertwined with what we are communicating, and bodies communicate in a variety of material ways. Alterity provides critics with a perspective that is sensitive to the idea that *who we are not* operates simultaneously to shape the body's rhetorical messages. Alterity is a particularly powerful lens for assessing ongoing debates about oppression by drawing attention to contested identities. Thus when critics consider the contours of identity within embodied rhetorical performance, we should be conscious of the ways that identity also constructs otherness. The bodies of SlutWalkers over its brief history from 2011 to the present have shifted in identity, a fact that the alterity rhetorics of the sex wars shed light upon. These shifts in identities have important consequences for how we read the material symbols of the march, particularly as they signify women's erotic bodies.

SlutWalk, particularly as we can understand it via the debates that surround it, illustrates some of the most tenacious tensions with regard to erotic performance. In particular, it illustrates the ways that feminism and race influence the criticism of cis and trans women's erotic body rhetorics. As we've seen with the various rhetorical acts throughout this book, any approach to body criticism is only a framework for the critic. These frameworks are useful for identifying and critiquing the combination of discursive and material rhetorics that constitute embodied communication, yet no approach can encompass all of the issues that influence the rhetorical body. Bodies are not value neutral, and this is especially apparent with regard to erotic performance where discourses of feminism and racism mediate critical analysis of embodied communication.

Like the other acts in this book, SlutWalk exists at the intersection between classic structural feminism and sex-positive feminism. SlutWalk calls attention to the neoliberal rhetorics of choice that tend to draw sex-positive women to neo-burlesque, SlutWalk marches, and pole-dancing classes and push them away from structural feminist critiques. In her criticism of SlutWalk's neoliberal rhetoric, Kathy Miriam argues:

> The structural causes of how women dress and adorn ourselves *as a class* are obfuscated by the emphasis on *individual* self-determination. Thus a main slogan of SlutWalk—most often trumpeted by women dressed in Victoria's Secret lace and stilettos—is that women should be free to choose how they dress, and it's not an invitation to rape. While rape is of course never invited, this statement only makes sense from the most one-dimensional, flattened perspective—one that removes the individual woman from the matrices of social relations through which our choices are structured. If the choice of sexual self-presentation for women were such a free, unconstrained choice, why does it seem to come in only one flavor, namely, some preconceptualized variant of the patriarchal construct of "slut"? And why does corporate patriarchy have such a mammoth investment in this construct? In light of these questions, a main claim of SlutWalk, "I have the pussy, so I make the rules" seems more like a declaration of self-deception than—as intended—self-determination.[58]

I quote Miriam at length here to illustrate persistent arguments about women's rights with regard to erotic performances, whether they be on a stage or in the street. From a structural feminist standpoint, patriarchy has already removed the choice from women so that one can never choose to do certain work, identify in certain ways, or make certain art without shoring up patriarchy. Interestingly, rhetorics of choice, a vanguard of feminist political thought about the body, becomes a sticking point in these debates. Thus sex-positive feminists see *my body, my choice* as an imperative that is relevant not only to motherhood but also to sexual behavior. In this passage from Miriam, we also gain insight into the most contentious areas of the contemporary sex wars. "Women dressed in

Victoria's Secret lace and stilettos" is derisively used metonymically to represent the material symbolic of erotic body rhetorics. The claim that "sexual self-presentation" comes in "one flavor" is similarly revealing. The diversity in pro-sex self-presentations can be considered "one flavor" only when those expressions are understood exclusively through the lens of patriarchy, rendering the woman whose body is speaking through these material symbols mute. This suggests that context is irrelevant with certain forms of dress: it is either patriarchal or not. Miriam's use of "most often" before the phrase is also telling, as firsthand accounts of SlutWalk[59] and detailed studies[60] make it clear that only some women choose to dress like sluts. Still, criticisms of SlutWalk by white feminists persistently focus on dress, as vocal SlutWalk critic/anti-trans/anti–sex work/anti-burlesque blogger and radical feminist Meghan Murphy screams in her title: "Breaking! Slutwalk Is About Spectacle, Individual Empowerment, Wearing Sexy Lingerie, Says Everyone with Eyes and Brains." Even in the new iteration of the Amber Rose SlutWalk, with its celebrity-driven focus on theatrical dress, slut wear is not *de rigeur*, but slut style does make good copy and has been both boon and bane to SlutWalk. Mendes's analysis of media coverage of SlutWalk events illustrates the ways that the mainstream media focused almost exclusively on those SlutWalkers in provocative dress.[61] These images helped shape and bolster feminist criticisms, which, like the mainstream media, focus primarily on the problems presented by rhetorics of sluthood via reclaiming slurs and dressing in clothes and cosmetics that second-wave feminists critics have classified as oppressive tools of patriarchy. That is, clothing that reveals or emphasizes the breasts, butt, and legs is clothing that arouses heterosexual male desire. It is a means by which women are mass marketed as sexual objects for men's consumption, and therefore these symbols cannot be mobilized in different ways. This critique is strengthened by media and bystander preoccupation with those marchers in slut wear. Structural feminists opposed to SlutWalk focus on these to the exclusion of other issues (like challenging rape culture). This focus signals that certain items of dress, in particular, makeup and other markers of high-femme style cannot be anything but patriarchal. This stance is particularly detrimental to those queer femme women and trans women for whom such symbols are powerful signifiers of subaltern identities.

Writing of her identification as a femme, Lisa Walker claims it as "not just an adjective," but also an identity, one that is "decidedly queer, encompassing gender, style, sexual practice, and alliance with other queers."[62] The hyperfocus on high-femme symbols, whether it be in regard to SlutWalk or feminist critiques of neo-burlesque (which is largely populated with queer femme women and is structured around communicating via material symbols of femininity), reflects femmephobia, which Laura Brightwell argues "has a historical lineage that originates in the lesbian-feminist community."[63] Indeed, critiques of butch-femme identities—identities that had been central to lesbian communities in the mid-twentieth century[64]—were a central part of late twentieth-century lesbian sex wars and deeply divided communities of lesbians. Many lesbian-feminists saw butch-femme identities as ways of emulating patriarchal roles that were oppressive to women and argued for wearing androgynous styles, which were supposedly gender neutral but left no place for femmes who express their identity through traditionally feminine styles, to dress in any way other than the masculine. Because what was feminine was equated with oppression, the masculine style symbolized freedom and was embraced.

The rejection of femme aesthetics is not a simple rejection of patriarchy, however. It also rejects identities that were (and continue to be) important signifiers for women of color and working-class and poor women. It is not only structural feminisms that reject femme identification. Julia Serano argues at length in *Whipping Girl* that queer theory's focus on gender transgressions has constructed binary gender identities as "conservative" or "hegemonic."[65] Via this process, we find yet another way that transgender people, at least those with binary gender identities, particularly feminine trans women, are shunted. Thus whether it is through classic second-wave feminism, in which feminine identities and symbols are linked to patriarchy, or through queer theory's refusal of masculine-feminine binaries, "the trend of devaluing femmes, transwomen, and feminine gender expressions is consistent across lesbian, lesbian feminist, and 'queer/trans' communities."[66] Thus feminism and queer theory, frequently at theoretical odds themselves, both problematize feminine embodied rhetoric, in particular, those kinesthetic, sartorial, and cosmetic symbols that have long been coded as limiting and patriarchal. This criticism or outright dismissal of the femme material symbolic bolsters the negative discourses of women's erotic performances, whether those performances be art, work, or politics.

Racist ideology and white supremacy also inform erotic performance. Even when those performances are not specifically addressing issues of race, the erotic body is always communicating in racialized ways. Black feminists have persistently identified the ways that white feminism universalizes the middle-class white woman's experience while ignoring the ways that gender oppression is inflected by race and class.[67] For SlutWalk, a movement that was sparked as an anti-rape movement rather than one for sexual liberation, the original organizers showed little understanding of the ways that rape as a tool of social control affects women of color differently than white women. Women of color are less likely to report rape and more likely to have deep distrust of a perpetually racist criminal justice system. As Bogado points out, white feminist SlutWalkers assumed they could march to educate the police about victim blaming, while women of color know from experience that racist policing enforces the dehumanizing practices of rape culture. Thus feminists of color and white feminists have often forged separate activist paths around the issue of rape.[68]

The critiques of SlutWalk by feminists of color demonstrate that "otherness ... is neither simplistic, nor monolithic" but "coalitional," requiring critical attention to multiple cultural and symbolic codes of identity.[69] Like other feminist movements, the original SlutWalk deployed embodied activist rhetorics in the name of women, without acknowledging the complexity of the lived experiences of women. And yet when the SlutWalk movement was declared dead by the media,[70] it was a woman of color who reignited it, focusing particularly on those aspects that most invited critique: the reclamation/reappropriation of the word *slut* and the style of dress that communicates sexuality. Pictures from Rose's SlutWalks show women of all races, including Rose, dressed in slut wear: lingerie, bras, fishnets and garters, heeled boots, and fetish wear. Thus Rose's take on SlutWalk with its corporate sponsorship embraces those aspects that feminist critics found most offensive, and she does so unapologetically. In an article on *HuffPost*—which probably made white feminist Meghan Murphy want to stab "[herself] in the eye"[71]—Rose slides among the criticisms of SlutWalk demonstrating both her dogged insistence on identifying as feminist and her developing political consciousness. Interestingly, while the original SlutWalk struggled to keep focus on its anti-rape message, Rose's preoccupation with slut shaming and sexual liberation came first, and she has since shown an increasing commitment to feminist politics. At one moment in the interview, Rose proclaims that "feminism is literally doing whatever the hell you want and not living up to society norms and what people want you to do," a definition that seems tailor made for SlutWalk critics, as it is literally not a representative definition of feminism. In the same article, however, as part of defining her own sex-positive feminism, she discusses her infamous "bush picture" that she posted on Instagram. Taking a page from 1970s-era lesbian-feminism and '90s-era beauty-myth rhetorics, Rose tells *HuffPost*:

It's healthier for us to have pubic hair, but men and other women will scrutinize us and say that we're unclean, that we smell funny, that we're unkept or we're poor. . . . You don't want to *have* to do that but we do that because society taught us that we had to, that it makes us cleaner. It makes us smell better. It makes us more kept and it's all bullshit. That's why I do stuff like that. I cause the controversy, I get people to talk, I get people to talk shit and I'm cool with it. But there's a bigger picture. There's more of a conversation that happens after the fact and that's the conversation that changes things.[72]

Although Rose's brand of sex-positive, "choice" feminism would defend a woman's right *to* shave, in this section, she indicates an awareness of structural constraints on women's bodies. Her noting "there's a bigger picture . . . after the fact" nods to more than the moment of exposure, more than just an individual thrill of being slutty. As a woman who grew up poor and black and who is one of the most visibly slut-shamed woman of the past decade, Rose embodies much of the SlutWalk controversy. She is a prime alter-feminist subject, and it is a subject position that many with feminist sensibilities that don't fit radical or structural models flock to. Her media-savvy spectacle, sex-positive feminist rhetorics, and corporate-sponsored activism are all of the things that structural and radical feminists despise (or at the very least disdain) about the politics of SlutWalk and other sites where femme/feminine style is celebrated. Yet Rose's SlutWalk also articulates a different identity for the movement via the bodies she has courted, making her march one that is not subject to the *same* critiques by feminists of color. The trans women, sex workers, and women of color she has drawn do not collude with the police. Rose often speaks of the importance of inclusion, demonstrating a commitment to coalition politics, particularly with regard to sex workers, trans women, and queer people, people who are used to being "fully defined by negative sexual referents" to quote Cooper.[73] As someone who is regularly reviled for her sluttiness—which sparked her interest in the movement to begin with—Rose proclaims that *slut* is not a slur relevant only to white women. This is not to say that there remain no grounds for black feminists to critique SlutWalk (the corporate sponsorship alone invites criticism). *Blavity* writer Miatta Williams explains why "even as a feminist, [she] can't get behind Amber Rose's SlutWalk."[74] While she makes it clear that she "co-exists" between the pro- and anti- SlutWalk crowds, the moniker *slut* is still open to the same critiques that black feminists made when SlutWalk emerged. Its associations with depravity and debauchery make it "a difficult feat" for "black women, who are too often over-sexualized and regarded/addressed as body parts." Williams questions whether or not "there's a way to reconcile the vocabulary and the essence of the Slut Walk." Alterity politics suggests that reconciliation will not happen, but that these micro-cohorts of feminism will continue to, like Williams, coexist and will continue to use alterity rhetorics to grapple over the formation and denial of feminist identity.

Many feminist theorists and postcolonial scholars have theorized the function of "the other" in both discursive and material manifestations. The *alter*, the *not me*, is a position, integral not only to structures of domination and control but also to any manifestation of identity. Frequently, alter-identities occupy spaces of oppression, dominated into positions of silence, but this is not always the case. Rhetorics of alterity can co-opt a range of experiences into an ideological position and from that position the other can make claims to agency. In the making of feminist sexuality, rhetorics of alterity have been used to define and delimit the assertions of social movements that claim to represent an identity called feminist. Thirty years of the sex wars, thirty years of *we* versus *they*—we are not sluts, they are not feminists; we are proud sluts, they are not feminists—thirty years of identity politics deployed through alterity rhetorics, these demonstrate that warring is a fundamental part of the making of feminist sexuality.

Conclusion | Embodied Erotic Rhetoric's Acceptance and Rejection

I pull up to Isabella's house. When I walk in the living room, she's sitting with three friends, all strippers, all women I know from the club. We all exchange Hey's and nod. They're passing both a joint and the final paper from my rhetorical analysis class called "Dirty Girls and Stinky Guys: A Fantasy-Theme Analysis." It was, at the time, my magnum opus. A harbinger of my assured success as a rhetorical critic. I was so proud of it. The paper features Isabella heavily, as did all of the papers from that class. She was funny, clever, and I was sprung beyond belief on her. I very nearly worshipped her and constantly sought her approval. When I gave her the paper to read, I was all puffed up, assuming she would be impressed by my brilliance. I may not be the type of bar-fighting butch dyke she liked, but look . . . brains! I figured that had to count for something.

I stood for a moment taking in the scene. Puff, puff, pass. Pass the joint, pass a page. Isabella spoke:

"We're reading your little story."
<inhale>
"It's hilarious."
Acceptance. Rejection.

Criticizing the Erotic Body

Historically, rhetoricians and communications scholars have largely been disciplined in analysis of linguistic communication, thus criticism of the body has tended toward textual analysis of discourses *about*, rather than the material symbolic communication *of* the body. Recent inter- and transdisciplinary scholarship has brought rhetoric and communication together with performance studies—in which the breathing, sweating, moving body has always been central—to expand theories and analysis of meaning and communication. The resulting collaborations yield an understanding that rhetoric of the body is always a multicoded rhetoric. Although critics can attend to any one symbolic aspect to theorize the body, understanding that it is always impacted by others is necessary to move criticism beyond text-only paradigms that flatten embodied practices. Thus critical methodologies that are attendant to these multiple realms and their interplay are imperative to unpacking complexities of the body's symbolic communication.

In this book, I've provided a series of analytical frameworks that can productively examine the interplay of linguistic and material symbols, and I have applied each to a different site of women's public erotic performance, sites of embodied rhetoric. I've followed one such erotic body—the stripping woman—through club and theater performances, into the streets, and as a cultural symbol, weaving through both discursive and material symbolic forms of embodied rhetoric. The first of these frameworks—delivery—offers an ancient link between rhetoric and performance showing the long-standing connections between the two. Delivery in itself offers an expansive way of criticizing embodied rhetorics because it is composed of various "common topics" or *topoi*—body, genre, space, and audience—that are each applicable to communication in varied symbolic realms. Delivery can provide an overall way of conceiving embodied rhetoric that other theories can enrich. The *topos* of the body includes material symbolic codes related to movement and adornment and also discursive codes including identity and persona. In various chapters, I have tracked the body *topos* through these realms, including movement and adornment in chapters 1, 2, and 3 and discussions of discourses that make and remake identities in chapters 4 and 5. I take up the genre *topos* explicitly in chapter 2, but as genre itself is composed of various parts—situation, substance, style—encouraging distinct affective responses in participants and yielding various social actions, genre is always shaping and shaped by communicating bodies. I've also taken up the space *topos* in both literal and metaphorical ways throughout. In the first part of the book, I analyze spatial differences between clubs and theaters (chapters 1 and 2), and in chapter 4 I illustrate that situating the stripping body in different spaces—protest spaces versus performance spaces—is part of how identities get dis- and rearticulated. In chapter 5, space is metaphorically invoked as a way to understand how movements, like SlutWalk, that embrace the material symbolic codes associated with sex work, are perceived as either opening or closing spaces for women of color. Finally, the *topos* of audience is at the heart of all of the critical work in this book. Relationships with audiences create both genres (chapter 2) and rhetorical forms (chapter 3). Audiences also have the power to shape rhetors' identities in ways that are fundamentally at odds with the rhetors' own (chapters 4 and 5).

Genre criticism, while primarily concerned with written texts in rhetoric and communication studies, has lately been embodied, largely through the theories of Joshua Gunn, who, drawing on film theory, connects genre to affect. Because rhetorical genres of the body often get collapsed into one another under vast labels—sports, acting, dance, stripping—genre offers critics a way to discern the particular and specific affective dimensions of individual types of body rhetoric. For example, as chapter 2 argues, topless dancing in clubs and neo-burlesque share many symbolic methods of communication but fundamentally differ in the ways that the audience body—both as individuals and as a collective—participate in the performances.

In addition to the application of corporeal-friendly concepts for body criticism like delivery and genre, embodied rhetoric also benefits from applying typically discursive theories because discourse shapes the ways that audiences and rhetors understand performance. One such theory, seduction, is particularly useful to embodied erotic rhetoric, especially when seduction operates both as it is popularly understood as arousing desire and as it is theoretically proposed as encompassing those rhetorical forms that operate outside of rationality and purpose-driven discourse.

Identity, understood in this book as various ideological elements joined into a named unity, is a fundamental part of embodied rhetorics. Articulation theory, because it is designed to look at the joining of parts into wholes, is a valuable approach to analyze what parts are made into which identities and what rhetorical work needs to be done to rejoin new parts into different identities. Because social movements engage in identity reconstitution in order to challenge oppressive ideologies, articulation is a productive conceptual tool for social-movement analysis. Further, articulation is an ideal theory for looking at both discursive and material symbols that are used to build and to communicate identities. Chapter 4 looked at *sex worker*—a symbolic remaking of identity intended to disarticulate ideologies of victimhood, criminality, and immorality from work in the sex trades; it also looked at the discourses that the sex-worker identity challenges, and the ways that material rhetoric of the body in protest is part of rearticulating this contested identity.

Alterity, like seduction, has a dense theoretical legacy and offers a way to understand not only the mechanisms but also the consequences of rhetorical operations. While alterity has been theorized as "extra-rhetorical," or "prior rhetorical," via the work of Diane Davis drawing on Emmanuel Levinas, in chapter 5 I propose that alterity can also provide a way to enrich criticism of identities, by showing how discursive and material symbols as they construct particular identities also exclude others. This fundamental pairing of "this is who we are" (identity) with "this is who we are not" (alterity) is a driver of contemporary social-movement rhetoric in which battles over identity form the core of rhetorical strategies.

This particular selection of concepts shows a range of critical approaches for analyzing rhetorics of the body. This combination of approaches makes clear that taking up one approach doesn't foreclose on another. As the preceding chapters explicate, linguistic and material symbols work together to create embodied rhetoric; thus critical methods must be capable of attending to both. The theories and methods highlighted in this book were also selected for their transdisciplinary utility due to their expansiveness. Although each chapter is intended to stand on its own as a coherent analysis, they are also intended to work together to show the robustness of what rhetoric of the body can entail. In addition to making an argument about body criticism, I make a more specific claim about the affordances of these theories and methods for analyzing embodied erotic rhetoric, in particular, public performances—here presented as entertainment and political actions—by women.

Another goal of this book is to advance conversations about women's erotic performances, which tend to get caught in circular arguments about either empowerment or oppression; such performances are, of course, neither/nor/both/and. By positioning these jobs and art forms within the realm of performance rhetoric, conversations about their cultural and social impacts can be moved beyond binary positions that close off further discussion. In the case of erotic performers and laborers, ignoring participants' own understandings of the workings of their acts is never in their best interest. Erotic performance as a type of performance rhetoric enables multiple new positions and perspectives that place the body and its contested contexts central. Taken together then, the analyses in this book yield the following insights about embodied erotic rhetoric:

1. Analysis of the body presents openings, not finalities.
2. Methods of criticism for embodied rhetoric should be able to accommodate the differences between the material and the discursive symbolic because rhetoric of the body is a production of both.

3. The body's material symbolic communication, such as the movement, costume, and adornment discussed in this book, cannot be separated from cultural contexts and the different somatic experiences of embodied identities, in particular, racial and gender identities.
4. Delivery provides a heuristic for understanding the multiple common topics of body rhetoric: body (identity), space, genre, audience, which are interdependent and tack between the material and the discursive.
5. As a particularly contested type of communication, the embodied erotic rhetoric of women vividly illustrates the ways that bodies are shaped by cultural discourses, the ways that bodies act as cultural symbols, and the ways that they communicate purposefully.

Beyond Burkean Burlesque

This book fundamentally aspires to advance understanding of methods, analyses, and ways of reading embodied erotic rhetoric, but it also aims to make a contribution to scholarly conversations concerning burlesque rhetoric, arising from Kenneth Burke's work on the burlesque—as a literary parody, not as erotic performance. Because erotic burlesque's origins derive from the same poetic category, however, and because erotic burlesque still relies heavily on mockery and parody, it has long been my goal to end this journey where I began: postulating what—if any—connections can be made between what scholars have theorized as *burlesque rhetoric* based on the literary form and erotic performance rhetoric. In *Attitudes Toward History*, Burke presents various poetic categories as a way of understanding human symbolic structures.[1] Burke classifies these categories as either frames of acceptance or frames of rejection, which reflect the symbolic action the text is undertaking, one that is either welcoming or combative.[2] Rhetoricians have been particularly interested in the differences of the modes of humor Burke categorizes, with comedy as a frame of acceptance and the burlesque as a frame of rejection: "comedy emphasizes acceptance by stressing positive aspects, whereas burlesque emphasizes rejection by stressing the negative."[3] Both modes allow rhetors to seek symbolic change, but rejection refuses symbols of authority in order to shift power.[4] Unlike comedy, which as a frame of acceptance emphasizes the oneness of the rhetor with the object of comedy in which all laugh together, frames of rejection stress separation between the burlesque rhetor and the target because the "burlesque rhetor wishes to decry the target and does so by rendering it absurd."[5] Burke makes his preference for symbolic change via frames of acceptance—not to be confused with passivity—clear: "Frames stressing the ingredient of *rejection* tend to lack the well-rounded quality of a *complete* here-and-now philosophy. They make for fanaticism, the singling-out of one factor above others in the chart of human relationships."[6] Burke illustrates the differences with the example of Thomas Aquinas and Karl Marx in terms of their attitudes toward class inequalities: Aquinas's discursive frames "accept the inevitability" of classes, whereas Marx "accepted the *need of eliminating classes*."[7] Burke defines the burlesque by its superficiality, by its preoccupation with peoples' behavior and not their minds. It is "reduction to absurdity"; it is "partial" and "partisan" and "*incomplete*"; it is something we must be "*greater than*." It is something we "enjoy . . . as an occasional dish, [but] no critic has ever been inclined to select it as the *pièce de résistance* for a steady diet."[8]

In chapter 1, I gave a brief introduction to what rhetorical scholars have done with Burke's concept of the burlesque with regard to rhetoric. Rhetorical scholars have been open to the persuasive affordances of this category's approach to social action, finding utility in Burke's definition, but retheorizing it for new contexts. A. Cheree Carlson theorizes the limits of the "charitable" openness of the comic frame of acceptance in "promoting peaceful social change."[9] In Carlson's analysis of "witty American women of the nineteenth century," she traces the shift in women's approach to humor from comedy to satire and ultimately to the burlesque, concurrent with the rise of women's fights for rights.[10] Contrary to Burke's insistence on the superiority of frames of acceptance, Carlson argues that such frames are of limited value in social movements because "when the strictures of the social order become totally unacceptable . . . a 'positive' frame will no longer suffice," as an acceptance frame "requires that the actor identify completely with the social order."[11] While she does not propose that the burlesque offers a complete solution to addressing inequality, Carlson's work invites women into the conversation of burlesque rhetoric, necessarily shifting assumptions about the potential values of acceptance and rejection depending on body and identity specific contexts.

Similarly, in his analysis of William F. Buckley Jr.'s burlesque rhetoric, Edward Appel argues that Burke's classification of *literary* categories, "require[s] adjustment" for rhetorical messages because the rhetorical situation "features the recommendation of an action for practical, realistic purposes" as opposed to "artistic or entertainment purposes."[12] He persuasively argues that burlesque as rhetoric is more than the impoverished and partial frame that Burke shows with regard to literature. Instead, Appel concludes that burlesque rhetoric has the capacity "to adopt a frame of acceptance and a frame of rejection *at the same time*."[13] Thus rhetorical burlesque has the capacity both to reject and to humanize.[14] Although Appel offers a more capacious rendering of the burlesque than Burke's original poetic category, he separates the theatrical and the rhetorical: rhetoric is practical and theater is entertaining. This separation doesn't go very far in when the rhetorical is recognized as encompassing both the practical and the entertaining, but Appel's theory of deploying frames simultaneously is useful in thinking about the ways that the erotic performances in this book operate rhetorically.

As I claimed in chapter 1, scholarship on burlesque rhetoric has little to do with burlesque as it is taken up in this book, which begs the question: What do stripping women bring to our understanding of burlesque rhetoric? And perhaps more importantly, does it have to bring anything? What I mean by this is that at the end of this project, I am not convinced that Burke's poetic categories from the mid-twentieth century, drawn from terminology for seventeenth-century literary forms, usefully contribute to an understanding of women's erotic performance in the twenty-first century. Yet the concept of burlesque rhetoric remains tantalizing to me as a rhetorician studying erotic dance; I keep finding myself drawn back to it, looking for connection, perhaps just looking to be the type of rhetorician who references Kenneth Burke. As an art form, neo-burlesque retains the spirit of mockery and farce that ties it to the literary genre, but conceptualizing the burlesque as partial and impoverished doesn't feel at all appropriate to the complex rhetorical communication of erotic dance and its contexts presented throughout this book.

In analyzing the rhetorical bodies of erotic dancers, mobilized in performance, mobilized in protest, mobilized as cultural symbol, various frames of rejection are apparent, because they are operating within contexts that are hostile to or at the very least misunderstanding of erotic bodies, particularly women's. Like Carlson's "witty women," erotic performers have no choice but to reject their antagonists, and like Appel's reclassification of the burlesque, they simultaneously adopt frames of acceptance and rejection. But with erotic performers, acceptance and humanizing aspects of rhetorical performance are designed to claim power for the self and those in coalition, accompanied by rejection of antagonists. The neo-burlesque performer mocks and ridicules, rejecting limits regarding the supposed proper places and spaces for women to engage in humorous and erotic spectacle. Neo-burlesque's insistence that any *body*—regardless of age, gender, race, or ability—can belong in burlesque wholeheartedly rejects norms of appropriateness. Neo-burlesque is also often overtly political, especially as relates to feminist, sex radical, and queer politics. Where neo-burlesque does *not* resemble literary burlesque is in where its rhetors place themselves. Unlike the burlesquers who laugh at others and emphasize their own superiority, neo-burlesque performers include themselves in on the joke, being the first to laugh at themselves and burlesque themselves along with other targets. By insisting that funniness and sexiness are not mutually exclusive, neo-burlesque embraces inclusiveness, opening up the category.

Similarly, topless dancers in clubs simultaneously adopt frames of acceptance and rejection in their performance rhetoric. Discourses about the proper place for women's bodies, particularly their erotic bodies, more particularly, their erotic bodies in commerce, make rejection a fundamental frame for club strippers. Rejection of entrenched sexist attitudes about visibility of women's sexuality is one aspect of this type of performance, often accompanied by self-acceptance. Many strippers of all types speak about the valuation of their own body as a result of erotic dance. This is not a simplistic "Love your body as is!" mentality. Modifications, cosmetics, enhancing clothes of all types are included in seeing one's own body—not as an object, but as an act, as an art, as having material worth. Dual frames of acceptance and rejection are also at work in the complex performances between customers and dancers. As researchers consistently note, the cultivating of sustaining relationships with regulars often requires a stance of fantasy acceptance paired with rejection in reality.

For erotic dancers who are also activists, either because of long-standing commitments to sex-work activism or because attacks on their employment demand it, rejection is a potent rhetorical frame. When the dominant social order and its symbolic world insist that a particular identity doesn't exist, this is an untenable situation, and a frame of acceptance is not useful or acceptable.[15] As demonstrated in chapter 4, dis- and rearticulation of an identity like *sex worker*, requires rejecting dominant social discourses about that work. Any who hold an antagonistic position toward this identity are rejected as a means of constructing frames of acceptance for the identity. For example, sex-worker activists reject discourses that say they don't exist, that they are always victims and criminals, and rearticulate their identities to show not only that they exist, but also how they exist: as workers, as activists, as tax-paying citizens, as humans.

Thus radical rearticulation as a rhetorical process rejects identities made by others and accepts those made by the group. Antagonists are placed into the position to accept or reject the new proffered identity. Therefore, the acceptance/rejection pairing is at work in political performances as well.

Finally, with regard to the erotic dancer as cultural symbol, whose material rhetoric becomes adopted as a representation of sexual freedom, inclusion, and anti-rape action, we see an amalgamation of these acceptance/rejection framings: the rejection of cultural norms about women's erotic bodies and denials of subjectivity and the acceptance of self/comrades and identities that insist, not only on existence but also on presence.

As these examples show, Burke's conception of the burlesque that has thus far been the basis of rhetorical scholarship on the form has limited value for the embodied erotic performances under study in this book, but his theories of orientations of acceptance and rejection toward dominant symbolic orders provides a compelling way to categorize the rhetorics presented here. Although Burke's attitude toward resolving social differences through acceptance of one's antagonists is understandable, the contexts of his work and his life are, naturally, so different from the women in this book that it would be shortsighted to assume that this attitude has to fit vastly different social actors and actions. Drawing on Carlson's argument that rejection is often the only available option for those with no or limited social power and Appel's argument that these frames can operate simultaneously, I propose that a rejection/acceptance pairing is a useful way to understand the symbolic operations of erotic performance and other similarly complicated rhetorical systems. As I have stressed throughout, rhetoric of the body is multicoded, operating in various material and symbolic universes. Therefore, understanding orientations *toward* those symbolic universes as similarly complicated—rejection, acceptance, both, neither—can help to uncover the rhetorical features that can be hidden in complex communication. When our rhetorical theories and methods don't fit the subjects of our analysis, the rhetorical tradition has been unable to see them. Embodied rhetorical scholarship that focuses on multicoded bodies and performances—like the performances explored in this book—has the potential to remake rhetorical scholarship from the outside in. By starting with those rhetorically complex performances that exceed a single mode of analysis or theoretical approach, we can make our theory responsive to those who actually practice it. If we fail to do so, we risk erasing remarkable rhetorical performers and performances. We also will continue to generate theory that does not adequately respond to the most powerful rhetorics of the present—those that are trying to remake the world while living in it.

This is my performance. I manipulate my readers. I seduce. I give the illusion of stripping myself down with my confessions. If only someone would give me some dollars.

Notes

Introduction

1. Selzer, "Habeus Corpus," 10.
2. Alexander and Rhodes, "What's Sexual," 1.
3. Ibid., 8.
4. Ibid., 12.
5. Hawhee, "Rhetoric's Sensorium," 5–6.
6. Ibid., 10.
7. See Corbett, "Open Hand"; Corbett, "Rhetoric of Protest"; Griffin, "Rhetorical Structure"; Haiman, "Rhetoric of the Streets."
8. Madison and Hamera, "Introduction," xii.
9. Ibid., xii.
10. Conquergood, "Ethnography, Rhetoric, and Performance," 80.
11. Bell, "Toward a Pleasure-Centered Economy," 99.
12. My starting point for embodied rhetoric was Patterson and Corning's "Researching the Body," but it's now twenty years old. My own bibliography on the rhetorical body is publicly accessible: https://www.zotero.org/groups/1851873/embodied_rhetoric.
13. Examples of each include: Butterworth, "'Katie Was Not Only a Girl'"; DeLuca, "Unruly Arguments"; Dickson, "Reading Maternally"; Holmes, "Working"; Martin, *Flexible Bodies*.
14. The study of "performance rhetoric" in particular has emerged to take up the theoretical and methodological intersections between the two fields. See, for example, Gencarella and Pezzullo, *Readings on Rhetoric and Performance*, and *Text and Performance Quarterly*'s special issue "Performance and Rhetoric," edited by Fenske and Goltz.
15. Selzer, "Habeus Corpus," 9.
16. Ibid., 9–10.
17. Butler, *Bodies That Matter*.
18. I'm borrowing this phrase from Clifford Geertz, who in "From the Native's Point of View" argues that a "continuous dialectical tacking" between global and local perspectives is at the core of critical analysis (43).
19. Celeste Condit, in Enos et al., "Symposium," 371.
20. Butterworth, "'Katie Was Not Only a Girl,'" 261.
21. Ibid., 262.
22. See, for example, Barton, "Literacy in (Inter)Action."; Butterworth, "'Katie Was Not Only a Girl'"; Jordan, "Reshaping the 'Pillow Angel'"; Singer, "Anti-Corporate Argument"; Mortensen, "Figuring Illiteracy."
23. Wilson and Lewiecki-Wilson, "Disability, Rhetoric, and the Body," 3.
24. Blair, "Reflections on Criticism and Bodies," 271.
25. Ibid., 273.
26. Hawhee, *Moving Bodies*, 10.
27. Ibid., 128.

28. Olomo, "Performance and Ethnography," 340.
29. Schechner, *Performance Studies*, 4.
30. Goltz, *Comic Performativities*, 16.
31. Ibid., 17.
32. Throughout this book, I use "burlesque" as an umbrella term to refer generally to theatrical erotic performance, and I use "neo-burlesque" to refer specifically to the revival of burlesque in the last thirty years. However, these terms are slippery, partial, and open to interpretation. Thus guided by advice from author and headmistress of the New York School of Burlesque, Jo Weldon, I attempt to avoid "preclud[ing] the flexibility of terms and multiple meanings," understanding that the "the purpose of language is not to be pedagogically correct but to communicate effectively" (phone call with author, June 20, 2019).
33. Ott and Dickinson, "Entering the Unending Conversation," 3.
34. Conquergood, "Ethnography, Rhetoric, and Performance," 81.
35. Blair, "Reflections on Criticism and Bodies," 273.
36. See for example, Ott and Keeling, "Cinema and Choric Connection," and Crable, "Symbolizing Motion."
37. I prefer this term to the more common "exotic dance." Appeals to the "exotic" are rather off-putting because they're steeped in classed and racialized power imbalances. Also, the ubiquity of corporate-managed gentlemen's clubs and the resurgence of burlesque just make "exotic" a term that no longer seems appropriate.
38. Special thanks to Penn State University Press acquisitions editor Ryan Peterson for helping me work through this framing, understanding what I was doing even when I did not.
39. I highly recommend Judith Hanna's "Dance and Sexuality: Many Moves" for an excellent overview of "manifestations of sexuality in Western theater art and social dance, plus ritual and non-Western social dance" (212).
40. Ibid., 212.
41. Ibid., 213.
42. The idea of choice for any wageworker is vexed as economic constraints often dictate choices for workers.
43. Brueggemann, "Still-Life," 26.
44. Bormann, "Symbolic Convergence Theory," 128.
45. King, "What Writing Is," 95.
46. Pelias and VanOosting, "Paradigm for Performance Studies," 221–22.
47. Wosick-Correa and Joseph, "Sexy Ladies Sexing Ladies," 203.
48. See, in particular, the works of Katherine Frank and Danielle Egan, who have written on strip clubs collaboratively and individually.
49. Shields, "Symbolic Convergence," 417.
50. Ibid., 416–17.
51. Gingrich-Philbrook, "Autoethnography's Family Values," 308.
52. Ibid., 307, 310.
53. Ibid., 311.
54. See, for example, Dodds, "Embodied Transformations in Neo-Burlesque"; Erickson and Tewksbury, "'Gentlemen' in the Club"; Manaster, "Treading Water"; Nally, "Grrrly Hurly Burly; Wosick-Correa and Joseph, "Sexy Ladies Sexing Ladies," and all of Danielle Egan and Katherine Frank's research on strippers and strip clubs.
55. Ellis, Adams, and Bochner, "Autoethnography," 273.
56. Tedlock, "From Participant Observation to the Observation of Participation."
57. Ellis, Adams, and Bochner, "Autoethnography," 278.

58. Ibid., 278.
59. Miller and Taylor, "Constructed Self," 170.
60. Branstetter, "Promiscuous Approaches," 18.
61. Ibid., 19.
62. Ibid., 20.
63. Crowley, *Toward a Civil Discourse*, 29.
64. Phone call with author, June 22, 2015. Weldon has made this point in various places throughout her career. I heard her make it at a BurlyCon panel in 2013, and followed up on the point by phone in 2015.
65. Nally, "Grrrly Hurly Burly," 639–40 (emphasis added).
66. Crowley, *Toward a Civil Discourse*, 59.
67. Johnson, "Black Performance Studies," 446.
68. Flores, "Rhetorical 'Realness' of Race," 94–95.
69. Happe, "Body of Race," 132.
70. Ibid., 133.
71. Baudrillard, *Seduction*.

Chapter 1

1. A version of this chapter originally appeared in *Rhetoric Review* 36, no. 1 (January 2017): 44–59.
2. Although Bettie Page, a pin-up and fetish model in the 1950s, did not perform burlesque, her looks—in particular, dark hair and red lipstick—are popular in neo-burlesque.
3. Legs Malone, "Bettie Page Tribute," *!BadAss! Burlesque: Black and Red Party*, prod. Velocity Chyaldd, host, Jonny Porkpie, Burlesque at the Beach, Coney Island, Brooklyn, NY, September 27, 2013.
4. Harris Ramsby, "Drama as Rhetorical Critique," 406 (emphasis added).
5. Fredal, *Rhetorical Action*, 21.
6. Fredal, "Language of Delivery," 255.
7. Goltz, *Comic Performativities*, 18.
8. Fenske and Goltz, "Disciplinary Dedications," 5.
9. Calafell, "Performance," 116.
10. Young, "Review of Readings on Rhetoric and Performance," 452.
11. In Pelias and VanOosting's "A Paradigm for Performance Studies," the authors theorize what rhetoricians regard as a rhetorical situation—text, event, performer, and audience—in order to delineate a specific performance studies approach to communication (221).
12. Conquergood, "Ethnography, Rhetoric, and Performance," 86.
13. Nadeau, "Delivery in Ancient Times," 54.
14. Mountford, *Gendered Pulpit*; Buchanan, *Regendering Delivery*.
15. Buchanan, *Regendering Delivery*, 160.
16. Siebler, "What's So Feminist About Garters and Bustiers?," 11.
17. The claim that neo-burlesque draws mixed-sex audiences, often dominated by women, is referred to frequently in the literature and in the lore of neo-burlesque (see, for example, Mansbridge, "Popular Bodies"; Nally, "Grrrly Hurly Burly"; and Willson, *Happy Stripper*). The actual percentage of women in audiences, however, is "subject to wide variation" (Harris, "Ghosts of New Burlesque," 148).
18. Butler, *Bodies That Matter*, 4–12.
19. Battaglia and Simmons, "Writing on the Wall," 15.

20. My separation of the material from the linguistic is intended to draw attention to the fact that linguistic practices are only one way that bodies communicate symbolically.
21. Crable, "Symbolizing Motion," 122.
22. Fredal, *Rhetorical Action*, 192, 201.
23. Pflugfelder, "Rhetoric's New Materialism," 447.
24. Nadeau, "Delivery in Ancient Times," 53.
25. Buchanan, *Regendering Delivery*, 159.
26. Mountford, *Gendered Pulpit*, 152.
27. Ibid., 4.
28. Gencarella and Pezzullo, "Introduction," 2.
29. Buchanan, *Regendering Delivery*, 159.
30. Kirsch, "Gertrude Stein Delivers," 266.
31. Rude, "Toward an Expanded Concept of Rhetorical Delivery," 273.
32. Levy, *Female Chauvinist Pigs*.
33. Burke, *Attitudes Toward History*, 52–56.
34. Ibid., 56.
35. Appel, "Burlesque Drama," 281–82.
36. See Appel, "Burlesque Drama"; Carlson, "Limitations on the Comic Frame"; Hubbard, "Reassessing Truman"; Moore, "'Quayle Quagmire.'"
37. Allen, *Horrible Prettiness*.
38. Ibid., 186.
39. Ibid., 189.
40. "Stripper Dixie Evans," YouTube video (site discontinued).
41. Baldwin, *Burlesque and the New Bump-n-Grind*, 18–19.
42. Ibid., 38.
43. Allen, *Horrible Prettiness*, 26 (emphasis added).
44. Buchanan, *Regendering Delivery*, 162; Porter, "Recovering Delivery," 220.
45. For example, Lindal Buchanan theorizes those delivery *topoi* that are relevant to women's oratory, and James Porter offers a different set for digital communication.
46. Bazerman, "Genre and Identity," 13.
47. Buchanan, *Regendering Delivery*, 161–62.
48. Porter, "Recovering Delivery," 212.
49. Graver, "Actor's Bodies," 222.
50. Crable, "Symbolizing Motion."
51. Weldon, *Burlesque Handbook*, 130.
52. Vanguri, "Introduction," 6.
53. Allen, *Horrible Prettiness*, 146.
54. Derksen, "'Attack Behind the Invitation,'" 236.
55. Vanguri, "Introduction," 1.
56. Stob, "Terministic Screens," 148.
57. At the 2013 Follies Fromage on Coney Island, headmistress of the New York School of Burlesque Jo Weldon shared that she advises students who can't think of a name to pick their favorite flower and favorite cheese. (I would be Daisy Havarti.)
58. Names vary for both strippers and burlesquers. Feature dancers, who travel and headline at different strip clubs, often share qualities with neo-burlesquers, including theatrical names and elaborate acts.
59. Mountford, *Gendered Pulpit*, 16–17.
60. Di Benedetto, "Body as Fluid Dramaturgy," 7.
61. Ibid., 7.

62. Allen, *Horrible Prettiness*.
63. Hanna, "Undressing the First Amendment," 44.
64. Pheterson, "Whore Stigma," 60.
65. Blair, "Reflections on Criticism and Bodies," 283.
66. Malone, "Burlesque Exposed."
67. Porter, "Recovering Delivery," 217.
68. See Mansbridge, "Popular Bodies"; Nally, "Grrrly Hurly Burly"; Willson, *Happy Stripper*.
69. Pelias and VanOosting, "Paradigm for Performance Studies," 226–27.
70. Ibid., 227.
71. Porter, "Recovering Delivery," 218.
72. Tease, "How To Burlesque."
73. Di Benedetto, "Body as Fluid Dramaturgy," 12.
74. Schneider, *Explicit Body in Performance*, 22 (emphasis added).
75. *America's Got Talent*, season 4, episode 5. The couple has since divorced and no longer performs together.
76. The Shanghai Pearl, interview by Legs Malone.
77. *America's Got Talent*, season 1, episode 2.
78. Smith, "America's Got an Ass That Goes Pow."
79. Hawhee, *Moving Bodies*, 166.
80. Ibid., 166.
81. Weldon, *Burlesque Handbook*, 38.
82. Buchanan, *Regendering Delivery*, 160.
83. Chocolat The Extraordinaire, "Race and Burlesque."
84. Lewis, "Looking Forward to the Past," 183.
85. Ibid., 202.
86. Fredal, "Beyond the Fifth Canon," 32–33.

Chapter 2

1. Stockton, *Queer Child*, 11.
2. Gunn, "Maranatha," 368 (emphasis added).
3. Many of the claims I make in this chapter are also true for nude dancing. I focus on topless because it shares more genre characteristics with neo-burlesque in that the reveal of breasts is the climax of an act and because most of my own experiences as a customer were in topless clubs. When I refer to "club stripping," the claims apply to both kinds of clubs.
4. Middleton, Senda-Cook, and Endres, "Articulating Rhetorical Field Methods," 398.
5. Pollock, "Performing Writing," 80–96.
6. All names of club dancers are pseudonyms.
7. See Allen, *Horrible Prettiness*; Baldwin, *Burlesque and the New Bump-n-Grind*; Weldon, *Burlesque Handbook*.
8. Egan and Frank, "Attempts at a Feminist and Interdisciplinary Conversation," 298.
9. See Burana, *Strip City*; Egan, *Dancing for Dollars*; Frank, *G-Strings and Sympathy*; Hanna, "Exotic Dance Adult Entertainment"; Hanna, "Undressing the First Amendment"; Liepe-Levinson, *Strip Show*. Please note: there is a wealth of contemporary scholarship on stripping. These are just a few of the major works that have informed my own scholarship.
10. Noire, "Part One: Race and Burlesque—The Interviews."
11. Weldon, *Burlesque Handbook*, 222.

12. Ott and Dickinson, "Entering the Unending Conversation."
13. Bawarshi, "Genre Function"; Berkenkotter and Huckin, *Genre Knowledge*; Campbell and Jamieson, "Form and Genre"; Devitt, "Generalizing About Genre"; Freadman, "Traps and Trappings of Genre Theory"; Gunn, "Maranatha"; Miller, "Genre as Social Action."
14. Bawarshi, "Genre Function," 352.
15. Ibid., 353.
16. Gunn, "Maranatha," 364.
17. Ibid., 369.
18. Clover, "Her Body, Himself," 189.
19. Williams, "Film Bodies," 4.
20. Ibid., 4.
21. Gunn, "Maranatha," 379.
22. Bawarshi, "Genre Function," 338.
23. Gunn, "Maranatha," 369.
24. I wrote the original version of this narrative back in 2006. Recently, I found the following excerpt from a Latina stripper describing how she appropriates customers' fantasies of the exotic other: "I whisper to them in Spanish ... the hilarious thing is they don't understand what I am saying ... so sometimes I just fuck with them ... you know like telling them some lines from the *telenovelas* ... or just like what I did that day ... it's not always erotic if you know what I mean ... [laughing]" (Egan, "I'll Be Your Fantasy Girl," 114).
25. Miller, "Genre as Social Action," 155.
26. Campbell and Jamieson, "Form and Genre," 20.
27. Ibid., 21–25.
28. Miller, "Genre as Social Action," 157.
29. For clarity's sake, throughout this analysis I will use the term "dancer" to refer to topless performers and "performer" to refer to neo-burlesque performers.
30. Egan, "I'll Be Your Fantasy Girl," 112.
31. For a description of dancer assets, see Ronai and Ellis, "Turn-Ons for Money," 276.
32. Egan, "I'll Be Your Fantasy Girl"; Frank, "Exploring the Motivations."
33. More specific and detailed taxonomies of customers exist in the literature. For example, Judith Hanna describes nine patron types: lonely/unhappy men, hostile men, bachelor party, pleasure-seeking men, macho men, victimized men, female companions of men, bachelorette party / young women, and lesbians. Although I find the category of "lesbian" far too narrow to reflect the breadth and complication of women's queer desire in clubs, overall the taxonomy coheres nicely with the literature (*Naked Truth*, 268–69). In contrast, Erickson and Tewksbury's study of strip-club goers in the late '90s yielded six distinct types of men: the Lonely, Socially Impotent, Bold Lookers, Detached Lookers, Players, and Sugar Daddies ("'Gentlemen' in the Club," 280–81). This piece is highly problematic for a number of reasons, including the ways in which data were gathered. The taxonomy also relies largely on stereotypes and assumptions rather than close ethnographic study. For a more detailed (and entertaining) critique of Erickson and Tewksbury, see Egan and Frank, "Attempts as an Interdisciplinary Conversation About Strip Clubs."
34. Egan, *Dancing for Dollars*, 13.
35. Egan and Frank, "Attempts at an Interdisciplinary Conversation," 304.
36. Frank, "Exploring the Motivations," 491.
37. I recommend the work of Katherine Frank and Danielle Egan for insight into regulars at strip clubs, in particular, Frank's *G-Strings and Sympathy* and Egan's *Dancing for Dollars*.
38. Hanna, "Dance and Sexuality," 230.
39. Frank, "Just Trying to Relax," 72.

40. Liepe-Levinson, *Strip Show*, 4.
41. Frank, "Exploring the Motivations," 490.
42. Egan, "I'll Be Your Fantasy Girl," 109; Frank, "Exploring the Motivations," 490.
43. I use "excesses" here in accordance with Williams to refer to the centrality of particular bodily responses over a particular narrative.
44. As with all of the features that I describe here, there are some instances where neo-burlesque performers accept tips or interact individually with an audience member. At my first neo-burlesque show at the Slipper Room on the Lower East Side of NYC, I tipped Julie Atlas Muz. *She's famous y'all.*
45. Baldwin, *Burlesque and the New Bump-n-Grind*; Ferreday, "'Showing the Girl'"; Harris, "Ghosts of New Burlesque"; Sally, "'It Is the Ugly That Is So Beautiful'"; Willson, *Happy Stripper.*
46. Ferreday, "'Showing the Girl,'" 61.
47. Willson, *Happy Stripper*, 33.
48. Harris, "Ghosts of New Burlesque," 154.
49. In some arenas, the transactional distinction between neo-burlesque and club stripping becomes more ambiguous. On the website Patreon.com, fans can become patrons to participating performers, including Sydni Deveraux. The more you pay, from $1 to $15 a month, increases what you see. But even Patreon does not cultivate the individual relationship that topless dance does.
50. Hanna, "Language of Dance," 41.
51. Michelle Mynx and Katrina Dohl.
52. Hanna defines the vocabulary of dance as its "steps and gestures." Dance also has grammar (the rules for combining these) and meaning. Together these compose the language of dance ("The Language of Dance," 41).
53. Weldon details ten different ways to twirl in *Burlesque Handbook.*
54. Lewis, "Looking Forward to the Past," 191.
55. Ibid., 191.
56. Egan, *Dancing for Dollars*; Frank, *G-Strings and Sympathy*; Lewis, "Lap Dancing," 378.
57. Lewis, "Lap Dancing," 378.
58. Hanna, "Dance and Sexuality," 230.
59. Hanna, "Undressing," 44.
60. Frank, "Exploring the Motivations," 490.
61. Even in the neo-burlesque subgenre of boylesque that features performances of diverse masculinities, common material symbols of neo-burlesque like Swarovski crystals, glitter, glam makeup, and form-fitting clothes are popular.
62. Weldon, *Burlesque Handbook*, 130.
63. Jones, "Lunch with Legs."
64. The 2013 Burlesque Hall of Fame (BHoF) exhibition "Not-So-Hidden Histories: Performers of Color in Burlesque" sketches out the legacy of women of color in burlesque.
65. Vesey, "How Performers of Color."
66. Harrington, "New Perspective."
67. Siobhan Brooks's *Unequal Desires: Race and Erotic Capital in the Stripping Industry* argues that Black and Latina women have lower "erotic capital" (that is, they are systematically undervalued, resulting in lower pay than white women) because of their hypersexualization. This comes about as a result of systemic racism yet is often cast as a matter of taste and free market choice.
68. Weldon, *Burlesque Handbook*, 226–27.
69. Ibid., 224.

70. Miller, "Genre as Social Action," 159.
71. Ibid., 158.
72. Bazerman, "Genre and Identity," 13.
73. See Bakhtin, "Problem of Speech Genres"; Bawarshi, "Genre Function"; Bazerman, "Genre and Identity"; Freedman and Medway, "Locating Genre Studies"; Kress, "Genre in a Social Theory of Language"; Miller, "Genre as Social Action"; Paré, "Genre and Identity."
74. Gunn, "Rhetoric of Exorcism," 18.
75. Ibid., 6.
76. Bawarshi, "Genre Function," 335.
77. Laqueur, *Making Sex*, 11.
78. Gunn, "Maranatha," 368.
79. Ibid., 369.
80. Williams, "Film Bodies," 5.
81. Egan, *Dancing*, 13.
82. Gunn, "Maranatha," 368.

Chapter 3

1. A persona of Slipper Room owner James Habacker.
2. A condensed version of this chapter was published in *Present Tense: A Journal of Rhetoric in Society* in 2015.
3. Villadsen, "Rhetoric of Seduction," 14.
4. Ballif, *Seduction, Sophistry*; Erickson and Thomson, "Seduction Theory."
5. Throughout this chapter, I use "seductive" as an adjective to modify rhetoric. This is meant to reflect the ways that I am using seduction to classify the type of rhetorics that display features of seduction, rather than using "seduction" as a description of all rhetoric.
6. Ferreday, "Showing the Girl," 50.
7. For an extended discussion of third sophistic rhetoric, see Vitanza, "'Some More' Notes," 133.
8. In the Freudian psychoanalytic tradition, "seduction" refers to the theory that Freud developed and later abandoned suggesting that hysteria in post-adolescents was the result of childhood sexual abuse by their parents. As Freud continued to develop his later and better-known theories of sexuality, he would abandon this early theory (Hunter, introduction to *Seduction and Theory*, 1–3). While investigations into seduction theory inevitably lead to and from Freud, the term "seduction" is neither descriptive nor reflective of Freud's early theory about the connection between childhood sexual abuse and hysteria. The term "seduction theory" was not applied to Freud's work until 1950 when Ernst Kris "invented the label . . . in propagation of the legendary claim that the Oedipus complex, representing the full blossoming of psychoanalysis and purportedly based in a universal fantasy of parental seduction, had originated in 1896" (Triplett, "Misnomer," 651–52). Freudian seduction theory is not, for these reasons, reflective of the seduction and the seductive rhetoric I mobilize here.
9. Lu, "Simple Pickup."
10. Ratchford, "I Tried to Find Out."
11. Felman, *Literary Speech*, 30.
12. Ibid., 31.
13. Ibid.
14. Crowley, "Plea for the Revival of Sophistry," 328.
15. Ibid., 328.

16. Gorgias, *Encomium of Helen*, 44–46.
17. Porter, "Seductions of Gorgias," 274.
18. Kelley, "Rhetoric as Seduction," 78.
19. Ibid., 78–79.
20. Ballif, *Seduction*, 5.
21. Crowley, "Plea for the Revival of Sophistry," 328.
22. Baudrillard, *Seduction*, 2; Ballif, *Seduction, Sophistry*, 11–12.
23. Ballif, *Seduction, Sophistry*, 11.
24. Baudrillard, *Seduction*, 7–8.
25. Here I depart from Michelle Ballif, who writes that seduction requires a "shift *beyond* epistemology" because seduction is not concerned with structuring and defining ways of knowing (*Seduction, Sophistry*, 11, emphasis added).
26. Baudrillard, *Seduction*, 79.
27. Ballif, *Seduction, Sophistry*, 179.
28. Ibid., 193.
29. Baudrillard, *Seduction*, 34.
30. Ibid., 54.
31. Ott, "Television as Lover, Part I," 39.
32. Vitanza, "Abandoned to Writing."
33. Wilson and Lewiecki-Wilson, "Disability, Rhetoric, and the Body," 3.
34. Baudrillard, *Seduction*, 10.
35. Ballif, *Seduction, Sophistry*, 17, 19.
36. Ibid., 29.
37. Ibid., 19.
38. Ibid., 2.
39. Ibid., 2, 19.
40. Erickson and Thomson, "Seduction Theory," 302, 312.
41. Ibid., 302.
42. Ballif, *Seduction, Sophistry*, 145.
43. Goshorn, "Valorizing 'the Feminine,'" 258.
44. Gallop, "French Theory," 113.
45. Baudrillard, *Seduction*, 8.
46. See Ahmed, *Differences That Matter*; Chaput, "Identity, Postmodernity"; Gallop, "French Theory"; Goshorn, "Valorizing 'the Feminine'"; Ross, "Baudrillard's Bad Attitude."
47. Goshorn, "Valorizing 'the Feminine,'" 272; See also Ballif, *Seduction, Sophistry*; Erickson and Thomson, "Seduction Theory"; Grace, *Baudrillard's Challenge*; Ross, "Baudrillard's Bad Attitude."
48. Ferreday, "'Showing the Girl,'" 50, 51.
49. Ibid., 50.
50. Rachel E. Mansfield's 2006 MA thesis "Trend and Aftermath: The Iconography and Rhetoric of Neo-Burlesque" contains excellent examples of the rhetoric of feminist empowerment in neo-burlesque. According to the author, "Neo-burlesque performance is classified as feminist because its celebrants claim the form as such" (ii), which we can read both as critique and as acknowledgment of how feminists claim space for specific cultural practices.
51. Siebler, "What's So Feminist About Garters and Bustiers?"
52. Prelli, "Rhetorics of Display," 2.
53. Erickson and Thomson, "Seduction Theory," 303.
54. See Pasko, "Naked Power: The Practice of Stripping as a Confidence Game." See also chapter 2.

55. Allen, *Horrible Prettiness*, 49 (emphasis added).
56. Ibid., 81.
57. Baudrillard, *Seduction*, 53.
58. Erickson and Thomson, "Seduction Theory," 304.
59. While distinction needs to be made between burlesque and strip-club dancing because they are different persuasive and performative arts, I find that stressing this difference risks pathologizing both strippers and their customers, and it is not my intent to romanticize burlesque and degrade strippers.
60. Baudrillard, *Seduction*, 34.
61. Weldon, *Burlesque Handbook*, 221.
62. See Egan, *Dancing for Dollars*; Erikson and Tewksbury, "'Gentlemen' in the Club"; Frank, *G-Strings and Sympathy*; Hanna, "Dance and Sexuality"; Pasko, "Naked Power"; Wosick-Correa and Joseph, "Sexy Ladies Sexing Ladies."
63. Baudrillard, *Seduction*, 153, 159.
64. Ibid., 13.
65. Ibid., 8.
66. Miss Indigo Blue, "Amazon Damsels in Bondage," Fisher Center for the Study of Gender and Justice, Winn-Seeley Theater, Hobart and William Smith Colleges, Geneva, New York, September 25, 2013. Accompanying photos are from a different performance of this same routine.
67. Actress Barbara Stanwyck is rumored to have had sexual relationships with women.
68. Baudrillard, *Seduction*, 21.
69. Ibid., 103–5.
70. Analysis based on my viewing of his performance in 2015. Photo is from a different performance in 2007.
71. Haraway, "Cyborg Manifesto," 170.
72. Ibid., 154. Ballif argues that Haraway's theorization of the cyborg "embodies" Third Sophistic Rhetoric.
73. Nally, "Grrrly Hurly Burly," 626.
74. Baudrillard, *Seduction*, 34.
75. Ibid., 32.
76. Weldon, *Burlesque Handbook*, 43.
77. Analysis based on an online video: Miss Indigo Blue, "Blue Gloves," YouTube video, Photos are from Burlesque Behind the Pink Door, Seattle, WA.
78. Dame CuchiFrita, email message to author, June 5, 2014.
79. Willson, *Happy Stripper*, 131.
80. Dame CuchiFrita, "Untitled with Mask," *The Slipper Room Show: Mel Frye's Pre-Existing Condition*, Perf. Mel Frye, Dame Cuchifrita, Legs Malone, Julie Atlas Muz, The Slipper Room, New York, August 1, 2013.
81. Ferreday, "'Showing the Girl,'" 55.
82. Debra Ferreday discusses the use of props as a *framing*, rather than a concealing device, in classic burlesque. I contend, however, that props are generally used both to conceal and frame, alternating to provide what Barthes calls the "flash … which seduces" (ibid.; see Barthes, *Pleasure of the Text*, 10).
83. Cheeky Lane's Instagram features several pictures and videos of this act. The video found at https://www.instagram.com/p/Bry7pswlEnE demonstrates the mechanisms of the costume particularly well.
84. Legs Malone, "Bettie Page Tribute."

85. Ferreday, "'Showing the Girl,'" 59.
86. Baudrillard, *Seduction*, 8.
87. Gencarella and Pezzullo, "Introduction," 2.
88. Erickson and Thomson, "Seduction Theory," 303.
89. Ibid., 304.
90. Davis, *Inessential Solidarity*, 68.
91. Ibid., 78.
92. Vitanza, "'Some More' Notes,"133.
93. Ballif, *Seduction, Sophistry*, 183.
94. Ibid., 189–92.
95. Dolmage, *Disability Rhetoric*, 152.
96. Ibid., 166.
97. Felman, *Literary Speech Act*, 28.

Chapter 4

1. Grant, *Playing the Whore*, 125.
2. Snow et al., "Frame Alignment Processes," 475.
3. Slack, "Communication as Articulation."
4. Kevin DeLuca's analyses of the embodied protest rhetoric of EarthFirst!, ACT UP, and Queer Nation ("Unruly Arguments") in the late '90s and more recently Dan Brouwer and Aaron Hess's analysis of the Westboro Baptist Church ("Making Sense") demonstrate articulation's flexibility as a method for analyzing social-movement rhetoric, which often finds bodies as generators of argument.
5. Jackson, "Framing Sex Worker Rights."
6. Harris-Perry, *Sister Citizen*, 38.
7. Jackson, "Framing Sex Worker Rights."
8. Griffin, "Rhetorical Structure of the 'New Left' Movement"; Haiman, "Rhetoric of the Streets"; Corbett, "Open Hand"; Corbett, "Protest."
9. Corbett, "Open Hand," 288.
10. Hawhee, *Bodily Arts*, 58 (emphasis added).
11. Dolmage, "Metis," 6.
12. Jung, "Textual Mainstreaming," 161.
13. Brouwer and Hess, "Making Sense of 'God Hates Fags'"; DeLuca, "Unruly Arguments"; Makus, "Stuart Hall's Theory of Ideology."
14. Angus, "Politics of Common Sense," 538.
15. Ibid., 541.
16. Ibid., 548.
17. Brouwer and Hess, "Making Sense of 'God Hates Fags,'" 70.
18. DeLuca, "Unruly Arguments."
19. Melucci, *Nomads of the Present*, 75 (emphasis added).
20. Chateauvert, *Sex Workers Unite*, 13.
21. Ibid.; Weitzer, "Prostitutes' Rights"; Jackson, "Framing Sex Worker Rights."
22. Activists differ in their approaches to the decriminalization/legalization issue. Some argue that full regulation is not ideal because it will interfere with the workers' right to determine what they will perform and where and when and under what conditions.
23. Lorey, "Governmental Precarization."

24. Alexander and Rhodes, "What's So Sexual About Rhetoric," 1.
25. The history of these riots illustrates the erasure rhetorics faced by trans people and by sex workers. The Compton's riots, although preceding Stonewall by three years, have been largely ignored in LGBQ history in favor of the Stonewall myth. People of color, trans people, and sex workers have been written out of or tokenized in both riots. Armstrong and Crage write, "Street queens and hustlers—marginalized by class, gender presentation, and often race—were more willing than others to confront police, and were important in the riots at both Compton's and the Stonewall Inn" ("Movements and Memory," 744).
26. Leigh, "Inventing Sex Work," 230.
27. Grant, *Playing the Whore*, 19–22.
28. Ditmore, "Use of Raids," 6.
29. National Human Trafficking Hotline, "Myths and Facts."
30. Grant, *Playing the Whore*, 93–94.
31. DeVries, "Red Umbrella."
32. For example, when I was researching topless dancers, I found (a finding that recurs in the literature on stripping) that many women with children stripped because they made more money in less time than other jobs. This in turn meant less money spent on day care. More than one woman I interviewed shook off the question of choice if I asked it. Asking it signaled that I didn't get it.
33. DeVries, "Red Umbrella."
34. NSWP, "History."
35. Snow and Benford, "Ideology, Frame Resonance, and Participant Mobilization," 198.
36. Because *sex work* and *sex worker* signify differently—the labor and the laborer are not the same—I use both throughout this essay.
37. Grant, *Playing the Whore*, 20.
38. Herndl and Licona, "Shifting Agency," 138.
39. Ibid., 145.
40. While it is not my focus here, these debates get played out starkly and bitterly in public forums on social media, in particular, on Twitter with little nuance and with maximum hostility. The circular debates, flattening of arguments, and *ad hominem* (or perhaps *ad feminam* is more accurate) attacks are similar to the still-raging sex wars among different types of feminists. Many of these arguments concern who gets the right to identify as a feminist.
41. "Open Letter Rejecting 'Sex Work' as AP Term."
42. CATW has a more extensive analysis of the term as part of a report to the UN; see Leidhold, "Presentation to UN Special Seminar on Trafficking." It is important for me to acknowledge that I use the term *sex worker* consciously and politically in my work. By doing so I suggest to some antagonists "that not only [am I an] apologis[t] for the sex industry; [I am] complicit with it" (Leidhold, "Presentation to UN").
43. NSWP, "History."
44. "Open Letter Rejecting 'Sex Work' as AP Term."
45. I use the term *women* here to reflect the position of CATW as expressed on their website http://www.catwinternational.org, which very clearly defines consumers as men and victims as women and children. Trans women are not explicitly mentioned, so it is unclear whether CATW includes them in the term *women* or not.
46. Jackson, "Framing Sex Worker Rights."
47. Ibid., 33.
48. Ibid., 35.
49. Benford and Snow, "Framing Processes and Social Movements," 613.

50. Although Don't Ask, Don't Tell was ended in 2011, allowing for the open military service of LGB people, trans people were still banned until 2016 when the ban was ended under President Obama, including a one-year review phase. In 2017, amid much misinformed rhetoric delivered via Twitter—our administration's official system for unilaterally crafting and delivering and instituting policy—the Trump-Pence administration reinstated the ban. At the time of this writing, the issue is still being litigated.

51. Hayward, "Don't Exist," 191.

52. Figure 12 shows the EDL's protest against the *LA Times*. Burlesque Hall of Fame Executive Director Dustin M. Wax notes that while the protest was supposedly in response to a "blackout" policy for strippers' advertisements that would forbid showing anything other than a headshot, that there is "some question whether this was an actual policy or whether it was ginned up to give the EDL an excuse to make a public display for publicity." Email message, February 7, 2018.

53. "Exotic Dancers League."

54. These were not straightforward victories, however, as clubs continued to engage in actions, such as declaring bankruptcy to avoid paying dancers (Brooks, "Exotic Dancing and Unionizing," 63).

55. Chateauvert, *Sex Workers Unite*, 144–48; Gall, *Sex Worker Union Organising*. 67–72.

56. Dancers at the Lusty Lady were classified as employees, rather than independent contractors, and joined the Service Employee International Union (SEIU) in 1996. Siobhan Brooks, a black dancer who worked at the Lady and was part of the effort to unionize writes: "The main issue that led women at the Lusty Lady to unionize was the videotaping of dancers by customers without their consent, a situation that the management would not change" ("Exotic Dancing and Unionizing," 63). Brooks goes on to stress, however, that white women and women of color had different priorities, and that unionization did little to stem systemic racism at the club, racism exacerbated by white workers and by management.

57. Covert, "Strip Clubs Get Away with Exploiting Dancers."

58. Grant, "New Orleans Strip Club Workers Battle 'Age Ban.'"

59. Williams, "Can Louisiana Enforce Strip Club Age Ban?"

60. Litten, "Track."

61. Grant, "Trafficking in Vagaries."

62. Ibid.

63. Clark, "Strippers Protest New Orleans Police."

64. Ibid.

65. DeLuca, "Unruly Arguments," 13.

66. Lunceford, *Naked Politics*, 5.

67. Stromquist, "Strip Club Workers." (Disneyfication—seen in Times Square when the closing of sex and strip clubs paved the way for an influx of chain stores and restaurants aimed at families, distinguishable from tourist traps all over the US only in its massive size—aims to remodel Bourbon Street as a family-friendly tourist destination by closing sex clubs and small and local businesses and bringing in corporate developments. While Hurricane Katrina brought renewed attention to this particular kind of gentrification, historian J. Mark Souther tracks it throughout the twentieth century in 2007's "The Disneyfication of New Orleans: The French Quarter as Facade in a Divided City.")

68. Archer, "Criminalizing Strippers' Work."

69. Martinez, "A Plea for Critical Race Theory Counterstory," 38.

70. Ibid., 38.

71. Litten, "Rick's Cabaret"; Clark, "Strippers Protest New Orleans Police."

72. Sauvage and White, "Bourbon Street Strippers Are Fighting."

73. Bourbon Alliance of Responsible Entertainers (BARE), "[The police] laughed."

74. Bourbon Alliance of Responsible Entertainers, press release, March 4, 2018.

Chapter 5

1. Crable, "Symbolizing Motion"; DeLuca, "Unruly Arguments"; Hauser, "Body Rhetoric"; Lunceford, *Naked Politics*.

2. Muñoz, *Disidentifications*, loc. 314 of 5327.

3. Nealon, *Alterity Politics*, 2.

4. Ibid., 3.

5. Hill, "SlutWalk as Perifeminist Response," 31.

6. Chateauvert, *Sex Workers Unite*.

7. Carr, "SlutWalk Movement"; Dow and Wood, "Repeating History"; Hill, "SlutWalk as a Perifeminist Response"; O'Keefe, "My Body Is My Manifesto!"; Pollitt, "Talk the Talk"; Reger, "Story of a Slut Walk"; Traister, "Ladies, We Have a Problem."

8. See Levy, *Female Chauvinist Pigs*.

9. Dow and Wood, "Repeating History," 27.

10. Hill, "SlutWalk as Perifeminist Response," 31.

11. Borah and Nandi, "Reclaiming the Feminist Politics," 419 (emphasis added).

12. Thompson, "Amber Rose Talks Sex."

13. McDonald, "Complicated Feminism."

14. The analysis of the Amber Rose SlutWalk presented here was written in 2018. The online presence for the event on Facebook, Twitter, and Instagram has been nonexistent since the last SlutWalk LA in October 2018. Rose is pregnant with her second child and announced on Instagram on May 27, 2019, that she has hyperemesis, a pregnancy complication causing her "extreme nausea, vomiting, and dehydration." She also says that she is "really really tired" and spends most of her time sleeping. On August 13, 2019, Rose announced on her Instagram that the 2019 march would be canceled in order to protect her "energy and peace" (quoted in "Amber Rose Cancels Annual SlutWalk").

15. Evans, "Amber Rose's Slutwalk"; Finley, "Amber Rose On Slut-Shaming."

16. Dow and Wood, "Repeating History," 23; Reger, "Micro-Cohorts," 59–61; Reger, "Story of a Slut Walk," 95.

17. Reger, "Micro-Cohorts," 51.

18. Dow and Wood, "Repeating History," 31.

19. Mendes, *Slutwalk*.

20. De Saussure, *Third Course of Lectures*.

21. Connolly, *Identity, Difference*, 64.

22. Burke, *Rhetoric of Motives*, 22.

23. This is not to say that alphabetic text is one-dimensional.

24. Davis, *Inessential Solidarity*, 53–54.

25. Bernstein, "Celebration and Suppression"; Gamson, "Must Identity Movements Self-Destruct?"; Kauffman, "Anti-Politics of Identity"; Melucci, *Nomads of the Present*; Pichardo, "New Social Movements"; Snow and Benford, "Ideology."

26. Anderson, *Identity's Strategy*, 4.

27. Nealon, *Alterity Politics*, 140.

28. Mendes, *Slutwalk*, 71–72.

29. Although my purpose here is to look at sexuality debates among feminists specifically, it is important to note that "although feminists comprise a large segment of the pro-sexuality movement, some pro-sex activists, including transgender, gay, bisexual, and S/M radicals, do not align themselves with feminism at all" (Glick, "Sex Positive," 20).

30. Reger, "Micro-Cohorts," 59.

31. Glick, "Sex Positive," 21–22.
32. Kapur, "Pink Chaddis," 4,
33. Vance, "Ninth Scholar," 443.
34. Vance et al., "Petition," 451.
35. Bright, *Susie Sexpert's Lesbian Sex World*, 13.
36. Hanscombe, "In Among the Market Forces?," 217.
37. Ibid., 218.
38. Denying the existence of another identity is a marker of alterity rhetorics and a common one within radical feminist discourse, which also strenuously denies the existence of sex workers and trans people.
39. Rubin, "Thinking Sex," 301.
40. Ibid., 302–3.
41. Moraga, "Barnard Sexuality Conference," 23.
42. Ibid.
43. This information was taken from http://www.slutwalktoronto.com/about/faqs; the site is no longer active.
44. Mendes identifies nine priorities for the movement: challenging rape culture / victim blaming; reappropriating "slut"; challenging "asking for it" rhetorics; encouraging a "do not rape" culture; improve police practices around sexual assault; providing education, support, and outreach; promoting respect for individual choices; fighting for women's rights; and including all "genders, ages, ethnicities, classes and sexual orientations" (*Slutwalk*, 4).
45. Dines and Murphy, "SlutWalk Is Not Sexual Liberation."
46. Rapp et al., "Internet as a Tool," 256. (See also Mendes, *Slutwalk*.)
47. See Mendes for a detailed analysis of critiques of SlutWalk.
48. Blay, "Reclaiming the Word 'Slut.'"
49. I've chosen the most widely cited critiques in order to demonstrate their persuasive power via the ways that their arguments are articulated using rhetorics of alterity.
50. The commentary following Bogado's post is a particularly rich site for analyzing the issue of race and SlutWalk.
51. Gaucher, Hunt, and Sinclair, "Can Pejorative Terms?," 129.
52. Bogado, "SlutWalk: A Stroll Through White Supremacy."
53. Cooper, "SlutWalks v. Ho Strolls."
54. Collins, *Black Sexual Politics*, 27.
55. Global Women's Strike, "Women of Colour Respond."
56. Plaid, "Does SlutWalk Speak to Women of Color?"
57. Nealon, *Alterity Politics*, 3.
58. Miriam, "Feminism, Neoliberalism, and SlutWalk," 262–63.
59. See for example, Carr, "SlutWalk Movement"; Dow and Wood, "Repeating History"; McCormack and Prostran, "Asking for It"; Reger, "Story of a Slut Walk."
60. Mendes, *Slutwalk*, 60.
61. Ibid., 60.
62. Walker, "Future of Femme," 795.
63. Brightwell, "Exclusionary Effects," 15.
64. See Faderman, *Odd Girls and Twilight Lovers*; Kennedy and Davis, *Boots of Leather, Slippers of Gold*.
65. Serano, *Whipping Girl*, 347.
66. Brightwell, "Exclusionary Effects," 22.
67. Collins, *Black Sexual Politics*.
68. Mendes, *Slutwalk*, 18–19.

69. Nakayama, "Show/Down Time," 370.
70. Mendes, *Slutwalk*.
71. Murphy, "Breaking!"
72. Finley, "Amber Rose On Slut-Shaming."
73. Cooper, "SlutWalks v. Ho Strolls."
74. Williams, "Why, Even as a Feminist."

Conclusion

1. Burke, *Attitudes Toward History*, 34.
2. Ibid., 4.
3. Moore, "'Quayle Quagmire,'" 112.
4. Burke, *Attitudes*, 21–22.
5. Bonnstetter, "Mel Brooks Meets Kenneth Burke," 25.
6. Burke, *Attitudes*, 28–29.
7. Ibid., 20–21.
8. Ibid., 54, 55.
9. Carlson, "Limitations on the Comic Frame," 310.
10. Interestingly, though it is not a part of Carlson's analysis, the period in which she identifies women's humor as moving into the burlesque—1870 to 1880—coincides with Lydia Thompson's 1868 arrival in the US and the popularizing of burlesque as a women-centric performance genre, not just a literary one.
11. Carlson, "Limitations on the Comic Frame," 314–15.
12. Appel, "Burlesque Drama as a Rhetorical Genre," 269, 280.
13. Ibid., 270.
14. Ibid., 280.
15. Carlson, "Limitations on the Comic Frame," 314.

Bibliography

Ahmed, Sara. *Differences That Matter: Feminist Theory and Postmodernism*. Cambridge: Cambridge University Press, 1998.

Alexander, Jonathan, and Jacqueline Rhodes, eds. *Sexual Rhetorics: Methods, Identities, Publics*. New York: Routledge, 2015.

———. "What's So Sexual About Rhetoric, What's Rhetorical About Sex?" In *Sexual Rhetorics: Methods, Identities, Publics*, edited by Jonathan Alexander and Jacqueline Rhodes, 1–13. New York: Routledge, 2015.

Allen, Robert C. *Horrible Prettiness: Burlesque and American Culture*. Chapel Hill: University of North Carolina Press, 1991.

"Amber Rose Cancels Annual SlutWalk." *Vibe*, August 13, 2019. Accessed March 2, 2020. https://www.vibe.com/2019/08/amber-rose-cancels-slutwalk.

America's Got Talent. Season 1, episode 2. Featuring Piers Morgan, Brandy Norwood, and David Hasselhoff. Aired June 28, 2006. NBC.

———. Season 4, episode 5. Featuring Piers Morgan, Sharon Osbourne, and David Hasselhoff. Aired July 7, 2009. NBC.

Anderson, Dana. *Identity's Strategy: Rhetorical Selves in Conversion*. Columbia: University of South Carolina Press, 2007.

Angus, Ian. "The Politics of Common Sense: Articulation Theory and Critical Communication Studies." *Annals of the International Communication Association* 15, no. 1 (1992): 535–70.

Appel, Edward C. "Burlesque Drama as a Rhetorical Genre: The Hudibrastic Ridicule of William F. Buckley, Jr." *Western Journal of Communication* 60, no. 3 (1996): 269–84.

Archer, Lynn. "Criminalizing Strippers' Work Makes Young Women More Vulnerable." *Times-Picayune/NOLA.com/New Orleans Advocate*, February 6, 2018. https://www.nola.com/opinions/article_603274cf-3833-5aa2-88e6-624c6149ab9f.html.

Armstrong, Elizabeth A., and Suzanna M. Crage. "Movements and Memory: The Making of the Stonewall Myth." *American Sociological Review* 71, no. 5 (2006): 724–51.

Bakhtin, Mikhail. "The Problem of Speech Genres." In *Speech Genres and Other Late Essays*, edited by Caryl Emerson and Michael Holquist, 60–102. Austin: University of Texas Press, 1986.

Baldwin, Michelle. *Burlesque and the New Bump-n-Grind*. Denver: Speck Press, 2004.

Ballif, Michelle. *Seduction, Sophistry, and the Woman with the Rhetorical Figure*. Carbondale: Southern Illinois University Press, 2001.

Barthes, Roland. *The Pleasure of the Text*. Translated by Richard Miller. New York: Hill and Wang, 1975.

Barton, Ellen. "Literacy in (Inter)Action." *College English* 59, no. 4 (1997): 408–37.

Battaglia, Adria, and Jake Simmons. "The Writing on the Wall: Metonymy, Pulse, and the Disciplinary Intersections of Rhetoric and Performance Studies." *Text and Performance Quarterly* 34, no. 1 (2014): 9–27.

Baudrillard, Jean. *Seduction*. New York: St. Martin's Press, 1990.

Bawarshi, Anis. "The Genre Function." *College English* 62, no. 3 (2000): 335–60.

Bazerman, Charles. "Genre and Identity: Citizenship in the Age of the Internet and the Age of Global Capitalism." In *The Rhetoric and Ideology of Genre: Strategies for Stability and Change*, 13–37. Cresskill, NJ: Hampton, 2002.
Bell, Elizabeth. "Toward a Pleasure-Centered Economy: Wondering a Feminist Aesthetics of Performance." *Text and Performance Quarterly* 15, no. 2 (1995): 99–121.
Benford, Robert D., and David A. Snow. "Framing Processes and Social Movements: An Overview and Assessment." *Annual Review of Sociology* 26 (2000): 611–39.
Berkenkotter, Carol, and Thomas N. Huckin. *Genre Knowledge in Disciplinary Communication: Cognition, Culture, Power.* Hillsdale, NJ: Lawrence Erlbaum, 1995.
Bernstein, Mary. "Celebration and Suppression: The Strategic Uses of Identity by the Lesbian and Gay Movement." *American Journal of Sociology* 103, no. 3 (1997): 531–65.
Black Women's Blueprint. "An Open Letter from Black Women to the SlutWalk." Accessed October 24, 2015. https://doi.org/10.1177/0891243215611868.
Blair, Carole. "Reflections on Criticism and Bodies: Parables from Public Places." *Western Journal of Communication* 65, no. 3 (2001): 271–94.
Blay, Zeba. "Reclaiming the Word 'Slut' Is an Entirely Different Beast for Black Women." Huffington Post, October 5, 2015. https://www.huffingtonpost.com/entry/reclaiming-the-word-slut-is-an-entirely-different-beast-for-black-women_us_56128706e4b0af3706e14d49.
Bogado, Aura. "SlutWalk: A Stroll Through White Supremacy." *To the Curb*. Accessed October 24, 2015. https://tothecurb.wordpress.com/2011/05/13/slutwalk-a-stroll-through-white-supremacy.
Bonnstetter, Beth E. "Mel Brooks Meets Kenneth Burke (and Mikhail Bakhtin): Comedy and Burlesque in Satiric Film." *Journal of Film and Video* 63, no. 1 (2011): 18–31.
Borah, Rituparna, and Subhalakshmi Nandi. "Reclaiming the Feminist Politics of 'SlutWalk.'" *International Feminist Journal of Politics* 14, no. 3 (September 2012): 415–21.
Bormann, Ernest G. "Symbolic Convergence Theory: A Communication Formulation." *Journal of Communication* 35, no. 4 (1985): 128–38.
Bourbon Alliance of Responsible Entertainers (BARE). Press release, March 4, 2018.
———. "[The police] laughed and said, 'You lost your right to decency when you became a stripper. I looked at him and was like, 'Every person has the right to decency.''" Anonymous NOLA dancer @NOPDNews. Twitter, January 29, 2018. 3:38 p.m. https://twitter.com/bare_nola/status/958076927142694913.
Branstetter, Heather Lee. "Promiscuous Approaches to Reorienting Rhetorical Research." In *Sexual Rhetorics: Methods, Identities, Publics*, edited by Jonathan Alexander and Jacqueline Rhodes, 17–30. New York: Routledge, 2015.
Bright, Susie. *Susie Sexpert's Lesbian Sex World*. Berkeley, CA: Cleis, 1990.
Brightwell, Laura. "The Exclusionary Effects of Queer Anti-Normativity on Feminine-Identified Queers." *feral feminisms*, no. 7 (Spring 2018): 15–24.
Brooks, Siobhan. "Exotic Dancing and Unionizing: The Challenges of Feminist and Antiracist Organizing at the Lusty Lady Theater." In *Feminism and Antiracism: International Struggles for Justice*, edited by France Winddance Twine and Kathleeen M. Blee, 59–70. New York: New York University Press, 2001.
———. *Unequal Desires: Race and Erotic Capital in the Stripping Industry.* Albany: State University of New York Press, 2010.
Brouwer, Daniel C., and Aaron Hess. "Making Sense of 'God Hates Fags' and 'Thank God for 9/11': A Thematic Analysis of Milbloggers' Responses to Reverend Fred Phelps and the Westboro Baptist Church." *Western Journal of Communication* 71, no. 1 (2007): 69–90.

Brueggemann, Brenda Jo. "Still-Life: Representations and Silences in the Participant-Observer Role." In *Ethics and Representation in Qualitative Studies of Literacy*, edited by Peter Mortensen and Gesa E. Kirsch, 17–39. Urbana, IL: NCTE, 1996.
Buchanan, Lindal. *Regendering Delivery: The Fifth Canon and Antebellum Women Rhetors*. Carbondale: Southern Illinois University Press, 2005.
Burana, Lily. *Strip City: A Stripper's Farewell Journey across America*. New York: Miramax Books, 2003.
Burke, Kenneth. *Attitudes Toward History*. 2nd ed. Boston: Beacon, 1961.
———. *A Rhetoric of Motives*. Berkeley: University of California Press, 1950.
Butler, Judith. *Bodies That Matter: On the Discursive Limits of Sex*. New York: Routledge, 1993.
Butterworth, Michael L. "'Katie Was Not Only a Girl, She Was Terrible': Katie Hnida, Body Rhetoric, and Football at the University of Colorado." *Communication Studies* 59, no. 3 (2008): 259–73.
Calafell, Bernadette Marie. "Performance: Keeping Rhetoric Honest." *Text and Performance Quarterly* 34, no. 1 (2014): 115–17.
Campbell, Karlyn Kohrs, and Kathleen Hall Jamieson. "Form and Genre in Rhetorical Criticism: An Introduction." In *Form and Genre: Shaping Rhetorical Action*, edited by Karlyn Kohrs Campbell and Kathleen Hall Jamieson, 9–32. Falls Church, VA: The Speech Communication Association, 1978.
Carlson, A. Cheree. "Limitations on the Comic Frame: Some Witty American Women of the Nineteenth Century." *Quarterly Journal of Speech* 74, no. 3 (1988): 310–22.
Carr, Joetta L. "The SlutWalk Movement: A Study in Transnational Feminist Activism." *Journal of Feminist Scholarship* 4 (2013): 24–38.
Chaput, Catherine. "Identity, Postmodernity, and an Ethics of Activism." *JAC* 20, no. 1 (2000): 43–72.
Chateauvert, Melinda. *Sex Workers Unite: A History of the Movement from Stonewall to Slut-Walk*. Boston: Beacon Press, 2013.
Chocolat The Extraordinaire. "Race and Burlesque: The Curious Case of the Performer of Colour." *21st Century Burlesque Magazine*, February 7, 2013. http://21stcenturyburlesque.com/race-and-burlesque-the-curious-case-of-the-performer-of-colour.
Clark, Jess. "Strippers Protest New Orleans Police." *Weekend Edition Saturday*, February 3, 2018. https://www.npr.org/2018/02/03/582968713/strippers-protest-new-orleans-police.
Clover, Carol J. "Her Body, Himself: Gender in the Slasher Film." *Representations*, no. 20 (1987): 187–228.
Collins, Patricia Hill. *Black Sexual Politics: African Americans, Gender, and the New Racism*. New York: Routledge, 2004.
Connolly, William E. *Identity, Difference: Democratic Negotiations of Political Paradox*. Minneapolis: University of Minnesota Press, 2002.
Conquergood, Dwight. "Ethnography, Rhetoric, and Performance." *Quarterly Journal of Speech* 78, no. 1 (1992): 80–97.
Cooper, Brittany. "SlutWalks v. Ho Strolls." *Crunk Feminist Collective*, May 23, 2011. Accessed October 24, 2015. https://crunkfeministcollective.wordpress.com/2011/05/23/slutwalks-v-ho-strolls.
Corbett, Edward P. J. "The Rhetoric of Protest." *Rhetoric Society Newsletter* 4, no. 2 (1974): 4.
———. "The Rhetoric of the Open Hand and the Rhetoric of the Closed Fist." *College Composition and Communication* 20, no. 5 (1969): 288–96.
Covert, Brice. "Strip Clubs Get Away with Exploiting Dancers Every Day, but These Strippers Are Fighting Back." *ThinkProgress*, November 4, 2015. https://thinkprogress.org

/strip-clubs-get-away-with-exploiting-dancers-every-day-but-these-strippers-are-fighting-back-fb3a204bcc5a.

Crable, Bryan. "Symbolizing Motion: Burke's Dialectic and Rhetoric of the Body." *Rhetoric Review* 22, no. 2 (2003): 121–37.

Crowley, Sharon. "A Plea for the Revival of Sophistry." *Rhetoric Review* 7, no. 2 (1989): 318–34.

———. *Toward a Civil Discourse: Rhetoric and Fundamentalism*. Pittsburgh: University of Pittsburgh Press, 2006.

Davis, Diane. *Inessential Solidarity: Rhetoric and Foreigner Relations*. Pittsburgh: University of Pittsburgh Press, 2010.

DeLuca, Kevin Michael. "Unruly Arguments: The Body Rhetoric of Earth First!, ACT UP, and Queer Nation." *Argumentation and Advocacy* 36, no. 1 (1999): 9–21.

Derksen, Céleste. "The 'Attack Behind the Invitation': Gender Parody in Karen Hines's *Pochsy's Lips*." In *Performing Gender and Comedy: Theories, Texts, and Contexts*, edited by Shannon Hengen, 233–46. New York: Routledge, 2013.

De Saussure, Ferdinand. *Third Course of Lectures on General Linguistics (1910–1911)*. New York: Pergamon, 1993.

Devitt, Amy J. "Generalizing About Genre: New Conceptions of an Old Concept." *College Composition and Communication* 44, no. 4 (1993): 573–86.

DeVries, Maggie. "The Red Umbrella: Sex Work, Stigma, and the Law." Filmed 2014 at TEDxSFU. Video, 17:38. https://www.youtube.com/watch?v=RUfcouJch7U&feature=youtube_gdata_player.

Di Benedetto, Stephen. "The Body as Fluid Dramaturgy: Live Art, Corporeality, and Perception." *Journal of Dramatic Theory and Criticism* 16, no. 2 (2002): 4–15.

Dickson, Barbara. "Reading Maternity Materially: The Case of Demi Moore." In *Rhetorical Bodies*, edited by Jack Selzer and Sharon Crowley, 297–313. Madison: University of Wisconsin Press, 1999.

Dines, Gail, and Wendy J. Murphy. "SlutWalk Is Not Sexual Liberation." *Guardian*, May 8, 2011, sec. Opinion. https://www.theguardian.com/commentisfree/2011/may/08/slutwalk-not-sexual-liberation.

Ditmore, Melissa. "The Use of Raids to Fight Trafficking in Persons." Sex Workers Project, 2009. http://sexworkersproject.org/downloads/swp-2009-raids-and-trafficking-report.pdf.

Dodds, Sherril. "Embodied Transformations in Neo-Burlesque Striptease." *Dance Research Journal* 45, no. 3 (2013): 75–90.

Dolmage, Jay. *Disability Rhetoric*. Syracuse, New York: Syracuse University Press, 2014.

———. "Metis, Mêtis, Mestiza, Medusa: Rhetorical Bodies Across Rhetorical Traditions." *Rhetoric Review* 28, no. 1 (2009): 1–28.

Dow, Bonnie J., and Julia T. Wood. "Repeating History and Learning from It: What Can SlutWalks Teach Us About Feminism?" *Women's Studies in Communication* 37, no. 1 (2014): 22–43.

Egan, R. Danielle. *Dancing for Dollars and Paying for Love: The Relationships Between Exotic Dancers and Their Regulars*. New York: Palgrave Macmillan, 2006.

———. "I'll Be Your Fantasy Girl, If You'll Be My Money Man: Mapping Desire, Fantasy, and Power in Two Exotic Dance Clubs." *Journal for the Psychoanalysis of Culture and Society* 8, no. 1 (2003): 109–20.

———. "The Phenomenology of Lap Dancing." In *Flesh for Fantasy: Producing and Consuming Exotic Dance*, 19–33. New York: Thunder's Mouth, 2006.

Egan, R. Danielle, and Katherine Frank. "Attempts at a Feminist and Interdisciplinary Conversation About Strip Clubs." *Deviant Behavior* 26, no. 4 (2005): 297–320.
Ellis, Carolyn, Tony E. Adams, and Arthur P. Bochner. "Autoethnography: An Overview." *Historical Social Research* 36, no. 4 (2011): 273–90.
Enos, Richard Leo, Karlyn Kohrs Campbell, Andrew King, Celeste M. Condit, Richard J. Jensen, Sonja K. Foss, Martin J. Medhurst, and David Zarefsky. "Symposium: Interdisciplinary Perspectives on Rhetorical Criticism." *Rhetoric Review* 25, no. 4 (2006): 357–87.
Erickson, David, and Richard Tewksbury. "The 'Gentlemen' in the Club: A Typology of Strip Club Patrons." *Deviant Behavior: An Interdisciplinary Journal* 21 (2000): 271–93.
Erickson, Keith V., and Stephanie Thomson. "Seduction Theory and the Recovery of Feminine Aesthetics: Implications for Rhetorical Criticism." *Communication Quarterly* 52, no. 3 (2004): 300–19.
Evans, Polly. "Amber Rose's Slutwalk: Is the Controversial Feminist Movement Still Relevant?" *New Statesman*, September 28, 2017. https://www.newstatesman.com/politics/feminism/2017/09/amber-roses-slutwalk-controversial-feminist-movement-still-relevant.
"The Exotic Dancers League." *Burlesque Hall of Fame*, November 21, 2010. https://www.burlesquehall.com/the-exotic-dancers-league.
Faderman, Lillian. *Odd Girls and Twilight Lovers: A History of Lesbian Life in Twentieth-Century America*. New York: Penguin, 1992.
Felman, Shoshana. *The Literary Speech Act: Don Juan with J. L. Austin, or Seduction in Two Languages*. Ithaca: Cornell University Press, 1983.
Fenske, Mindy, and Dustin Bradley Goltz. "Disciplinary Dedications and Extradisciplinary Experiences: Themes on a Relation." *Text and Performance Quarterly* 34, no. 1 (2014): 1–8.
———, eds. "Performance and Rhetoric." Special Issue, *Text and Performance Quarterly* 34 no. 1 (2014).
Ferreday, Debra. "'Showing the Girl': The New Burlesque." *Feminist Theory* 9, no. 1 (2008): 47–65.
Finley, Taryn. "Amber Rose on Slut-Shaming, Sex Positivity, and Talking to Her Son About Her Period." *Huffington Post*, October 11, 2017. https://www.huffingtonpost.com/entry/amber-rose-slutwalk_us_59dbc371e4b00377980ae5fd.
Flores, Lisa A. "The Rhetorical 'Realness' of Race, or Why Critical Race Rhetoricians Need Performance Studies." *Text and Performance Quarterly* 34, no. 1 (2014): 94–96.
Frank, Katherine. "Exploring the Motivations and Fantasies of Strip Club Customers in Relation to Legal Regulations." *Archives of Sexual Behavior* 34, no. 5 (2005): 487–504.
———. *G-Strings and Sympathy: Strip Club Regulars and Male Desire*. Durham: Duke University Press, 2002.
———. "'Just Trying to Relax': Masculinity, Masculinizing Practices, and Strip Club Regulars." *Journal of Sex Research* 40, no. 1 (2003): 61–75.
———. "'The Management of Hunger': Using Fiction in Writing Anthropology." *Qualitative Inquiry* 6, no. 4 (2000): 474–88.
Freadman, Anne. "The Traps and Trappings of Genre Theory." *Applied Linguistics* 33, no. 5 (2012): 544–63.
Fredal, James. "Beyond the Fifth Canon: Body Rhetoric in Ancient Greece." PhD diss., Ohio State University, 1998.
———. "The Language of Delivery and the Presentation of Character: Rhetorical Action in Demosthenes' *Against Meidias*." *Rhetoric Review* 20, nos. 3–4 (2001): 251–67.

———. *Rhetorical Action in Ancient Athens: Persuasive Artistry from Solon to Demosthenes.* Carbondale: Southern Illinois University Press, 2006.
Freedman, Aviva, and Peter Medway. "Locating Genre Studies: Antecedents and Prospects." In *Genre and the New Rhetoric*, edited by Aviva Freedman and Peter Medway, 2–18. Bristol, PA: Taylor & Francis, 1994.
Gaucher, Danielle, Brianna Hunt, and Lisa Sinclair. "Can Pejorative Terms Ever Lead to Positive Social Consequences? The Case of SlutWalk." *Language Sciences* 52 (2015): 121–30.
Gall, Gregor. *Sex Worker Union Organising: An International Study.* New York: Palgrave Macmillan, 2006.
Gallop, Jane. "French Theory and the Seduction of Feminism." In *Men in Feminism*, edited by Alice Jardine and Paul Smith, 111–15. New York: Routledge, 1989.
Gamson, Joshua. "Must Identity Movements Self-Destruct? A Queer Dilemma." *Social Problems* 42, no. 3 (1995): 390–407.
Geertz, Clifford. "'From the Native's Point of View': On the Nature of Anthropological Understanding." *Bulletin of the American Academy of Arts and Sciences* 28, no. 1 (1974): 26–45.
Gencarella, Stephen Olbrys, and Phaedra C. Pezzulo. "Introduction: Body Politics, Social Drama, and Public Culture." In *Readings on Rhetoric and Performance*, edited by Stephen Olbrys Gencarella and Phaedra C. Pezzulo. State College, PA: Strata, 2010.
———, eds. *Readings on Rhetoric and Performance.* State College, PA: Strata, 2010.
Gingrich-Philbrook, Craig. "Autoethnography's Family Values: Easy Access to Compulsory Experiences." *Text and Performance Quarterly* 25, no. 4 (October 2005): 297–314.
Glick, Elisa. "Sex Positive: Feminism, Queer Theory, and the Politics of Transgression." *Feminist Review* 64 (2000): 19–45.
Global Women's Strike. "Women of Colour Respond to Black Women's Blueprint Attack on Slutwalk." Accessed October 24, 2015. http://www.globalwomenstrike.net/content/women-colour-respond-black-women's-blueprint-attack-slutwalk.
Goltz, Dustin Bradley. *Comic Performativities: Identity, Internet Outrage, and the Aesthetics of Communication.* New York: Routledge, 2017.
Gorgias. *Encomium of Helen.* In *The Rhetorical Tradition: Readings from Classical Times to the Present*, edited by Patricia Bizzell and Bruce Herzberg, 44–46. 2nd ed. Boston: Bedford/St. Martin's, 2001.
Goshorn, A. Keith. "Valorizing 'the Feminine' While Rejecting Feminism? Baudrillard's Feminist Provocations." In *Baudrillard: A Critical Reader*, edited by Douglas M. Kellner, 257–91. Oxford: Blackwell, 1994.
Grace, Victoria. *Baudrillard's Challenge: A Feminist Reading.* New York: Routledge, 2000.
Grant, Melissa Gira. "New Orleans Strip Club Workers Battle 'Age Ban' in Federal Court." *Appeal*, February 12, 2018. https://theappeal.org/new-orleans-strip-club-workers-battle-age-ban-in-federal-court-4b0bf8d6419c.
———. *Playing the Whore: The Work of Sex Work.* London: Verso Books, 2014.
———. "Trafficking in Vagaries: How a Times Picayune Series That Found Only 'Trafficking Opportunity' in Strip Clubs Paved the Way for a Bourbon Street Crackdown." *Appeal*, February 12, 2018. https://theappeal.org/trafficking-in-vagaries-how-a-times-picayune-series-that-found-only-trafficking-opportunity-in-strip-clubs-paved-the-way-for-a-bourbon-street-crackdown.
Graver, David. "The Actor's Bodies." *Text and Performance Quarterly* 17, no. 3 (1997): 221–35.
Greene, Robert. *The Art of Seduction.* London: Profile Books, 2001.
Griffin, Leland M. "The Rhetorical Structure of the 'New Left' Movement: Part I." *Quarterly Journal of Speech* 50, no. 2 (1964): 113–35.

Gunn, Joshua. "Maranatha." *Quarterly Journal of Speech* 98, no. 4 (2012): 359–85.
———. "The Rhetoric of Exorcism: George W. Bush and the Return of Political Demonology." *Western Journal of Communication* 68, no. 1 (2004): 1–23.
Haiman, Franklyn S. "The Rhetoric of the Streets: Some Legal and Ethical Considerations." *Quarterly Journal of Speech* 53, no. 2 (1967): 99–114.
Hanna, Judith Lynne. "Dance and Sexuality: Many Moves." *Journal of Sex Research* 47, nos. 2–3 (2010): 212–41.
———. "Exotic Dance Adult Entertainment: A Guide for Planners and Policy Makers." *Journal of Planning Literature* 20, no. 2 (2005): 116–34.
———. "The Language of Dance." *Journal of Physical Education, Recreation, and Dance* 72, no. 4 (2001): 40–45.
———. *Naked Truth: Strip Clubs, Democracy, and a Christian Right*. Austin: University of Texas Press, 2012.
———. "Undressing the First Amendment and Corsetting the Striptease Dancer." *Drama Review* 42 (1998): 38–69.
Hanscombe, Gillian. "In Among the Market Forces?" In *An Intimate Wilderness: Lesbian Writers on Sexuality*, edited by Judith Barrington, 216–20. Portland: Eighth Mountain, 1991.
Happe, Kelly E. "The Body of Race: Toward a Rhetorical Understanding of Racial Ideology." *Quarterly Journal of Speech* 99, no. 2 (2013): 131–55.
Haraway, Donna. "A Cyborg Manifesto: Science, Technology, and Socialist-Feminism in the Late Twentieth Century." In *Simians, Cyborgs, and Women: The Reinvention of Nature*, 149–81. New York: Routledge, 1991.
Harrington, Cora. "A New Perspective on an Icon: My Review of Dita von Teese's 'Strip Strip Hooray!' Show." *Lingerie Addict—Expert Lingerie Advice, News, Trends, and Reviews*, June 5, 2012. https://www.thelingerieaddict.com/2012/06/dita-von-teese-strip-strip-hooray-review.html (article no longer available on this site).
Harris, Geraldine. "The Ghosts of New Burlesque." In *A Good Night Out for the Girls: Popular Feminisms in Contemporary Theatre and Performance*, edited by Elaine Aston and Geraldine Harris, 135–57. New York: Palgrave Macmillan, 2013.
Harris-Perry, Melissa V. *Sister Citizen: Shame, Stereotypes, and Black Women in America*. New Haven: Yale University Press, 2011.
Harris Ramsby, Fiona. "The Drama as Rhetorical Critique: Language, Bodies, and Power in Angels in America." *Rhetoric Review* 33, no. 4 (2014): 403–20.
Hauser, Gerard A. "Body Rhetoric: Conflicted Reporting of Bodies in Pain." In *Deliberation, Democracy, and the Media*, edited by Simone Chambers and Anne Costain, 135–53. Lanham, MD: Rowan and Littlefield, 2000.
Hawhee, Debra. *Bodily Arts: Rhetoric and Athletics in Ancient Greece*. Austin: University of Texas Press, 2004.
———. *Moving Bodies: Kenneth Burke at the Edges of Language*. Columbia: University of South Carolina Press, 2009.
———. "Rhetoric's Sensorium." *Quarterly Journal of Speech* 101, no. 1 (2015): 2–17.
Hayward, Eva S. "Don't Exist." *TSQ: Transgender Studies Quarterly* 4, no. 2 (2017): 191–94.
Herndl, Carl G., and Adela C. Licona. "Shifting Agency: Agency, Kairos, and the Possibilities of Social Action." In *Communicative Practices in Workplaces and the Professions: Cultural Perspectives on the Regulation of Discourse and Organizations*, edited by Mark Zachry and Charlotte Thralls, 133–53. Amityville, NY: Baywood, 2007.
Hill, Annie. "SlutWalk as Perifeminist Response to Rape Logic: The Politics of Reclaiming a Name." *Communication and Critical/Cultural Studies* 13, no. 1 (2016): 23–39.

Holmes, Martha Stoddard. "Working (with) the Rhetoric of Affliction: Autobiographical Narratives of Victorians with Physical Disabilities." In *Embodied Rhetorics: Disability in Language and Culture*, edited by James C. Wilson and Cynthia Lewiecki-Wilson, 27–44. Carbondale: Southern Illinois University Press, 2001.

Hubbard, Bryan. "Reassessing Truman, the Bomb, and Revisionism: The Burlesque Frame and Entelechy in the Decision to Use Atomic Weapons Against Japan." *Western Journal of Communication* 62, no. 3 (1998): 348–85.

Hunter, Diane. Introduction to *Seduction and Theory: Readings of Gender, Representation, and Rhetoric*, edited by Diane Hunter, 1–10. Urbana: University of Illinois Press, 1989.

Jackson, Crystal A. "Framing Sex Worker Rights: How US Sex Worker Rights Activists Perceive and Respond to Mainstream Anti–Sex Trafficking Advocacy." *Sociological Perspectives* 59, no. 1 (2016): 27–45.

Johnson, E. Patrick. "Black Performance Studies: Geneologies, Politics, Futures." In *The Sage Handbook of Performance Studies*, edited by D. Soyini Madison and Judith Hamera, 446–63. Thousand Oaks: SAGE, 2006.

Jones, Tangerine. Interview by Legs Malone. *Lunch with Legs Podcast*. June 18, 2014. Audio, https://www.legsmalone.com/lunchwithlegs/2014/6/18/ep-24-tangerine-jones.

Jordan, John W. "Reshaping the 'Pillow Angel': Plastic Bodies and the Rhetoric of Normal Surgical Solutions." *Quarterly Journal of Speech* 95, no. 1 (2009): 20–42.

Jung, Julie. "Textual Mainstreaming and Rhetorics of Accommodation." *Rhetoric Review* 26, no. 2 (2007): 160–78.

Kapur, Ratna. "Pink Chaddis and SlutWalk Couture: The Postcolonial Politics of Feminism Lite." *Feminist Legal Studies* 20, no. 1 (2012): 1–20.

Kauffman, L. A. "The Anti-Politics of Identity." *Socialist Review* 20, no. 1 (1990): 67–80.

Kelley, William G. "Rhetoric as Seduction." *Philosophy and Rhetoric* 6, no. 2 (1973): 69–80.

Kennedy, Elizabeth Lapovsky, and Madeline D. Davis. *Boots of Leather, Slippers of Gold: The History of a Lesbian Community*. New York: Penguin, 1994.

King, Stephen. "What Writing Is." In *On Writing: A Memoir of the Craft*. 95–99. New York: Pocket Books. 2000.

Kirsch, Sharon J. "Gertrude Stein Delivers." *Rhetoric Review* 31, no. 3 (2012): 254–70.

Kress, Gunther. "Genre in a Social Theory of Language: A Reply to John Dixon." In *The Place of Genre in Learning: Current Debates*, edited by Ian Reid, 35–45. Geelong, AUS: Deakin University Press, 1988.

Laqueur, Thomas. *Making Sex: Body and Gender from the Greeks to Freud*. Cambridge: Harvard University Press, 1990.

Leidhold, Dorchen A. "Presentation to UN Special Seminar on Trafficking, Prostitution, and the Global Sex Industry: Position Paper for CATW: Part Two." *Coalition Against Trafficking in Women*, July 12, 2011. http://www.catwinternational.org/Home/Article/59-presentation-to-un-special-seminar-on-trafficking-prostitution-and-the-global-sex-industry-postion-paper-for-atw-part-two. (Site no longer active.)

Leigh, Carol. "Inventing Sex Work." In *Whores and Other Feminists*, edited by Jill Nagle, 225–31. Hoboken: Taylor and Francis, 2013.

Levy, Ariel. *Female Chauvinist Pigs: Women and the Rise of Raunch Culture*. New York: Free Press, 2006.

Lewis, Jacqueline. "Lap Dancing: Personal and Legal Implications for Exotic Dancers." In *Prostitution: On Whores, Hustlers, and Johns*, 376–89. Amherst, NY: Prometheus Books, 1998.

Lewis, Sydney Fonteyn. "Looking Forward to the Past: Black Women's Sexual Agency in 'Neo' Cultural Productions." PhD diss., University of Washington, 2012.

Liepe-Levinson, Katherine. *Strip Show: Performances of Gender and Desire*. New York: Routledge, 2002.

Litten, Kevin. "Rick's Cabaret Becomes 5th Strip Club Targeted by State Authorities." *Times-Picayune/NOLA.com/New Orleans Advocate*, January 25, 2018. https://www.nola.com/news/politics/article_4b9248f0-ef41-535a-810e-67a4bd9842a8.html.

———. "The Track: How Sex Trafficking Has Taken Hold of Bourbon Street." *Times-Picayune/NOLA.com/New Orleans Advocate*, October 18, 2017. https://www.nola.com/news/politics/article_f2a2e0eb-5128-5976-abbc-99eaee9b0b2b.html.

Lorey, Isabell. "Governmental Precarization." *eipcp.net*, January 2011. https://transversal.at/transversal/0811/lorey/en.

Lu, Peter. "Simple Pickup: Are These the Greatest Pickup Artists of All Time?" *Salon*, September 20, 2011. https://www.salon.com/2011/09/20/greatest_pickup_artists_of_their_generation.

Lunceford, Brett. *Naked Politics: Nudity, Political Action, and the Rhetoric of the Body*. Lanham, MD: Lexington Books, 2012.

Madison, D. Soyini, and Judith Hamera. "Introduction: Performance Studies at the Intersections." In *The Sage Handbook of Performance Studies*, edited by D. Soyini Madison and Judith Hamera, xi–xxv. Thousand Oaks: SAGE, 2006.

Makus, Anne. "Stuart Hall's Theory of Ideology: A Frame for Rhetorical Criticism." *Western Journal of Speech Communication* 54, no. 4 (1990): 495–514.

Malone, Legs. "Bettie Page Tribute." *!BadAss! Burlesque: Black and Red Party*. Produced by Velocity Chyaldd. Hosted by Jonny Porkpie. Burlesque at the Beach, Coney Island, Brooklyn, NY, September 27, 2013

———. "Burlesque Exposed: Exclusive Interview with Legs Malone, 'The Girl with the 34 and a Half Inch Inseam,'" interview by Maria Vultaggio, *International Business Times*, April 4, 2013. http://www.ibtimes.com/burlesque-exposed-exclusive-interview-legs-malone-girl-34-half-inch-inseam-1170423.

Manaster, Shelley. "Treading Water: An Autoethnographic Account(ing) of the Lap Dance." In *Flesh for Fantasy: Producing and Consuming Exotic Dance*, edited by R. Danielle Egan, Katherine Frank, and Merri Lisa Johnson, 3–17. New York: Thunder's Mouth, 2006.

Mansbridge, Joanna. "Popular Bodies, Canonical Voices: Paula Vogel's Hot 'n' Throbbing as Performative Burlesque." *Modern Drama Modern Drama* 52, no. 4 (2009): 469–89.

Mansfield, Rachel E. "Trend and Aftermath: The Iconograhpy and Rhetoric of Neo-Burlesque." MA thesis, Tufts University, 2006.

Martin, Emily. *Flexible Bodies: Tracking Immunity in American Culture from the Days of Polio to the Age of AIDS*. Boston: Beacon Press, 1994.

Martinez, Aja Y. "A Plea for Critical Race Theory Counterstory: Stock Story Versus Counterstory Dialogues Concerning Alejandra's 'Fit' in the Academy." *Composition Studies* 42, no. 2 (2014): 33–55.

McCormack, Clare, and Nevena Prostran. "Asking for It: A First-Hand Account from Slutwalk." *International Feminist Journal of Politics* 14, no. 3 (2012): 410–14.

McDonald, Soraya Nadia. "The Complicated Feminism of Amber Rose's SlutWalk." *Washington Post*, October 5, 2015, sec. Arts and Entertainment. https://www.washingtonpost.com/news/arts-and-entertainment/wp/2015/10/05/the-complicated-feminism-of-amber-roses-slutwalk.

Melucci, Alberto. *Nomads of the Present: Social Movements and Individual Needs in Contemporary Society*. London: Hutchinson Radius, 1989.

Mendes, Kaitlynn. *Slutwalk: Feminism, Activism, and Media*. New York: Palgrave Macmillan, 2015.

Middleton, Michael K., Samantha Senda-Cook, and Danielle Endres. "Articulating Rhetorical Field Methods: Challenges and Tensions." *Western Journal of Communication* 75, no. 4 (2011): 386–406.

Miller, Carolyn R. "Genre as Social Action." *Quarterly Journal of Speech* 70, no. 2 (1984): 151–67.

Miller, Lynn C., and Jacqueline Taylor. "The Constructed Self: Strategic and Aesthetic Choices in Autobiographical Performance." In *The SAGE Handbook of Performance Studies*, edited by D. Soyini Madison and Judith Hamera, 169–87. Thousand Oaks: SAGE, 2006.

Miriam, Kathy. "Feminism, Neoliberalism, and SlutWalk." *Feminist Studies* 38, no. 1 (2012): 262–66.

Miss Indigo Blue. "Blue Gloves." YouTube video, 5:53, "thetwirlygirl," March 12, 2009. https://www.youtube.com/watch?v=hbqejgQufCw.

Moore, Mark P. "'The Quayle Quagmire': Political Campaigns in the Poetic Form of Burlesque." *Western Journal of Communication (Includes Communication Reports)* 56, no. 2 (1992): 108–24.

Moraga, Cherríe. "Barnard Sexuality Conference: Played Between White Hands." *off our backs*, 1982.

Mortensen, Peter. "Figuring Illiteracy: Rustic Bodies and Unlettered Minds in Rural America." In *Rhetorical Bodies*, edited by Jack Selzer and Sharon Crowley, 143–70. Madison: University of Wisconsin Press, 1999.

Mountford, Roxanne. *The Gendered Pulpit: Preaching in American Protestant Spaces*. Carbondale: Southern Illinois University Press, 2005.

Muñoz, José Esteban. *Disidentifications: Queers of Color and the Performance of Politics*. Minneapolis: University of Minnesota Press, 1999. Kindle edition.

Murphy, Meghan. "Breaking! Slutwalk Is About Spectacle, Individual Empowerment, Wearing Sexy Lingerie, Says Everyone with Eyes and Brains." *Feminist Current*, August 9, 2012. https://www.feministcurrent.com/2012/08/09/breaking-slutwalk-is-aboutspectacle-individual-empowerment-wearing-sexy-lingerie-says-um-everyone-with-eyes-and-brains.

Nadeau, Ray. "Delivery in Ancient Times: Homer to Quintilian." *Quarterly Journal of Speech* 50, no. 1 (1964): 53–60.

Nakayama, Thomas K. "Show/Down Time: 'Race,' Gender, Sexuality, and Popular Culture." In *The Routledge Reader in Rhetorical Criticism*, edited by Brian L. Ott and Greg Dickinson, 367–79. New York: Routledge, 2013.

Nally, Claire. "Grrrly Hurly Burly: Neo-Burlesque and the Performance of Gender." *Textual Practice* 23, no. 4 (2009): 621–43.

National Human Trafficking Hotline. "Myths and Facts." Polaris Project. https://humantraffickinghotline.org/what-human-trafficking/myths-misconceptions.

Nealon, Jeffrey Thomas. *Alterity Politics: Ethics and Performative Subjectivity*. Durham: Duke University Press, 1998.

Noire, Perle. "Part One: Race and Burlesque — The Interviews." *21st Century Burlesque Magazine*, February 25, 2013. https://21stcenturyburlesque.com/race-and-burlesque-the-interviews-perle-noire-la-cholita-coco-framboise-and-marianne-cheesecake-13.

"Not-So-Hidden Histories: Performers of Color in Burlesque." *Burlesque Hall of Fame*. Accessed June 30, 2018. http://www.burlesquehall.com/not-so-hidden-histories-performers-of-color-in-burlesque.

NSWP. "History." *Global Network of Sex Work Projects*. October 13, 2010. https://www.nswp.org/history.

O'Keefe, Theresa. "My Body Is My Manifesto! SlutWalk, FEMEN, and Femmenist Protest." *Feminist Review*, no. 107 (2014): 1–19.
Olomo, Olorisa Omi Osun. "Performance and Ethnography, Performing Ethnography, Performance Ethnography." In *The Sage Handbook of Performance Studies*, edited by D. Soyini Madison and Judith Hamera, 339–46. Thousand Oaks: SAGE, 2006.
"Open Letter Rejecting 'Sex Work' as AP Term." Letter to David Minthorn, October 31, 2014. http://www.catwinternational.org/Home/Article/587-over-300-human-rights-groups-and-antitrafficking-advocates-worldwide-weigh-in-on-sex-work-terminology-in-media. (Site no longer active.)
Ott, Brian L. "Television as Lover, Part I: Writing Dirty Theory." *Cultural Studies ←→ Critical Methodologies* 7, no. 1 (2007): 26–47.
Ott, Brian L., and Greg Dickinson. "Entering the Unending Conversation: An Introduction to Rhetorical Criticism." In *The Routledge Reader in Rhetorical Criticism*, edited by Brian L. Ott and Greg Dickinson, 1–13. New York: Routledge, 2013.
Ott, Brian L., and Diane Marie Keeling. "Cinema and Choric Connection: *Lost in Translation* as Sensual Experience." *Quarterly Journal of Speech* 97, no. 4 (2011): 363–86.
Paré, Anthony. "Genre and Identity: Individuals, Institutions, and Ideology." In *The Rhetoric and Ideology of Genre*, Strategies for Stability and Change, edited by Richard M. Coe, Lorelei Lingard, and Tatiana Teslenko, 57–71. Cresskill, NJ: Hampton Press, 2002.
Pasko, Lisa. "Naked Power: The Practice of Stripping as a Confidence Game." *Sexualities* 5, no. 1 (2002): 49–66.
Patterson, Randi, and Gail Corning. "Researching the Body: An Annotated Bibliography for Rhetoric." *Rhetoric Society Quarterly* 27, no. 3 (1997): 5–29.
Pelias, Ronald J., and James VanOosting. "A Paradigm for Performance Studies." *Quarterly Journal of Speech* 73, no. 2 (1987): 219–31.
Perle Noire. Interview by Chocolat the Extraordinaire. *21st Century Burlesque Magazine*, February 25, 2013. http://21stcenturyburlesque.com/race-and-burlesque-the-interviews-perle-noire-la-cholita-coco-framboise-and-marianne-cheesecake-13.
Pflugfelder, Ehren Helmut. "Rhetoric's New Materialism: From Micro-Rhetoric to Microbrew." *Rhetoric Society Quarterly* 45, no. 5 (2015): 441–61.
Pheterson, Gail. "The Whore Stigma: Female Dishonor and Male Unworthiness." *Social Text*, no. 37 (1993): 39–64.
Pichardo, Nelson A. "New Social Movements: A Critical Review." *Annual Review of Sociology* 23 (1997): 411–30.
Plaid, Andrea. "Does SlutWalk Speak to Women of Color?" *Alternet*, June 22, 2011. https://www.alternet.org/story/151390/does_slutwalk_speak_to_women_of_color.
Pollitt, Katha. "Talk the Talk, Walk the SlutWalk." *Nation*, June 28, 2011. https://www.thenation.com/article/talk-talk-walk-slutwalk.
Pollock, Della. "Performing Writing." In *The Ends of Performance*, edited by Peggy Phelan and Jill Lane, 73–103. New York: New York University Press, 1998.
Porter, James E. "Recovering Delivery for Digital Rhetoric." *Computers and Composition* 26, no. 4 (2009): 207–24.
Porter, James I. "The Seductions of Gorgias." *Classical Antiquity* 12, no. 2 (1993): 267–99.
Prelli, Lawrence J. "Rhetorics of Display: An Introduction." In *Rhetorics of Display*, edited by Lawrence J. Prelli, 1–38. Columbia: University of South Carolina Press, 2006.
Rapp, Laura, Deeanna M. Button, Benjamin Fleury-Steiner, and Ruth Fleury-Steiner. "The Internet as a Tool for Black Feminist Activism: Lessons from an Online Antirape Protest." *Feminist Criminology* 5, no. 3 (July 2010): 244–62.

Ratchford, Sarah. "I Tried to Find out If Pick Up Artists Are Still Influential in 2017." *Vice*, August 25, 2017. https://www.vice.com/en_au/article/j55bxd/i-tried-to-find-out-if-pick-up-artists-are-still-influential-in-2017.

Reger, Jo. "Micro-Cohorts, Feminist Discourse, and the Emergence of the Toronto SlutWalk." *Feminist Formations* 26, no. 1 (2014): 49–69.

———. "The Story of a Slut Walk: Sexuality, Race, and Generational Divisions in Contemporary Feminist Activism." *Journal of Contemporary Ethnography* 44, no. 1 (2015): 84–112.

Ronai, Carol Rambo, and Carolyn Ellis. "Turn-Ons for Money: 'Interactional Strategies of the Table Dancer.'" *Journal of Contemporary Ethnography* 18, no. 3 (1989): 271–98.

Ross, Andrew. "Baudrillard's Bad Attitude." In *Seduction and Theory: Readings of Gender, Representation, and Rhetoric*, edited by Dianne Hunter, 214–25. Urbana: University of Illinois Press, 1989.

Rubin, Gayle S. "Thinking Sex: Notes for a Radical Theory of Sexuality." In *Pleasure and Danger: Exploring Female Sexuality*, edited by Carol S. Vance, 267–319. New York: Routledge, 1984.

Rude, Carolyn D. "Toward an Expanded Concept of Rhetorical Delivery: The Uses of Reports in Public Policy Debates." *Technical Communication Quarterly* 13, no. 3 (2004): 271–88.

Sally, Lynn. "'It Is the Ugly That Is So Beautiful': Performing the Monster/Beauty Continuum in American Neoburlesque." *Journal of American Drama and Theatre* 21, no. 3 (2009): 5–23.

Sauvage, Brooke, and Avery L. White. "Bourbon Street Strippers Are Fighting Intrusive Regulations." *VICE*, February 9, 2018. https://www.vice.com/en_us/article/7x7vmd/bourbon-street-strippers-are-fighting-intrusive-regulations.

Schechner, Richard. *Performance Studies: An Introduction.* 3rd. ed. London: Routledge, 2013.

Schneider, Rebecca. *The Explicit Body in Performance.* New York: Routledge, 1997.

Selzer, Jack. "Habeas Corpus: An Introduction." In *Rhetorical Bodies*, edited by Jack Selzer and Sharon Crowley, 3–15. Madison: University of Wisconsin Press, 1999.

Serano, Julia. *Whipping Girl: A Transsexual Woman on Sexism and the Scapegoating of Femininity.* 2nd edition. Berkeley, CA: Seal Press, 2016.

Shanghai Pearl. Interview by Legs Malone. *Lunch with Legs Podcast.* May 21, 2014. Audio, 46:03. https://www.legsmalone.com/lunchwithlegs/2014/5/21/ep-22-shanghai-pearl.

———. "'It's Complicated': More on Cultural Appropriation." Facebook, May 29, 2012. https://www.facebook.com/notes/shanghai-pearl/its-complicated-more-on-cultural-appropriation/380708325309457.

Shields, Donald C. "Symbolic Convergence and Special Communication Theories: Sensing and Examining Dis/Enchantment with the Theoretical Robustness of Critical Auto Ethnography." *Communication Monographs* 67, no. 4 (2000): 392–421.

Siebler, Kay. "What's So Feminist About Garters and Bustiers? Neo-Burlesque as PostFeminist Sexual Liberation." *Journal of Gender Studies*, February 28, 2014, 1–13.

Singer, Ross. "Anti-Corporate Argument and the Spectacle of the Grotesque Rhetorical Body in Super Size Me." *Critical Studies in Media Communication* 28, no. 2 (2011): 135–52.

Slack, Jennifer Daryl. "Communication as Articulation." In *Communication As . . . : Perspectives on Theory*, by Gregory Shepherd, Jeffrey St. John, and Ted Striphas, 223–31. Thousand Oaks, CA: SAGE, 2006.

Smith, Scott. "America's Got an Ass That Goes Pow." *Chicagoist.* June 29, 2006. http://chicagoist.com/2006/06/29/americas_got_an_ass_that_goes_pow.php.

Snow, David A., and Robert D. Benford. "Ideology, Frame Resonance, and Participant Mobilization." *International Social Movement Research* 1 (1988): 171–218.

Snow, David A., E. Burke Rochford, Steven K. Worden, and Robert D. Benford. "Frame Alignment Processes, Micromobilization, and Movement Participation." *American Sociological Review* 51, no. 4 (1986): 464–81.

Souther, J. Mark. "The Disneyfication of New Orleans: The French Quarter as Facade in a Divided City." *Journal of American History* 94, no. 3 (2007): 804–11.

Stob, Paul. "Terministic Screens, Social Constructionism, and the Language of Experience." *Philosophy and Rhetoric* 41, no. 2 (2008): 130–52.

Stockton, Kathryn Bond. *The Queer Child, or Growing Sideways in the Twentieth Century.* Durham: Duke University Press, 2009.

Strauss, Neil. *The Game: Penetrating the Secret Society of Pickup Artists.* New York: HarperTorch, 2006.

"Stripper Dixie Evans." YouTube video, 4:22, "Voyenty," July 2019. https://www.youtube.com/watch?v=5uKpuHTULSI (site discontinued).

Stromquist, Kay. "Strip Club Workers Drown out Bourbon Street Infrastructure Press Conference." *Gambit*, January 31, 2018. https://www.bestofneworleans.com/thelatest/archives/2018/01/31/strip-club-workers-drown-out-bourbon-street-infrastructure-press-conference. (Site no longer active.)

Tease, Frankie. "How To Burlesque: Connecting with Your Audience." *Frankie Tease Magazine*, October 24, 2011. http://www.frankietease.com/2011/10/how-to-burlesque-connecting-with-your.html.

Tedlock, Barbara. "From Participant Observation to the Observation of Participation: The Emergence of Narrative Ethnography." *Journal of Anthropological Research* 47, no. 1 (1991): 69–94.

Thompson, Eliza. "Amber Rose Talks Sex, Stripping, and How the Internet Made Her a 'Feminist Monster.'" *Cosmopolitan*, June 8, 2015. https://www.cosmopolitan.com/entertainment/celebs/a40004/amber-rose-internets-most-fascinating.

Traister, Rebecca. "Ladies, We Have a Problem." *New York Times*, July 20, 2011, sec. Magazine. https://www.nytimes.com/2011/07/24/magazine/clumsy-young-feminists.html.

Triplett, Hall. "The Misnomer of Freud's 'Seduction Theory.'" *Journal of the History of Ideas* 65, no. 4 (2004): 647–65.

Vance, Carol S. "The Ninth Scholar and the Feminist Conference Concept Paper." In *Pleasure and Danger: Exploring Female Sexuality*, edited by Carol S. Vance, 443–46. New York: Routledge, 1984.

Vance, Carol S., et al. "Petition in Support of the Scholar and Feminist IX Conference." In *Pleasure and Danger: Exploring Female Sexuality*, edited by Carol S. Vance, 451–53. New York: Routledge, 1984.

Vanguri, Star Medzerian. "Introduction: Toward a Rhetorical Onomastics." In *Rhetorics of Names and Naming*, edited by Star Medzerian Vanguri, 1–11. New York: Routledge, 2018.

Vesey, Jordan. "How Performers of Color Are 'Revolutionizing' Burlesque." *PBS NewsHour*, August 18, 2015. https://www.pbs.org/newshour/arts/shimmying-beat-history-performers-color-burlesque.

Villadsen, Lisa Storm. "The Rhetoric of Seduction." PhD diss., Northwestern University, 2000.

Vitanza, Victor J. "Abandoned to Writing: Notes Toward Several Provocations." *Enculturation* 5, no. 1 (2003). http://www.enculturation.net/5_1/vitanza.html.

———. "'Some More' Notes, Toward a 'Third' Sophistic." *Argumentation* 5, no. 2 (1991): 117–39.

Walker, Lisa. "The Future of Femme: Notes on Femininity, Aging, and Gender Theory." *Sexualities* 15, no. 7 (2012): 795–814.
Weitzer, Ronald. "Prostitutes' Rights in the United States: The Failure of a Movement." *Sociological Quarterly* 32, no. 1 (1991): 23–41.
Weldon, Jo. *The Burlesque Handbook*. New York: It! Books, 2010.
Werner, Maggie M. "Deploying Delivery as Critical Method: Neo-Burlesque's Embodied Rhetoric." *Rhetoric Review* 36, no. 1 (2017): 44–59.
———. "Seductive Rhetoric and the Communicative Art of Neo-burlesque." *Present Tense: A Journal of Rhetoric in Society* 5 no. 1 (2015). http://www.presenttensejournal.org/category/volume-5/issue1-1-volume-5.
Williams, Jessica. "Can Louisiana Enforce Strip Club Age Ban? Judges Hear Arguments, Mull Decision." *Times-Picayune/NOLA.com/New Orleans Advocate*, February 7, 2018. https://www.nola.com/news/article_3952427a78bc5ec08b369aaa8d21be7a.html.
Williams, Linda. "Film Bodies: Gender, Genre, and Excess." *Film Quarterly* 44, no. 4 (1991): 2–13.
Williams, Miatta. "Why, Even as a Feminist, I Can't Get Behind Amber Rose's Slut Walk." *Blavity*, October 12, 2015. https://blavity.com/on-amber-roses-la-slut-walk-defining-the-meaning-of-her-movement.
Willson, Jacki. *The Happy Stripper: Pleasures and Politics of the New Burlesque*. New York: I. B. Tauris, 2008.
Wilson, James C., and Cynthia Lewiecki-Wilson. "Disability, Rhetoric, and the Body." In *Embodied Rhetorics: Disability in Language and Culture*, edited by James C. Wilson and Cynthia Lewiecki-Wilson, 1–24. Carbondale: Southern Illinois University Press, 2001.
Wosick-Correa, Kassia R., and Lauren J. Joseph. "Sexy Ladies Sexing Ladies: Women as Consumers in Strip Clubs." *Journal of Sex Research* 45, no. 3 (2008): 201–16.
Young, Vershawn Ashanti. "Review of Readings on Rhetoric and Performance." *Text and Performance Quarterly* 31, no. 4 (2011): 451–53.

Index

Italicized page references indicate illustrations. Endnotes are referenced with "n" followed by the endnote number.

acceptance, and understanding symbolic operations of erotic performance, 164–65
Act 395 ("age ban," 2016), 119
Adams, Tony, 16–17
"age ban" (Act 395, 2016), 119
agency, in sex work, 110, 111–13, 114–15, 124
  See also choice
Ahmed, Sara, 85
Alexander, Jonathan, 2–3
Allen, Robert, 33, 35, 86–87
alter-identity, 132, 134, 138, 156
alterity
  and analyzing body rhetorics, 150–56, 159–60
  politics of, 128
  rhetorical function of, 127–28
  as rhetorical strategy, 132–35
  sex wars and rhetorics of, 130–31, 135–40
  SlutWalk and rhetorics of, 140–50
"Amazon Damsels in Bondage" (Indigo Blue), 88–89
Amber Rose SlutWalk, 129–30, 143, 154–55, 180n14
America's Got Talent, 42–43
Anderson, Dana, 134
Angus, Ian, 103
antagonisms, 104
anti-feminist sexuality, 139–40
anti-trafficking rhetoric, 101, 104, 110–15, 119–25
Appel, Edward, 162–63
Aquinas, Thomas, 162
Archer, Lyn, 122
Aristotle, 28
Armstrong, Elizabeth A., 178n25
articulation, 100, 102–5, 159
artifice
  in neo-burlesque, 87–89
  and sophistic rhetoric, 77, 80, 81
artificial authenticity, 88

Art of Seduction, The (Greene), 78–79
assel twirling, 62–63
audience
  of neo-burlesque, 60, 72–73, 98, 173n44
  of strip clubs, 57–59, 172n33
audience *topos*, 40–43, 158–59
authenticity, artificial, 88
autoethnography, 15–17

Ballif, Michelle, 82, 83–84, 98, 175n25
Barbier, Carl, 119
Barnard College conference, 136–37, 139
Baudrillard, Jean, 23, 76, 77, 78, 81–82, 83, 85, 88, 89–90, 97
Bawarshi, Anis, 53, 70
Bazerman, Charles, 69
binaries, in seductive rhetoric, 83–85
Black Women's Blueprint (BWB), 147–49
Blair, Carole, 7, 10
Blay, Zeba, 143
"Blue Gloves" (Indigo Blue), 92
Bochner, Arthur, 16–17
bodies, criticism of, 5–9
body genre, 48–49, 54, 64, 71–73
body genre films, 54
body positivity, 57, 67, 164
body rhetoric, 102
body *topos*, 36–39, 158
Bogado, Aura, 144–47, 154
Borah, Rituparna, 129
Bormann, Ernest, 16
Branstetter, Heather Lee, 17
Breyer, Johanna, 116
Bright, Susie, 137
Brightwell, Laura, 153
British Blondes, 31
Brooks, Siobhan, 173n67, 179n56
Buchanan, Linda, 29, 30, 170n45
Burke, Kenneth, 7–8, 31, 132, 161–63

burlesque
    and audience participation / interaction *topos*, 41
    Burke's conception of, 161–63, 165
    as frame of rejection, 161–62
    history of, 31–35, 50–51
    neo-burlesque versus literary, 163–64
    rhetorical scholarship on, 31, 163–64
    and sex-work activism, 115–18
    use of term, 168n32
    whiteness and cultural appropriation's impact on, 21
    women of color's legacy in, 44–45, 65–66
    See also neo-burlesque
Burris, Autumn, 113
butch-femme identities, 153
Butterworth, Michael, 6

Campbell, Karlyn Kohrs, 55
Carlson, A. Cheree, 162, 182n10
Chateauvert, Melinda, 129
Cheeky Lane, 93–95
choice
    and feminism, 141, 151, 154–55
    in sex work, 108, 178n32
    See also agency, in sex work
Cicero, 29
classification, 55
coalition, 144–45, 147, 154
Coalition Against Trafficking in Women (CATW), 110–13, 178nn42,45
collusion, and SlutWalk, 144–45, 147
color, women of. *See* women of color
comedy, as frame of acceptance, 161
commercial erotic dancing, 12, 56–59, 68, 88, 178n32
    See also stripping; topless dance
communication
    as articulation, 100
    embodied, 26–27, 97–98
    and social-movement activism, 103
community, of neo-burlesque, 60
Compton's Cafeteria riot (1966), 106, 178n25
Connolly, William, 132
Conquergood, Dwight, 4
Cooper, Britany C. ("Crunktastic"), 146–47, 148, 155
coquette, in Greene's conception of seduction, 78
Corbett, Edward, 102
costuming, 37, 60, 64–65, 173n52
counterstories, 100, 101, 114–15, 119–25

covering and uncovering, in neo-burlesque, 91–96, 176n82
Crage, Suzanna M., 178n25
criminality, sex work and, 109
criticism of bodies, 5–9
Crowley, Sharon, 19
"Crunktastic" (Brittany C. Cooper), 146–47, 148, 155
CuchiFrita, Dame, 93
cultural appropriation, 66–67
customer experience, in neo-burlesque versus club stripping, 51–52
    See also audience

data collection, 11–17
Davis, Diane, 132, 133, 160
delivery, 27–28
    as critical method for embodied rhetoric, 45–46
    and dissimilarities between neo-burlesque and club stripping, 51–52
    and interplay of interdependent symbolic practices, 35–43
    and performance, 29, 158
    and rhetorical bodies, 28–31
    and spectacular made from mundane, 43–45
Deveraux, Sydni (The Golden Glamazon), 61
Dines, Gail, 141–42
disidentification, 128, 135
Dolmage, Jay, 98
Don't Ask, Don't Tell, 179n50

economic privilege, 143, 149
Egan, Danielle, 51
Ellis, Carolyn, 16–17
embodied communication, 26–27, 97–98
empowering, 19
erasure, politics of, 115
Erickson, David, 172n33
Erickson, Keith, 84
erotic dancing
    ethnographic research on, 12–16
    versus exotic dance, 168n67
    overview of, 11–12
    as type of performance rhetoric, 160–62
    See also burlesque; neo-burlesque; stripping; topless dance
ethnography, 9, 12–17
Evans, Dixie, 33, 34, 116
Exotic Dancers Alliance (EDA), 116–18
Exotic Dancers League (EDL), 115–16

fantasy
    and commercial aspect of strip clubs, 57–58, 68
    of exotic other, 172n24
Felman, Shoshana, 79–80
female sexuality, 135–39, 151–52
feminine, versus woman in postmodern theories of seduction, 83–84
feminism, 18–21
    and alterity rhetorics in sex wars, 135–39
    debates regarding, 178n40, 180n29
    lesbian feminists, 137–39, 153
    neo-burlesque's relationship to, 85–86
    rhetoric of feminist empowerment in neo-burlesque, 175n50
    Rose's definition of, 154–55
    seduction as antithetical to, 78–79
    seductive rhetoric's relationship to, 85
    sex-positive, 141, 151, 152
    versus sex work activism, 105, 106
    structural, 136, 141–42, 152
    See also sex wars; SlutWalk
"feminist stripping," neo-burlesque as, 43, 49
femme aesthetics, 152–53
femmephobia, 152–53
Ferreday, Debra, 60, 96, 176n82
Fight Online Sex Trafficking Act (FOSTA), 125
framing, rights-based, 114
Frank, Katherine, 51, 57–58
Fredal, James, 27, 46
Freud, Sigmund, 174n8

Gallop, Jane, 85
Game, The (Strauss), 79
gay rights movement, 105, 106, 115, 178n25, 179n50
Geertz, Clifford, 167n18
gender
    as lens for analyzing performance, 21–22
    performances in Greene's conception of seduction, 78
    and rearticulation of sex-worker identity, 111–12
genre
    defined, 55
    as embodied, 70
    and production of social identities, 69
    social aspects of, 69–70
    typified situations and coalescence into, 56–68
genre analysis, 48–49, 159
    as approach to classification, 55
    and author's study of topless dance and neo-burlesque, 73–74

context in, 52–53
    and dissimilarities between neo-burlesque and club stripping, 51–52
    and history of burlesque, 50–51
    as provocative and problematic approach, 52–54
    and social hierarchy of erotic dance, 73
    and typified situations of topless dance and neo-burlesque, 56–68
genre *topos*, 36, 158
Ginger Snapz, 62–63
Gingrich-Philbrook, Craig, 16
Glick, Elisa, 135
Global Network of Sex Work Projects (NSWP), 108–9
Global Women's Strike (GWS), 148–49
glove peel, 92
Golden Glamazon, The (Sydni Deveraux), 61
Goltz, Dustin Bradley, 8
Gorgias, 80
Grant, Melissa Gira, 108, 120
Gravity Plays Favorites, 61–62
Greene, Robert, 78–79
growing sideways, 48
Gunn, Joshua, 48, 53–54, 69, 70, 71, 72, 159

Hall, Stuart, 115
Hamera, Judith, 4
Hanna, Judith, 11, 172n33, 173n52
Hanscombe, Gillian, 137–38
Happe, Kelly, 22
Haraway, Donna, 90
Harris, Gerry, 60
Harrison, Michael, 120
Harris-Perry, Melissa, 101
hate terms, reclamation of, 141–42, 145–50, 154
Hawhee, Debra, 3, 7–8, 43
Head, Stacy, 119
Helen of Troy, 80
high-femme symbols, 152–53
Hill, Murray, 49
Hnida, Katie, 6
"House" (Cheeky Lane), 93–95

identity
    and agency in sex work, 110
    and alterity as rhetorical strategy, 132–33
    and alterity rhetorics in sex wars, 135–39
    and analyzing body rhetorics through alterity lens, 150–56, 159–60
    construction of, 127–28

identity (continued)
    genre and production of social, 69
    and hate term reclamation, 145–50
    as part of embodied rhetorics, 159
    politics of alterity and, 128
    rearticulation of sex-worker, 99–101, 111–15, 164–65
    SlutWalk and performance of slut, 140–41, 152
inclusiveness, in neo-burlesque, 57, 67, 164
independent-contractor status of strippers, 117–19, 179n56
Indigo Blue, 60–61, 88–89, 92
interaction *topos*, 40–43

Jackson, Crystal, 114
Jamieson, Kathleen Hall, 55
Johnson, E. Patrick, 21
Joseph, Lauren, 15

Kelley, William, 81
Kenison, Marc (Waxie Moon), 89–90
kinesthetic symbolic, 61
King, Stephen, 15
Kris, Ernst, 174n8

labor activism, 113
labor movement, 105–6
L'amour, Michelle, 42
Landrieu, Mitch, 120, 122
language
    and creation of alter-identity, 132
    and hate term reclamation, 145–50
    seductive power of, 80–81
lap dance, 58–59, 63
Laqueur, Thomas, 70
Lee, Jennie, 115
Leigh, Carol, 106, 112
lesbian feminists, 137–39, 153
Levinas, Emmanuel, 133, 160
Levy, Ariel, 131
Lewis, Sydney, 44–45, 62–63
LGBTQ social-movement activism, 105, 106, 115
linguistic critical approach, 5–9
Lusty Lady peep show, 118, 179n56

Madison, D. Soyini, 4
Malone, Legs, 25–26, 37, 95–96
Mansfield, Rachel E., 175n50
Marx, Karl, 162
material critical approach, 5–9

Mendes, Kaitlynn, 129, 135, 152, 181n44
military, LGBT service in, 179n50
Miller, Carolyn, 67
Miller, Lynn, 17
Miriam, Kathy, 151–52
misrecognition, 101
Moira, Fran, 139
Moraga, Cherríe, 139, 142–43
Mountford, Roxanne, 29–30
mundane, spectacular made from, 43–45
Muñoz, José, 128
Murphy, Meghan, 152, 154
Murphy, Wendy, 141–42

Nally, Claire, 19
Nandi, Subhalakshmi, 129
narrative ethnography, 16–17
Nealon, Jeffrey, 128, 134, 150
neo-burlesque
    and affordances of delivery in analyzing rhetoric of body, 28, 30–31
    artifice in, 88–89
    and audience participation / interaction *topos*, 40, 41–43
    audiences of, 25, 173n44
    and body *topos*, 37
    costuming in, 60, 65, 173n52
    delivery of embodied rhetoric in, 30
    embodied communication in, 26–27, 97–98
    ethnographic research on, 14–16
    features of seduction in, 77
    and feminism, 19, 43, 49, 85–86
    fusion of features of, 49
    genre analysis and author's study of, 73–74
    genre analysis and cultural value of, 70–71
    and genre *topos*, 36
    history of, 50–51
    interaction with audience in, 173n44
    versus literary burlesque, 163–64
    as mostly cis woman's art form, 21–22
    as not operating as "body genre," 48–49
    overview of, 12
    and persona *topos*, 38–39
    racism and cultural appropriation in, 66–67
    resurgence of, 51
    rhetorical function of nonlinguistic elements in, 27
    and rhetorical process, 96–98
    rhetoric of feminist empowerment in, 175n50
    scholarship on, 30
    seductive rhetoric of, 83

seductive strategies of teasing and withdrawal in, 86–96
as social action, 71–72
and space *topos*, 39–40
and spectacular made from mundane, 43–45
versus stripping, 49, 51–52
symbolic features of, 61–65
typified situations of, 56–68
use of term, 168n32
whiteness and cultural appropriation's impact on, 21
women of color in, 65–67
New Orleans, sex-work activism in, 101, 119–26, 180nn52,56,67
"new social movements" (NSMs), 104
Noire, Perle, 51
NOLA.com / *Times Picayune*, 119–20
Norwood, Brandy, 42

O'Farrell Theatre, 117–18
Opium Den routine (Von Teese), 66–67
oppressive, 19
other, the, 133
otherness, 132–35, 154, 172n24
See also alterity
Ott, Brian, 82–83

Page, Bettie, 95–96, 169n2
Pelias, Ronald, 40
Perelman, Chaïm, 121
performance
and delivery, 29, 158
erotic, as type of performance rhetoric, 160–61
seduction in neo-burlesque as, 86–87
of slut identity at SlutWalk, 140–41, 152
as transaction and production, 55
Performance Rhetoric, 27
performance studies, 4, 8, 27–28
persona *topos*, 36–39
pick-up artists, 78–80
Plaid, Andrea, 149–50
Plato, 81
pole dancing, 61–62
police
abuse of power by, 122–23, 124–25
SlutWalk and collusion with, 144–45, 147, 154
Pollock, Della, 49
Porter, James E., 41, 170n45
Presser, Dawn, 116
promiscuous research, 17
props, 37, 86, 93, 176n82

prostitution, 100, 105, 106–7, 108, 109, 111–13, 115
protest rhetoric, 5, 45, 177n4
See also sex-work activism

queer theory, 153

race and racism, 21, 22, 146–49, 173n67
See also women of color
rake, in Greene's conception of seduction, 78
rape and rape culture, 128–29, 140–50, 153–55, 181n44
Ratchford, Sarah, 79
rearticulation, 99–101, 105, 110, 111–15, 124, 164–65
reclamation, of hate terms, 141–42, 145–50, 154
Reger, Jo, 135
rejection, and understanding symbolic operations of erotic performance, 164–65
rhetoric
as muscle craft of self-fashioning and self-presentation, 27
and performance, 27–28
rise of new social movements and, 102
seduction and ancient, 80–81
rhetorical criticism, 6–7
rhetorical field methods, 49
rhetorical studies, performance studies and, 4
rhetoric of the body
alterity and analysis of, 150–56, 159–60
and construction of identity and alterity, 133–34
criticism of, 5–9
delivery and, 28–31, 45–46, 158
genre's applicability to, 53
as multicoded, 157–58, 165
scholarship on, 1–5
seductive rhetoric as lens for criticizing, 96–98
Rhodes, Jacqueline, 2–3
rights-based framing, 114
Rihanna, 6
Rose, Amber, 129–30, 143, 154–55, 180n14
Rubin, Gayle S., 138–39

Sanguinetti, Michael, 140
de Saussure, Ferdinand, 132
Savage X Fenty, 6
Schneider, Rebecca, 41
seduction, 76–77
Baudrillard on, 81–82
defining, 78
features of, in neo-burlesque, 77
in Freudian psychoanalytic tradition, 174n8

seduction (*continued*)
    literature on, 78
    popular legacy of, 78–80
    rhetorical applications of postmodern, 82
    and rhetorical process, 96–98
    and Sophistic rhetoric, 80–81
    strategies of teasing and withdrawal in neo-burlesque, 86–96
Seduction (Baudrillard), 85
seductive rhetoric, 76–77
    analyzing, 82–83
    binaries in, 83–85
    of neo-burlesque, 83
    relationship to feminism, 85
    and rhetorical process, 96–98
    strategies of teasing and withdrawal in neo-burlesque, 86–96
Selzer, Jack, 2
Serano, Julia, 153
sex-positive feminism, 141, 151, 152
sex trafficking, 101, 104, 107–8, 110–13, 114, 119–21, 123, 125
sexuality
    anti-feminist, 139–40
    female, 135–39, 151–52
    of white versus black women, 146–49
Sexual Rhetorics: Methods, Identities, Publics (Rhodes), 2–3
sex wars, 18
    alterity rhetorics in, 135–40
    and SlutWalk controversy, 130–31
    women of color and, 142–43
    See also feminism; SlutWalk
sex-work activism, 99–102
    and anatomy and implications of "sex workers," 105–13
    articulation and, 102–5
    emergence of, 113–19
    and erasure rhetorics faced by sex workers, 178n25
    versus feminism and gay liberation movements, 105–6
    mission of, 105
    in New Orleans, 101, 119–26, 179nn52,56,67
sex work and sex workers
    anatomy and implications of term, 105–13
    characterization of bodies of, 99–100
    choice in, 108, 178n32
    devaluation and criminalization of, 114, 122–25
    erasure rhetorics faced by, 178n25
    origin of term, 112
    rearticulation of sex-worker identity, 99–101, 111–15, 164–65
Sex Workers Outreach Project (SWOP) Seattle, 99
Shanghai Pearl, The, 42, 66, 67
Shields, Donald, 16
shoes, stripper, 64–65
sideways, growing, 48
sign play, 87, 88, 89–96
skill, 56
Slack, Jennifer, 100
slut
    and black feminism, 155–56
    reclamation of, 141–42, 145–50, 154
SlutWalk, 128–31
    and alterity as rhetorical strategy, 134–35
    and analyzing body rhetorics through alterity lens, 150–56
    backlash against, 141
    and defining anti-feminist sexuality, 139–40
    mission of, 181n44
    multicoded rhetoric of, 140–50
    See also Amber Rose SlutWalk
social-movement activism
    articulation and, 102–5
    strategic use of alterity in, 134
    See also sex-work activism
"someone for everyone," 57, 67, 164
Sophistic rhetoric, 80–81
space *topos*, 39–40, 158
spectacular, made from mundane, 43–45
stage names, 37–39
Stallybrass, Peter, 35
Stockton, Kathryn Bond, 48
Stonewall riots (1969), 106, 178n25
Stop Enabling Sex Traffickers Act (SESTA), 125
Strauss, Neil, 79
street–sex workers, 109–10
stripper shoes, 64–65
stripping
    audiences of, 57–59, 172n33
    and body *topos*, 37
    burlesque and, 33–35
    categories of, 12
    commercial aspect of, 56–59, 68, 88
    employment status of strippers, 117–19, 179n56
    ethnographic research on, 12–16
    fusion of features of, 49
    genre analysis and author's study of, 73–74

and genre *topos*, 36
versus neo-burlesque, 49, 51–52
neo-burlesque as "feminist," 43, 49
popularization of, 51
scholarship on, 51
and sex-work activism, 115–24
as social action, 68–74
and space *topos*, 40
See also topless dance
striptease, seduction in, 87–88
structural feminism, 136, 141–42, 152
symbolic practices
    delivery and interplay of interdependent, 35–43
    in topless dancing and neo-burlesque, 61–65

table dance, 58–59
tassel twirling, 62–63
Taylor, Jacqueline, 17
Tease, Frankie, 41
teasing, in neo-burlesque, 86–96
Tedlock, Barbara, 17
telepathy, 15
Tewksbury, Richard, 172n33
theatrical burlesque, 31–32
Thompson, Lydia, 31, 32, 182n10
Thomson, Stephanie, 84
topless dance
    commercial aspect of, 68, 178n32
    frames of acceptance and rejection in, 164–65
    genre analysis and cultural value of, 70–71
    as social action, 72
    symbolic features of, 61–65
    typified situations of, 56–68
    See also stripping
Toronto SlutWalk, 140–41
"Towards a Politics of Sexuality" conference (1982), 136–37, 139
"Track, The" (NOLA.com / *Times Picayune*), 119–20
trans women, 18, 21–22, 106, 110, 155, 178n45

Trixie Little and The Evil Hate Monkey, 42
typified situations, of topless dance and neo-burlesque, 56–68

"Untitled with Mask" (Dame CuchiFrita), 93

VanOosting, James, 40
vaudeville, 32–33
veiling and unveiling, 91–96, 176n82
vintage, 60, 65
Von Teese, Dita, 66–67

Walker, Lisa, 152
Wax, Dustin M., 179n52
Waxie Moon, 89–90
Weldon, Jo, 19, 37, 38, 51–52, 62, 168n32, 170n57
White, Allon, 35
White Angry Man (WAM), 134
white imperialism, 145
white privilege, 146–47, 154
white supremacy, 144–45, 146, 153–54
Williams, Linda, 48–49, 54, 71
Williams, Miatta, 155–56
Willson, Jacki, 60
withdrawal, in neo-burlesque, 86–96
woman / women
    versus feminine in postmodern theories of seduction, 83–84
    individuals included in category, 21–22
    as neo-burlesque audience, 60
    trans women, 18, 21–22, 106, 110, 155, 178n45
women of color
    and alterity rhetorics in sex wars, 139
    in burlesque and neo-burlesque, 44–45, 65–68
    erotic capital of, 173n67
    and sex work, 109–10
    and SlutWalk, 129–30, 142–50, 153–56
Wosick-Corea, Kassia, 15

Young, Vershawn, 27